791.06873 O'BRIEN
O'Brien, Tim.
The amusement park
guide : coast to coast

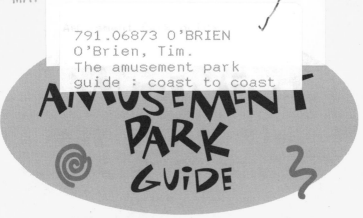

AMUSEMENT PARK GUIDE

"Tim is an industry insider. There are many people who write about theme parks and waterparks but there are few insiders who can write as he does. Tim is your inside ticket to great information!"

> — Chip Cleary, Vice President, Waterpark Division, Palace Entertainment

"As I travel each summer with my family, we always use *The Amusement Park Guide* when we visit parks. It helps us plan our visit and ensures that we see everything the park has to offer."

> — William Stevenson, Vice President of Publications, International Association of Amusement Parks & Attractions

"Nobody knows amusement parks better than Tim O'Brien. *The Amusement Park Guide* is the bible for park lovers, packed with details and rich with the distilled wisdom of O'Brien's many years following the industry . . ."

> — Gene Sloan, *USA Today*

"Tim's guidebook offers those rare and helpful insights that can only come from a skilled amusement park professional."

> — Janice Witherow, Public Relations Manager, Cedar Point

"Tim's attention to details an[d] training as a journalist. His c[ ] from his extensive knowledge o[f]

> — Sean Wood, *Fort Worth Star-Telegram* (Tex.)

"Tim's knowledge and experience in the amusement park industry is legendary."

> — Dick Kinzel, President and CEO, Cedar Fair, L.P.

HELP US KEEP THIS GUIDE UP TO DATE

Every effort has been made by the author and editors to make this guide as accurate and useful as possible. However, many things can change after a guide is published—parks close or new ones open, rides are added, management changes, etc.

We would love to hear from you concerning your experiences with this guide and how you feel it could be improved and be kept up to date. While we may not be able to respond to all comments and suggestions, we'll take them to heart and we'll also make certain to share them with the author. Please send your comments and suggestions to the following address:

The Globe Pequot Press
Editorial Department
P.O. Box 480
Guilford, CT 06437

Or you may e-mail us at:

editorial@globe-pequot.com

Thanks for your input, and enjoy the rides!

THE AMUSEMENT PARK GUIDE

Coast to Coast Thrills

Fifth Edition

TIM O'BRIEN

ALAMEDA FREE LIBRARY
2200-A CENTRAL AVENUE
ALAMEDA, CA 94501

The Globe Pequot Press

GUILFORD, CONNECTICUT

The prices listed in this guidebook were confirmed at press time. We recommend, however, that you call establishments before traveling to obtain current information.

Copyright © 1991, 1997, 1999, 2001, 2003 by Tim O'Brien

All rights reserved. No part of this book may be reproduced or transmitted in any form by any means, electronic or mechanical, including photocopying and recording, or by any information storage and retrieval system, except as may be expressly permitted by the 1976 Copyright Act or by the publisher. Requests for permission should be made in writing to The Globe Pequot Press, P.O. Box 480, Guilford, Connecticut 06437.

Text design by M. A. Dubé

This book makes reference to various Disney copyrighted characters, trademarks, and registered marks owned by The Walt Disney Company and Disney Enterprises, Inc.

ISBN 0-7627-2537-0

Manufactured in Canada
Fifth Edition/First Printing

To my daughters, Molly and Carrie,
who unselfishly volunteered to help me
research the amusement parks and
waterparks of North America,
and to my wife, Kathleen, for her
understanding and support when I leave
in the morning to go "to work."

The Globe Pequot Press and the author assume no liability for accidents happening to, or injuries sustained by, readers who engage in the activities described in this book.

CONTENTS

FOREWORD

FOR MORE THAN ONE HUNDRED years, one of the great summer traditions has been to pack up the family and head out to an amusement park for a day of fun, thrills, and memories. While much has changed at these parks over the past century, their basic appeal has pretty much remained the same.

Where else can you travel at speeds that would get you a ticket in the real world? Where else can you get soaked to the skin and not get yelled at by your mother? Where else can you sample such a delightful variety of food? Where else can you share that special moment when a loved one experiences a favorite ride for the first time? Yes, then as now, amusement parks provide a wonderful escape from the grind of everyday life and a basis for happy memories.

Today we are blessed with a huge variety of amusement parks, each with its own special personality and unique attractions to offer. The larger parks, such as Disneyland, Universal Studios, Cedar Point, and several Six Flags parks, are nearly a vacation unto themselves, with multi-million-dollar high-tech thrill rides.

But the smaller parks are also special and are not to be missed. Places like Kennywood, Lakeside, and Rye Playland offer nostalgic thrills on lovingly maintained historic rides that are quite rare in today's modern parks. Morey's Piers and Santa Cruz Beach Boardwalk still offer that classic seaside amusement park experience, while Knoebels and DelGrosso's offer some of the best food served in any amusement park.

That's what makes this book such a valuable resource. It gives you a chance to see what makes each park special. So whether you are heading out on a family vacation or just looking for a quick weekend getaway, take a look inside.

I have known Tim for more than ten years and our shared passion for amusement parks gives us a special bond. I always enjoy reading his books, as I believe he passes that passion to all of you. See you at the park!

Jim Futrell
Historian
National Amusement Park Historical Association

ACKNOWLEDGMENTS

AMUSEMENT PARK PEOPLE are indeed a unique bunch. They make their living by dedicating their lives to putting smiles on other people's faces while working virtually nonstop from spring through fall, with few hours or days away from the park. However, they are almost always eager to take time to share their little worlds with others, whether by providing a guided tour of their facility, or by talking in length on the phone.

Thanks to that spirit of sharing, my research team and I have been able once again to gather accurate and last-minute, up-to-date information for a new edition. We have received unprecedented help in putting this edition together and it is the largest, most comprehensive edition to date. Thanks to everyone out there who helped.

I have a lot of respect for my eagle-eyed research team of Adam Sandy, Jim Futrell, and Keith Miller. Their knowledge of this industry is staggering and I certainly was able to put together a better book because of their help. Thanks, guys!

And thanks to Joan Wheal, my editor, for her diligence and all the TLC.

INTRODUCTION

I'M OBVIOUSLY NOT ALONE in my passion for amusement and theme parks. In 2002, despite the drop in tourism and despite the dive in the economy, nearly 320 million visits were registered at North American parks. That's more than attended all professional football, basketball, baseball, and hockey games combined.

People often ask why I enjoy parks so much. That's a hard question to answer. I like the way they look. I like the way they sound. I like the way they smell, and I like what happens to me when I'm there. A park visit is a multisensory symphony and is truly one of the few experiences where I can escape from the cares of the outside world.

Even if I don't ride any rides, a park visit is a special experience. Parks are fabulous places to study mankind, to people watch. Sometimes that's more fun than a coaster ride. Few places offer the opportunity to observe so many people unabashedly enjoying themselves.

What exactly is the draw? Why are parks so popular, even in hard economic times? The simple answer is that they provide an experience that can't be replicated anywhere else. When you come through the turnstiles of a park, you are entering a unique atmosphere that you won't and can't find on the Internet, on TV, at the cinema, in the mall, or even at the county fair.

It's fantasy at its best and in the world today, true fantasy is hard to find. An amusement park is one of the few pieces of Americana still thriving today.

NEW STUFF!

Nearly all the listings in this Fifth Edition of The Amusement Park Guide *have been rewritten with new as well as updated material. More emphasis was placed on antique carousels and darkrides than in the past, and we provide a bit more specifics on coasters and other thrill rides this time around. Also, more than a dozen new listings have been added! Enjoy.*

As Senior Editor of *Amusement Business*, the leading business-to-business trade magazine for the international amusement park and theme park industry, I get the opportunity to visit the best the world has to offer and to meet and mingle with the greatest park pioneers of all time.

I visit parks mostly as part of my job, but even on assignment, with a camera and notepad in hand, I still experience the thrill of being there. I'm one of only two or three journalists in the entire world who get to chronicle parks on a full-time basis. I do for a living what other people do for vacations. Lucky, you say? You bet I am!

A Very Brief History of America's Amusement Parks

Most people today take for granted the sophisticated rides, shows, and attractions found in modern parks. With all the excitement a park has to offer, few people take the time to consider how the park or the rides came to be. Actually, the amusement park phenomenon has an interesting, albeit humble, beginning.

The roots of the amusement park industry go back to medieval times, when pleasure gardens began to spring up on the outskirts of major European cities. These gardens were forerunners of today's amusement parks, featuring live entertainment, fireworks, dancing, games, and even primitive amusement rides. Pleasure gardens remained extremely popular until the 1700s, when political unrest caused many of these parks to close. However, one of these parks remains: Opened in 1583, Bakken, north of Copenhagen, enjoys the status of being the world's oldest operating amusement park.

In the United States, during the nineteenth century, beach clubs were popular along the shores of New York. These clubs were gathering places to drink beer, play games, and socialize. By 1880, the Coney Island area of Brooklyn was becoming a popular resort area, and thousands made their way to the beaches every weekend during the summer. There was a plethora of entertainment pavilions at which those city folks who didn't want to swim could drink, socialize, and watch musical productions.

The first real "ride" didn't make it to the beach area until 1877, when a 300-foot-tall observatory from the Philadelphia Centennial Exposition was moved there and renamed the Iron Tower. Then in 1884, LaMarcus Thompson built a Switchback Railway ride, the forerunner of the roller coaster, in Coney Island. Others soon copied and improved

"The Howler," Holiday World and Splashin' Safari, Santa Claus, Indiana
Photo by Adam Sandy

on Thompson's railway idea. But it wasn't long until he was eager to enhance the concept even more. Two years later, in 1886, Thompson built a "real" roller coaster, and the success of that ride soon brought a steady stream of other amusement rides—and bigger crowds—to the beach.

By the late 1800s, the amusement park industry expanded to other areas in America. Following the Civil War, increased urbanization gave rise to electric traction (trolley) companies. At that time, utility companies charged the trolley companies a flat fee for the use of their electricity. As a result, the transportation companies looked for a way to stimulate weekend ridership. This resulted in the amusement park. Typically built at the end of the trolley line, amusement parks initially were simple operations consisting of picnic facilities, dance halls, restaurants, games, and a few amusement rides, often located on the shores of a lake or river. These parks were immediately successful and soon opened across America. Most survived the Great Depression, but by this time the automobile was increasing the scope of leisure time opportunities available to the public. The smaller parks started losing their weekend guests, who could now drive to a larger park, or to the beach 50 or 60 miles away.

Although many of the small parks closed, most of the strong, clean, well-run family operations continued to prosper. But by the early 1950s, only a small percentage of those early parks were still in operation, and many experts were writing death notices for the American amusement park. The parks couldn't compete, many thought, with motion pictures and television.

Along Came Walt

Then, in 1955, in southern California, Walt Disney combined color, fantasy, and excitement with food, rides, and shows, and put that combination into a safe, clean family environment. He called it Disneyland—and the theme park industry as we know it today was born.

When Disneyland first opened in 1955, many people were skeptical that an amusement park without any of the traditional attractions would succeed. But Disneyland was different. Instead of a midway, Disneyland offered five distinct themed areas, providing guests with the fantasy of travel to different lands and times. Disneyland was an immediate success.

Over the next several years, there were many failed attempts to copy Disneyland's success. It wasn't until 1961, when Six Flags Over Texas opened, that another theme park was successful. Throughout the 1960s and 1970s, theme parks were built in many major cities across America. Unfortunately, while these theme parks were opening, many of the grand old traditional amusement parks continued to close in the face of increased competition and urban decay.

During the same time, however, many of these traditional parks continued to thrive because the renewed interest in amusement parks in general brought people back to their local parks. Ironically, many of the older parks were able to borrow fresh ideas from the new theme parks and introduced new rides and attractions to their longtime patrons.

Although the large destination parks in the country today get most of the attention, the backbone of the industry is still the small, family-run park. On the whole, these parks are professional, well-run attractions but are unknown to most outside a small marketing area.

There are more of these small "traditional" parks, as they are called, than larger theme parks. Most often, though, they don't have themes and don't have many of the multimillion-dollar rides that are so abundant today. What they do have, however, is history, quaintness, and nostalgia. They are well-preserved examples of true Americana and provide visitors with great opportunities for low-key fun.

The Rides, Parks, and Other Things

Roller coasters are still the most popular rides in amusement parks, and the coaster resurgence of the late 1980s and early 1990s has left us with some mighty big, fast, and expensive thrill machines in the parks across America.

During the early 1990s, roller coaster designers, armed with new technology and powerful computers, were able to come up with all types of twists, turns, and rolls for the thrill-seekers. Riders were waiting for what the engineers could think of next to do to our bodies.

By 1992, engineers had developed the inverted roller coaster, one that allows riders to ride on the outside of the loop. Inverted coasters sit riders under the track, in a type of ski-lift seat that allows their feet to dangle beneath them as the coaster loops and twists its way along the track. Batman The Ride coasters at Six Flags were the first of these coasters.

By the mid-1990s, some of the emphasis turned away from twists and loops and a new trend toward speed and height became popular. Hypercoasters, 200-foot-tall superfast coasters with no inversions, began to challenge the super loopers for popularity. The Steel Force at Dorney Park, Allentown, Pennsylvania; Magnum XL200 at Cedar Point, Sandusky, Ohio; the Mamba at Worlds of Fun, Kansas City, Missouri; and The Wild Thing at Valleyfair!, Shakopee, Minnesota, are popular examples of the hypercoaster genre.

The creation of Linear Induction Motor–powered coasters allowed the traditional first-hill climb of a coaster to be eliminated, permitting greater speed and a larger coaster in a smaller footprint. With LIM power, coasters are catapulted out of the station; they reach 60 or 70 miles per hour in less than three or four seconds, giving the coaster train more than enough speed and momentum to go through the various elements.

Before this invention, the most common way a coaster could gain that kind of speed was to be pulled by chain to the top of a tall hill and then let gravity take over, creating the speed as it whooshed down the hill. Examples of LIM technology can be seen on the Flight of Fear coasters at two of the Paramount Parks and the Mr. Freeze coasters at two Six Flags parks.

In 1998, Journey to Atlantis at SeaWorld Adventure Park in Orlando, Florida, became the first roller coaster/water

"Haunted House," Camden Park, Huntington, West Virginia
Photo by Adam Sandy

flume combination ride. Passengers start out on what appears to be a traditional water flume ride, then the ride turns into a roller coaster, out of the water and on tracks. This technology allows for the best elements of both types of rides to be utilized. Ripshaw Falls at Silver Dollar City in Branson, Missouri, is another example of this type of ride.

In 1999, Six Flags Great Adventure in Jackson, New Jersey, premiered the new "floorless" coaster design. Riders on Medusa sit high on a pedestal on top of the train chassis with their feet dangling and no coaster car, per se, surrounding them. The ride, created by the same company that created the Batman inverted coaster, offers a totally new openness to the coaster experience.

Ushering in the new millennium, 2000 was a banner year for coaster innovations, and roller coaster designers outdid themselves. The first to open was Stealth, the first "flying" coaster, at Paramount's Great America in Santa Clara, California. Passengers climb aboard standing up, are turned 90 degrees, and experience the ride lying in a horizontal position as if they are flying. Paramount's Kings Island, near Cincinnati, Ohio, opened Son of Beast, the first wooden looping roller coaster since the Flip Flap experienced a short life during the early 1900s.

Cedar Point, in Sandusky, Ohio, premiered Millennium Force, the first continuous circuit roller coaster to top the 300-foot level. MF reaches 315 feet, offering a 300-foot drop at an astounding 80-degree angle. Passengers travel over 6,595 feet of track at 92 mph.

All coaster innovations in 2000 weren't high-speed thrill rides, however. The Nickelodeon Flying Super Saturator coaster at Paramount's Carowinds, Charlotte, North Carolina, is the first truly interactive roller coaster. The Rugrats-themed suspended coaster allows passengers to interact with the crowds below by dropping water bombs on them. Those on the ground can shoot water cannons at the coaster riders.

In spring 2001, Paramount's Kings Dominion, near Richmond, Virginia, debuted the world's first pneumatically launched coaster. The Hypersonic XLC propels riders, by air, from 0–80 mph in just 1.8 seconds. It's the first to be launched by air power, and it's the first to run on rubber aircraft tires instead of traditional steel or resin wheels.

In early 2002, the X coaster debuted at Six Flags Magic Mountain in Valencia, California. It provides the most innovative coaster ride ever created. Not only are passengers treated to a "normal" coaster ride, but along the way their individual seats flip forward 360 degrees when they least expect it!

The second generation of the flying coaster became a reality in 2002 with Six Flags Over Georgia, Atlanta, premiering the Superman–Ultimate Flight coaster to great success. Six Flags Elitch Gardens, Denver, Colorado, also premiered a smaller version of the flying coaster from a different manufacturer.

Indiana Beach, Monticello, Indiana, premiered the most innovative coaster in 2002, with the opening of the Lost Coaster of Superstition Mountain. The now defunct coaster company Custom Coasters created the ride, with an elevator lift, in the park's old darkride "mountain."

In 2003 more flying coasters were to premiere in Six Flags parks, and Cedar Point, Sandusky, Ohio, was to add its sixteenth coaster, Top Thrill Dragster, the world's first 400-foot-tall roller coaster. It only made sense; the park had already introduced to the world the first 200-foot-tall and the first 300-foot-tall coasters. Not to be outdone by Cedar Point, Six Flags Magic Mountain was to add its sixteenth coaster as well, a floorless coaster named Scream! Those two parks remain the coaster capitals with sixteen each, more than any other park on the planet.

Right behind roller coasters in popularity are the water-oriented rides found in so many parks today. More log flumes, raging rapids, and spill-water raft rides are being added each year. Usually equipped with a warning sign that proclaims YOU WILL GET WET, PROBABLY SOAKED, these rides offer a way to cool off during a hot summer's day at the park.

In addition to the amusement rides that run in and over the water, parks have been adding full-fledged waterparks and waterpark elements to their lineup of attractions. You must wear swimsuits to participate, and the parks have built bathhouses and locker rooms to accommodate the water lovers.

While some parks are building waterparks next door and charging a separate fee to get in, most are building water facilities within the gates of their existing parks and including them in the one-park admission. Parks have found that their repeat business and the sale of season passes have increased since adding the local "swimming holes" to their offerings.

The waterparks are great, especially during hot summers, when you would not ordinarily want to go to an amusement park. You can play in the water during the hot afternoon, and then as the sun goes down, go ride a few rides, have dinner, and enjoy the cooler evening in the ride park.

A good-size waterpark with dozens of elements can be built for the same cost as, or less than, a big roller coaster. Look for more parks to add waterparks in the future as part of their regular lineup.

Purpose of This Book

This book is intended to show off the parks of North America and to call attention to some of the great entertainment treasures hidden within our continent. Sure, you've probably heard of many of them, but unless you live near Valdosta, Georgia, chances are you've never heard of Wild Adventures Theme Park. And I'd wager that few people outside the Cleveland, Ohio, area are acquainted with the wonderful little Memphis Kiddie Park in the Brooklyn suburbs of that city. Have you ever heard of Lucy's Amusement Park in Minot, North Dakota? How about Cliff's Amusement Park in Albuquerque, New Mexico?

You'll be amazed and delighted by what's out there.

HOW TO USE THIS BOOK

IN AN EFFORT TO BE AS thorough as possible and to paint a realistic picture of amusement and theme parks, I've listed not only the larger, better-known facilities but also the small, family-owned parks offering just a few rides. Thus, you will find two types of listings in this book, major and minor.

The Minor Listings

The minor listings are for those parks that I feel are special enough to be included but that don't necessarily have as much to offer as the major parks. Some of these parks have only three or four rides, but because of their setting, theme, attractions, or activities, I felt they should be included.

✳ As you will discover, some of the neatest parks in the country have little more to offer than a few good rides and a great deal of atmosphere.

✳ Many of the waterparks listed in this book are located within amusement parks. If the waterpark is included in the admission price of the amusement park, its listing is included within that park's major listing. If a small water-park with only a few attractions is located within an amusement park, but still charges an extra fee, it is listed in that amusement park's listing, because of its size.

✳ If, however, an amusement park owns a major waterpark and either charges an additional price for its use, or if it is located away from the amusement park, the waterpark will have a separate listing, in alphabetical order, within that state.

✳ Most of the amusement park–owned waterparks listed in this volume that are not included in the admission price of the amusement park offer money-saving combination tickets that are good at both the waterpark and the amusement park.

The Major Listings

Most of the major listings are self-evident, but for a better overview, here are a few additional comments:

✳ Parks that are not year-round facilities are usually open on a weekend-only basis prior to Memorial Day and after Labor Day. I have listed the first and last days of seasonal operation; unless the listing specifies otherwise, assume the park is open only on weekends in the spring and fall.

✳ You will encounter three common types of admission policies. At pay-one-price parks, you'll pay one price at the gate that includes almost every ride, show, and attraction.

✳ Parks that charge general admission require you to pay one fee, usually less than $5.00, and then pay extra for rides and attractions. Quite often, general admission permits you to enjoy most of the live shows and productions; usually, a pay-one-price ride ticket is available once you get into the park, or you can play on a pay-as-you-go basis.

✳ Parks that allow free admission charge nothing to get in; you pay for anything you want to do as you go. Again, pay-one-price ride tickets are often available.

✳ Probably in no other business today do open hours fluctuate as much as in the amusement park industry. In listing these hours, I've tried to be as exact as possible; nevertheless, to list some parks' hours would take an entire paragraph. So if you plan to visit a park either early or late in the day, or before Memorial Day or after Labor Day, be sure to call first. Also, although the hours and admission fees listed in this guide were confirmed at press time, it's generally a good idea to call for the most current information before traveling.

✳ Those of you who aren't yet "parkies" (amusement park fanatics) need to know that roller coasters are shown with a "(W)" for wood and an "(S)" for steel. Parkies know these things.

Something Extra

You are holding in your hands the world's only animated, interactive amusement park guidebook! Turn it on its side, flip the pages, and watch the coaster zip down the page. You'll have to add your own screams, however. We haven't figured out a way to do that yet!

Tim's Ten Tips on How To Make Your Amusement Park Trip More Fun

HERE ARE TEN TOP TIPS on how to make your trip to an amusement park a bit easier, a little less tiring, and a lot more fun.

1. Wear comfortable shoes; you'll be walking a lot.

2. Plan your day. Pick up a guidebook when you buy your tickets and plot out what rides and shows you want to experience. Some shows are only performed once or twice during the day.

3. Dress for the day, but plan for cooler (warmer) and wetter weather. Bring backup clothes and shoes and keep them in your car or in a locker, just in case.

4. Use sunscreen, wear a hat, and drink lots of water.

5. Don't eat between noon and 2:30 P.M. That's when everyone else gets hungry and the lines are the longest. That means the ride lines are shorter, so go for it!

6. Make a mental note of the number of the car in which you ride. If you lose something, it makes retrieving it much easier.

7. Many larger parks sell their tickets off-premises at grocery stores, convenience stores, and hotels. You can usually get them there for less, plus it's one less line you'll need to stand in at the park.

THE AMUSEMENT PARK GUIDE

8. Use the park's virtual queue systems, which allow you to make a reservation or save you a spot in a queue. Some charge extra for the privilege, but it's usually worth it.

9. Follow the rules; they are made for safety reasons. In some states if you cause an accident or an injury, you can be held liable! Don't lock your brain in the trunk on your way in.

10. Check the Internet or call customer service before you head to the park to check out any special events that may be going on or promotional prices that may be available.

TiM'S TEN TiPS ON MAKING THE DAY HAPPIER AND SAFER FOR THE KIDS

IF YOU CAN HELP make the day more pleasant for the kids, chances are it will be a better day for you as well. With that in mind, here are ten hints to help you save the day.

1. If they are to go off on their own, give your kids specific information on when and where to meet you. Mark it on a map and they won't have an excuse.

2. Point out the park's uniformed employees and instruct your kids to report to one of those workers if they get lost or need any sort of help during the day.

3. Hauling around souvenirs can be an unpleasant experience. Instruct your family that they can each buy a souvenir, but only on their way out to the car after a day in the park.

4. Take them to the rest room before getting in a long waiting line. You know what will happen if you don't.

5. Make sure they understand what the ride does and how it works before spending time in line. It's frustrating if they decide not to ride after a long wait. Let them closely watch first.

6. Never force children to ride something they don't want to ride. It could leave a very bad impression on them and scare them off rides forever. Plus, it's just not a nice thing to do.

7. If your child wants to ride, but isn't quite sure, alert the ride attendant to watch the child and stop the ride if it appears to be traumatizing the child. You pay attention as well.

THE AMUSEMENT PARK GUIDE

8. Your visit is not a marathon. Chances are you're there for the kids, so listen to them and let them rest, eat, drink, or whatever when they need to.

9. Instruct the children on safety requirements. Explain height limitations, about not getting off before the ride comes to a complete stop, and about not standing up while the ride is in motion. Help them realize the rules are there for their own safety.

10. Many parks have child locater devices you can rent and at any time during the day, you can walk up to a monitor and scan the park for the location of your child. If you are worried about sending children off on their own, this device could give you some comfort.

Tim's Top Five Non-Roller-Coaster Rides

1. **Spider-Man Adventure,** Universal Orlando Resort's Islands of Adventure, Orlando, Florida (p. 65)

   The most technically advanced attraction in the world. It combines ride vehicles, 3-D film, live action, and special effects, all in one great indoor 1.5-acre adventure. It's an amazing high-tech experience that seems almost real! Watch out for the "sensory drop," a 400-foot plunge into total darkness. WOW!

2. **Pirates of the Caribbean,** The Disneyland Resort, Anaheim, California (p. 14) /Walt Disney World Resort, Lake Buena Vista, Florida (p. 67)

   A dark boat ride through the loud, crazy, and often scary life of the pirate. It's nicely paced, nice and cool, and marked by a great theme song.

3. **Cedar Downs,** Cedar Point Amusement Park & Resort, Sandusky, Ohio (p. 196)

   A large, fast carousel whose horses move back and forth and actually race one another as the ride spins. One of only two such rides left in the country, this one was built in 1925; the other one can be found at Playland Park, Rye, New York.

4. **Journey to Atlantis,** SeaWorld Adventure Park, Orlando, Florida (p. 60)

   This wonderfully themed ride is one of total surprises! First you're on the water, splashing along until you drop over a 60-foot-tall waterfall, then you're on a high-speed roller-coaster track, then you're back in the water. This is the first ride of its kind in the world and is a must-ride if you're in the area.

5. **Skooters,** Knoebels Amusement Resort, Elysburg, Pennsylvania (p. 231)

   There are two ways you can identify a quality bumper-car operation: First, you smell the graphite when you get within 20 feet of the place. Second, the cars must be the classic Lusse Skooter cars, in near-perfect condition. Knoebels passes the test on both counts.

THE CAROUSEL PRIMER

While there have been many carousel carvers through the years, most fit into one of three general categories:

* **The Philadelphia Style:** This was based on realism, with attention paid to translating the physical characteristics of the actual horses into wood.
* **The Coney Island Style:** This style combined the Philadelphia style with whimsy, adding more gold, characteristics, and flamboyance, much like the famous amusement area in which it evolved.
* **The County Fair Style:** This was the most simple of the three styles. Instead of focusing on artistry, the county fair carvers were concerned with simple interpretations of the horses.

The Most Notable Carousel Carvers

* **Dentzel,** 1870: Gustav Dentzel's company, the G.A. Dentzel, Steam and Horsepower Carousell Builder, started creating entire machines. He was known for elegant Philadelphia-style horses and unique menagerie figures. One of the company's best-kept machines is a 3-row 1909 carousel at Libertyland in Memphis, Tennessee. This was built the same year that Gustav passed away and his son William took over the business.
* **Looff,** 1876: Charles Looff, a carver and carousel entrepreneur, installed Coney Island's first carousel, a menagerie machine in Balmer's Bathing Pavilion. This was one of dozens that would soon dot the island. One of the carver's most famous machines still runs in Rhode Island. Built for Crescent Park in 1895, the ride operates with a Ruth & Sohn band organ and a ring machine. This Philadelphia-style machine was Looff's "working catalogue." He brought potential customers to the carousel from across the country to let them choose what they wanted on their machine.
* **Dare,** Circa 1890: Charles Dare moved his operations to Brooklyn. While the Coney Island carvers he lived near were known for expressive horses, Dare's were simple; he defined the county fair style. The oldest operating carousel in the country, the Flying Horses of Martha's Vineyard, opened in 1876 and was carved by

Dare. The 2-row machine has run in the Vineyard since 1884 and riders can still try to catch the brass ring.

✳ Herschell/Spillman Company, 1900: Allan Herschell re-formed with new partners as the Herschell/Spillman Company following the bankruptcy of the Armitage/Herschell Company. This company was not known for elaborate horses, but was productive and spread the county fair style throughout the United States. It built hundreds of carousels for both parks and carnivals, and many are still in operation today. One of the best-maintained carousels from the company is the 1915, 3-row menagerie machine at Myrtle Beach Pavilion in Myrtle Beach, South Carolina. The ride features horses as well as menagerie animals such as a giraffe, lion, rooster, and frog.

✳ William F. Mangels' Patents, 1901: The father of amusements, William Mangels, patented a device that allowed carousel horses to "gallop." While there were several other devices patented, Mangels' was the version adopted by most of the American amusement industry and it was improved upon in 1907. It helped put an end to carousels with standing-only horses. Mangels built frames and bought horses from carvers like Illions and Carmel. Today Mangels' B&B Carousell still spins on Surf Avenue at Coney Island only a few blocks from where his factory stood.

✳ The Philadelphia Toboggan Company, 1904: PTC was formed by Henry Auchy and Chester E. Albright and produced approximately 100 carousels between its inception and 1933, when the company stopped producing carousels. Throughout its history PTC employed great carvers like Leo Zoller, John Zalar, and Daniel Muller. Today the company's machines are common throughout the country at parks of all sizes. Two of the most famous are #17 at Six Flags Over Georgia (1908, 5-row) and #47 at Hersheypark (1919, 4-row). Both combine gorgeous horses with beautiful frames and showcase the elegant simplicity of which PTC was capable.

✳ Charles Carmel, 1905: Carmel opened his shop in Brooklyn, just south of Prospect Park. Carmel carved for many people and was able to freely float between styles; his horses had characteristics from both the Philadelphia and Coney Island formats. Sadly, there are few carousels left with only Carmel horses, with the surviving crown jewel from this master carver running at Playland Park in Rye, New York. The beautiful 4-row machine, sporting a Gavioli band organ, dates from 1915 and was moved to the park for the 1928 season. It is considered by many to be the most beautiful in the country.

✳ **Stein & Goldstein,** 1907: Solomon Stein and Harry Goldstein stopped freelancing for other manufacturers and opened their own shop, Stein & Goldstein Artistic Carousel Manufacturers. Although they only built carousels through 1918, their rides had an impact. The difference between these carvers and their contemporaries was that their carvings, while based loosely on the Coney Island style, were large. Many of their horses had huge structures, muscles, and floral arrangements on their bodies. Today the pair's rides run in several places around the country. One of the most famous is the Central Park Carousel in New York City; a 4-row machine that opened at the park in 1908 after being moved from Coney Island. Another fine example of their work is the beautiful 3-row machine at Bushnell Park in Hartford, Connecticut. This carousel has been beautifully restored and is the best example of Stein & Goldstein's work today.

✳ **M.C. Illions & Sons Inc.,** 1909: After collaborating with others in the amusement industry, Marcus Illions opened his own factory, which carved horses in the Coney Island style through 1929. Some of Illions's horses can be seen on the Dr. Floyd Moreland Carousel on the Casino Pier in Seaside Heights, New Jersey. These beautiful carvings are on a Dentzel frame and mixed with the works of other carvers. Another treasure is in Bonfante Gardens in Gilroy, California. This well-run machine is one of three Supreme carousels and was built shortly before Marcus stopped constructing new rides.

Courtesy: Adam Sandy

Ten of the Most Important Dates in Roller-Coaster History

✳ **1873,** The Mauch Chunk Railway, Mauch Chunk, Pennsylvania: This rail line, which originally carried coal, started carrying passengers in search of beautiful views of the mountains. Although it was not technically a roller coaster, the positive response and income the

Mauch Chunk earned was no doubt an inspiration to later designers. The ride ran down the mountainside until 1929 and had a perfect safety record.

✳ **1884,** The Switchback Railway, Brooklyn, New York: LaMarcus Adna Thompson, the father of the modern roller coaster, opened the Switchback Railway at Coney Island. The ride consisted of 2 parallel point-to-point tracks. During this time Coney Island was a place where many roller coaster designers built their own versions of the ride. Although recent patent evidence indicates that Thompson may not have built the first ride, the majority of primary sources still point to him as the creator of America's first roller coaster.

✳ **1901,** Loop the Loop, Brooklyn, New York: The first clothoid looped coaster was created by designer Edward Prescott. Several designers had built looping coasters before this time, and all had been unsuccessful. The problem was that many rides, such as the Flip Flap in Sea Lion Park at Coney Island, were built with circular loops. Prescott understood that the forces would be better applied to the human body if the track were built in the shape of a clothoid (elliptical) loop. Prescott used flat iron to make his track and built it along Coney Island's main thoroughfare at Surf Avenue and West 10th Street, the current location of Astroland Amusement Park.

✳ **June 6, 1907,** Drop the Dip, Brooklyn, New York: It stood 60 feet tall and had a series of drops and turns very different from the gentle rolling hills that were commonplace on the coasters of the day. Coaster historian Robert Cartmell writes that Christopher Feucht saw a model of this coaster in the office of his dentist, Dr. Welcome Mosley. Intrigued by the dentist's unusual design, Feucht partnered with him to build what most consider the first modern roller coaster.

✳ **1959, Matterhorn,** Disneyland, Anaheim, California: Using tubular steel, this was a watershed in coaster construction that made steel coasters popular as alternatives to the traditional wooden coaster. It also set the stage for the ability to create multiple ride elements, which only a steel-tracked ride could provide. Within two years of opening the park, Walt Disney wanted a family roller coaster. His Imagineers looked at many styles but eventually contacted Arrow Development, a company that had built many of Disneyland's darkrides, to build the coaster. To make the ride a smooth experience for the family, Arrow designed the new style of tubular steel track, one still used by most major designers today.

✳ **April 29, 1972,** The Racer, Kings Island, near Cincinnati, Ohio: The second golden age of roller coasters is said to have started on this day. Kings Island was the first modern-day theme park to open with a major wooden roller coaster. The ride featured 2 parallel white tracks that ran the length of the park's northern border. It quickly became a darling of the media and was seen in national newspapers, in magazines, and on television shows. The Racer helped the wooden roller coaster make a comeback after being sidelined by steel coasters for many years.

✳ **1975,** Arrow Corkscrews: Steel coasters grew in popularity during the 1960s and by the early 1970s park owners were asking for a unique take on the popular rides. Arrow Development came up with its corkscrew coasters. These were simple rides that featured only a drop and 2 corkscrews, but they were significant because they inverted riders for the first time since the early 1900s. Three opened for the 1975 season at Knott's Berry Farm in Buena Park, California, Old Chicago in Chicago, Illinois, and Opryland in Nashville, Tennessee.

✳ **June 15, 1985,** The Phoenix, Knoebels Amusement Resort, Elysburg, Pennsylvania: Owner Dick Knoebel wanted a wooden coaster for his park, but decided to buy an old one because a new one was out of his price range. After looking throughout the United States, Knoebel decided on the Rocket coaster at the defunct Playland Park in San Antonio, Texas. The ride was dismantled, moved, and rebuilt for a cost of $1.5 million. Today the Phoenix is recognized as one of the best wooden coasters in the country. The choice to move and rebuild a roller coaster, called impossible by many in the industry, showed other parks that this was an affordable option.

✳ **May 6, 1989,** Magnum XL200, Cedar Point, Sandusky, Ohio: This park shattered many records when this ride, its ninth coaster, opened. It was the fifth in the park from manufacturer Arrow Dynamics. The ride was inspired in part by the traditional out-and-back style of wooden roller coasters. The Magnum was the first coaster in the world to feature a 200-foot drop, while offering a series of hills that provided air time in abundance within a simple layout. It remains one of the most popular rides in the country.

✳ May 6, 1995, The Raven, Holiday World, Santa Claus, Indiana: While not the tallest or fastest wooden roller coaster, the Raven has proven that size does not matter. This park looked at various options for its first wooden coaster and eventually decided on one that used the terrain to its advantage. Owner Will Koch was inspired by many coasters, especially The Beast at Paramount's Kings Island, and wanted a coaster that stood out in the minds of riders. With its tunnel, lakeside turn, 60-foot drop midway through the ride, and mad dash back to the station, the Raven, built by Custom Coasters, was an instant success. It showed many small-park owners that a wooden roller coaster was an affordable investment that could build attendance.

Courtesy: Adam Sandy

Ten of the More Notable Theme/Amusement Parks

1. Busch Gardens, The Old Country,
Williamsburg, Virginia (p. 274)

Acres and acres of beautifully mature trees, colorful flowers, and intricate Old World theming, combined nicely with high-tech rides and attractions make it unique. Great shopping for quality gift items from Europe.

2. Cedar Point Amusement Park & Resort,
Sandusky, Ohio (p. 196)

More rides and more roller coasters than any other amusement park on the planet. One of the oldest continuously operated parks in the United States. Plenty of mature trees, classic rides, and turn-of-the-twentieth-century architecture.

3. The Disneyland Resort, Anaheim, California (p. 14)

The original Disneyland park now has a couple of sisters. Downtown Disney is a fun entertainment zone that you'll now pass through on your way to the original park and Disney's California Adventure, the new park full of great rides and some amazing

architecture. *Disneyland was great by itself—now there's even more to do.*

4. Holiday World and Splashin' Safari, Santa Claus, Indiana (p. 97)

Formerly known as Santa Claus Land, the 50-plus-year-old family-owned park is widely considered America's first theme park. The clean, beautifully kept park features three wooded, themed areas celebrating three holidays: Christmas, July 4th, and Halloween. The Raven is the only Edgar Allan Poe–themed roller coaster in the world.

5. Santa Cruz Beach Boardwalk, Santa Cruz, California (p. 31)

As the last surviving major seaside park in California, this mile-long collection of rides and attractions along the boardwalk has been providing entertainment for Northern Californians since 1907 and is truly a nostalgic gem. Both its circa 1924 wooden roller coaster and its circa 1911 carousel have been designated National Historic Landmarks. Now with more than 30 rides, the park's owners have blended the old and the new successfully into a unique experience.

6. Knoebels Amusement Resort, Elysburg, Pennsylvania (p. 231)

A traditional park at its finest, with free admission, plenty of classic rides, and beautiful surroundings. It has the best bumper cars in the world, and possibly the best pizza you'll ever eat!

7. Morey's Piers, Wildwood, New Jersey (p. 153)

This quintessential seaside resort has 4 piers, a boardwalk, and a lot of nostalgia. The Morey family has taken a grass-roots approach to building their amusement dynasty, building and creating a little bit more each year for more than fifty years. There are more than 100 rides and 2 waterparks on the piers, and because space is at a premium, the rides and attractions have been built over, under, and through all the others. Quite an engineering feat!

8. Wild Adventures, Valdosta, Georgia (p. 84)

In less than ten years, this privately owned, year-round park in south Georgia went from a tranquil, rural horse farm to a major family fun park with 55 rides including 7 roller coasters. Now drawing more than a million visitors a year, there are five parks here: a zoo, a ride park, a concert park with forty-plus major concerts a year, a family entertainment center with go-karts, and a waterpark.

9. Universal Orlando Resort, Orlando, Florida (p. 63)

Universal Studios Florida theme park has been joined by a new sister park, Islands of Adventure. Both fall under the umbrella of Universal Orlando. The "new" park has been built on a series of islands full of rides and themed areas and two world-class roller coasters. The "old" park, created both as a theme park and a working film studio, still has some of the best custom-created rides in the world. The two parks sit side-by-side, with the entertainment-packed City Walk serving as a gateway for both.

10. Walt Disney World Resort, Lake Buena Vista, Florida (p. 67)

The largest resort complex in the world continues to get larger. In 1998, the 500-acre Disney's Animal Kingdom was added to the other offerings within the 48-square-mile Disney complex. The "new species" of theme park joined Magic Kingdom, Epcot, and Disney–MGM Studio Theme Park in the list of the Top ten most-attended theme parks in the world.

North America's Oldest Operating Roller Coasters

(In operation at the same location)

1. **Leap the Dips,** Lakemont Park, Altoona, Pennsylvania, 1902 (p. 233)
2. **Jack Rabbit,** Clementon Amusement Park, Clementon, New Jersey, 1919 (p. 157)
3. **Jack Rabbit,** Seabreeze Amusement Park, Rochester, New York, 1920 (p. 180)
4. **Jack Rabbit,** Kennywood, West Mifflin, Pennsylvania, 1921 (p. 229)
5. **Roller Coaster,** Lagoon Park, Farmington, Utah, 1921 (p. 271)

Courtesy: National Amusement Park Historical Association

North America's Oldest Amusement Parks

(Continuously operated)

1. **Lake Compounce,** Bristol, Connecticut, 1846 (p. 49)
2. **Cedar Point,** Sandusky, Ohio, 1870, (p. 196)
3. **Idlewild Park,** Ligonier, Pennsylvania, 1878, (p. 228)
4. **Seabreeze Park,** Rochester, New York, 1879, (p. 180)
5. **Dorney Park,** Allentown, Pennsylvania, 1884, (p. 223)

Courtesy: National Amusement Park Historical Association

Three of the Most Notable Darkrides in North America

✳ **Knoebels Haunted Mansion/House,** Knoebels Amusement Resort, Elysburg, Pennsylvania: The Knoebels family showed the industry that a traditional darkride still has a place in today's amusement parks. From its in-house construction to the recycling of gags from defunct rides to the wonderful props constructed of cast-off items, this ride shows that a good darkride doesn't have to cost millions.

✳ **Disney's Haunted Mansion,** Disneyland, Anaheim, California, and Walt Disney World, Lake Buena Vista, Florida: This ride is the root of the modern darkride. Disney showed us how computers and animatronics can really bring a darkride to life. This ride blends modern electronics with century-old illusions into a fascinating family ride. Disney proved that the old-fashioned darkride has a place in a modern theme park and that it could be done with high capacity without sacrificing the quality of the ride.

✳ **The Old Mill,** Kennywood, West Mifflin, Pennsylvania: This is the granddaddy of many of today's attractions and is one of the last remaining "tunnels of love." This water darkride has entertained several generations of parkgoers during its century of operation. While the scenes have changed many times during its history, the ride's wooden troughs still offer a chance to relive the olden days and to discover that the darkness has the same appeal today as it did to young couples 100 years ago.

Courtesy: Darkride and Funhouse Enthusiasts

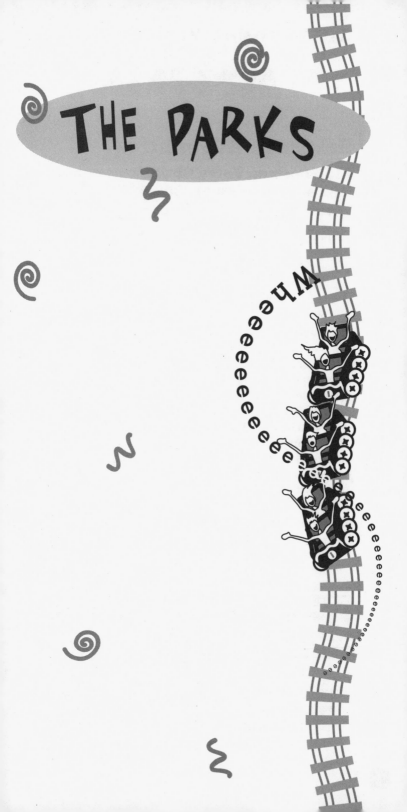

THE PARKS

Wheeeeeeeeeeeeeeeeeeeeeeeeeeeee

ALABAMA

Southern Adventures

**2150 Leeman Ferry Circle
Huntsville, AL (256) 880–6599
www.southernadventures.net**

There's a lot of punch in this small family park. During summer you can splash around at the Adventure Island waterpark, featuring three, 320-foot-long open flume slides and a 180-foot-long enclosed tube slide, as well as 2 kiddie slides and a children's playground. After drying off you can play Peg-Leg's Trail or the Alabama Amazon, both 18-hole miniature golf courses; test your mountaineering skills on The Rock, a new rock-climbing wall; or test your driving skills at 2 go-kart tracks. If you're a golfer try a different type of driving at the Full Swing, a golf simulator, or choose from bumper cars, batting cages, a MaxFlight coaster simulator, an arcade, a soft-play area for children, and 7 amusement rides, including 3 for kids.

Waterpark admission is under $13, with an after 5:00 P.M. price of $6.00, and admission to all other attractions is on a pay-as-you-go basis. There are also several special packages and special event prices from which to choose. The waterpark is open from Memorial Day through Labor Day, and the rest of the facility is open year-round. Operating hours change, so call ahead to see what's open the day you want to visit.

 TiM'S TRiViA

The most-attended theme park in the world is the Magic Kingdom at Walt Disney World in Florida, with approximately 15 million people visiting each year. The most-attended waterpark in North America is Blizzard Beach, at Walt Disney World, with attendance of nearly 2 million each year. Disney rules!

VisionLand Theme Park
Splash Beach Water Park
Magic Adventure Theme Park

5051 Prince Street
Bessemer, AL (205) 481–4750

Following several years of financial problems, capped off with a 2002 bankruptcy, the 35-acre park found a new owner in late 2002 who promises to reopen the park in 2003 and to reinvest in it. Team ProParks, the new owner, is adding a wave pool to the waterpark for 2003, it plans to separate the waterpark from the amusement park and charge individual admissions to both, with the Celebration Street area, which separates the two, having free admission.

The complex now includes Splash Beach and Magic Adventure, and includes more than 25 rides, including Rampage, the tallest and fastest wooden roller coaster in the state, and the Sky Wheel, a 120-foot-tall Ferris wheel that provides a great panoramic view of the park.

The Celebration Street entrance area was built to resemble a small Alabama town and includes everything from an old theater facade to a 1950s-era high school, which contains the park's 10,000-square-foot arcade. Marvel City is a great area for family rides including Marvel Mania, a kiddie roller coaster; crank cars; bumper cars; and a hot air balloon–shaped Ferris wheel. Celebration City contains the games and thrill rides area.

Splash Beach is a 7-acre waterpark themed as an early steel production facility. Its attractions include tube slides, interactive water play elements, an endless river, and an interactive family activity pool with a 1,000-gallon bucket that dumps water on everyone below every 10 minutes. Rides in the park include Hurricane Rapids, a rapids ride; Cahaba Falls, a log ride and Fender Bender bumper cars.

 Roller coasters: Rampage (W); Marvel Mania, kiddie (S).

The park is expected to reopen over Memorial Day weekend and remain open through September, with weekend operation in late August and September. Located 16 miles southwest of Birmingham. Take exit 108 off I–20/59 and follow signs to park.

Waterville USA

906 Gulf Shores Parkway
Gulf Shores, AL (251) 948–2106
www.watervilleusa.com

Once you enter the 14-acre complex you'll realize there's a lot more here than what the name implies. Sure, there's plenty of cool, clear water, but you'll also find a miniature golf course, a go-kart track, an indoor laser tag arena, a large games arcade, an Ejection Seat, a motion-based simulator, a Trampoline Thing, and 5 kiddie rides.

The waterpark has 9 slides, a wave pool, a lazy river, and a children's activity pool with slides and crawls.

Amusement park is open 10:00 A.M. to midnight. Waterpark open daily 10:00 A.M. to 6:00 P.M., Memorial Day through Labor Day. All activities on a pay-as-you-play basis, pay-one-price at the waterpark, under $22; after 3:00 P.M., under $15.

 Roller coaster: The Cannonball (W).

ALASKA

H₂Oasis Indoor Waterpark

1520 O'Malley Road
Anchorage, AK (907) 344–8610/
(888)–H2OASIS
www.h2oasiswaterpark.com

Billing itself as a "tropical island in the last frontier," this new indoor facility can easily make you forget you're in the frigid north. With all water heated to 84 degrees, this is a full-fledged action-packed waterpark.

It has a Master Blaster uphill water coaster, a 575-foot-long Lazy River, a wave pool that puts out 3- to 4-foot waves, a children's lagoon with a pirate ship and kiddie slides, enclosed body slides, a spa, tanning beds, a food court, and a game room.

Open daily, 10:00 A.M. to 10:00 P.M.; it's under $20 for a full-day visit.

Pioneer Park

Airport Way and Peger Road
Fairbanks, AK (907) 459-1087

In celebration of the hundredth anniversary of the purchase of Alaska from Russia, this 44-acre historical park was founded in 1967 as Alaskaland and changed its name to Pioneer Park in the early 2000s to better reflect its mission.

The eclectic offerings here include 2 family rides—the Crooked Creek and Whiskey Island Railroad, a narrow-gauge train trip around the park—and a circa 1911 antique carousel. Elsewhere in the park are a playground, a native village, a mining valley, an art gallery, and a miniature golf course.

A vaudeville-style show on the state's history is presented daily during peak season, and the park is home to the famous Alaska Salmon Bake, served daily. While some of the offerings are open year-round, the rides and outdoor activities operate daily, from Memorial Day to Labor Day, 11:00 A.M. to 9:00 P.M. Call for admission prices.

ARIZONA

Castles & Coasters

9445 Metro Parkway East
Phoenix, AZ (602) 997-7575
www.castlesncoasters.com

Both the castle and the coasters can be spotted as you pull up to this 7-acre complex, located across from the huge Metrocenter regional mall.

In addition to the state's only looping roller coaster, the park features a log flume, a Sea Dragon, several kiddie rides, a family roller coaster, bumper cars, a Magic Carpet ride, and a beautiful carousel with 60 hand-painted horses and circus animals. There are also a go-kart track, bumper boats, and 4 miniature golf courses.

The entrance is marked by a mammoth stucco castle with big blue fiberglass turrets, which houses the multitude of arcade games and a few smaller attractions.

Open 365 days a year. Golf opens at 10:00 A.M., rides open at noon. Closing times vary. Rides priced individually, or an all-day ride and golf pass may be purchased under $25.

 Roller coasters: Desert Storm, 2-loop (S); Patriot, junior (S).

Enchanted Island

In Encanto Park
1202 West Encanto Boulevard
Phoenix, AZ (602) 254–2020
www.enchantedisland.com

The circa 1948 Allan Herschell "Little Beauty" carousel, which has been here in Encanto Park since it was created, stands as the centerpiece of this top-notch little fun park created for families with young children. Occupying a 6-acre island, the amusement park is on the former site of the Encanto Kiddieland, which opened in 1933 and closed in 1987. Enchanted Island opened in 1991, with the Little Beauty completely renovated and raring to go.

Today there are 10 rides, including the carousel, a C.P. Huntington train, Parachute Tower, miniwheel, Red Baron airplanes, bumper boats, and a mini-Enterprise.

Open year-round; hours and days of operation vary greatly with the seasons and day of week. During the summer months, opening hours tend to be later, due to the heat. Admission is free, with rides on a pay-as-you-play basis, or an all-day wristband, under $11. Individual tickets cost $1, with each ride taking 1–3 tickets.

Old Tucson Studios

201 South Kinney Road
Tucson, AZ (520) 883–0100
www.oldtucson.com

Created in 1939 as the set for the film *Arizona*, and then the site for subsequent Western films, the studio today is a fun and action-packed family theme park with gunfight shows, cancan dancers, Western song sing-alongs, and a stunt show that reveals how the Hollywood stunt actors do their thing.

A summer-long concert series featuring top-name rock and country acts takes place in the 4,400-seat amphitheater, with the magnificent Tucson Mountains serving as a backdrop.

Through the years more than 350 films, TV shows, and commercials have been filmed here and it still serves as an active film studio. A film showing the history of the studio is part of the official tour.

Mechanical rides include a carousel, antique cars, a 15-minute ride on a C.P. Huntington train, the Iron Door Mine Adventure darkride, and a canoe adventure. In addition there are pony rides and a fun stagecoach ride that offers up a few surprises. Thirty-minute trail rides into the mountains and an opportunity to pan for gold are available for an extra fee.

Open year-round, with special Halloween and Christmas events and activities. Opens daily at 10:00 A.M., closes at various times depending on season. Pay-one-price, under $16. To find the park, take the Speedway Boulevard exit off I–10, go west 12 miles. When Speedway dead-ends, take a left, and the park is about ¼ mile on the left.

ARKANSAS

Burns Park Funland
Funland Drive
North Little Rock, AR (501) 753–7307

The folks of North Little Rock have quite the treasure with Burns Park, a 1,562-acre city park with all the amenities that you would expect from a large park of this sort.

Nestled into a few acres is a simple and traditional little amusement area. Funland opened in 1964 and several of its 12 rides, such as the traditional Pretzel darkride, The Spook House, date back to opening day. Among the other rides are a carousel, a great train ride, Flying Scooters, Tilt-A-Whirl, Scrambler, Tubs-O-Fun for the kids, and bumper boats.

Open March through mid-October; opens daily during the summer at 11:00 A.M., closing at 5:00 P.M. during the week,

6:00 P.M. on weekends. Free gate admission with everything on a pay-as-you-go basis. Take the Burns Park exit off I–40; follow signs to the park and then to Funland.

Magic Springs and Crystal Falls

**1701 East Grand Avenue
Hot Springs, AR (501) 624–0100
www.magicsprings.com**

You get three parks in one here. There's a full-scale waterpark, there's a 22-ride amusement park, and everything is located within the 4,700-acre Hot Springs National Park.

The old Magic Springs closed in 1995, but new owners came in, renovated, rebuilt, added new rides, attractions, and a waterpark, and in 2000 opened to the public to great success.

Developed on 140 heavily wooded rolling acres, the two parks offer a full day's worth of fun for the entire family. In 2003 a new amphitheater was to open in a natural bowl area of the park and a big-name concert series was to be held, with admission to the park being your ticket to the concert.

Between the two parks, there are a total of 80 rides and attractions, including 22 mechanical rides. Among the more popular rides are Dr. Dean's Rocket Machine, a 100-foot-tall shot and drop tower; Old No. 2 Logging Company log flume; Rum Runner pirate ship; Razorback Round-Up bumper cars; Magic Swings giant swing ride; and the Kit n' Kaboodle Express kiddie train ride.

 Roller coasters: Arkansas Twister (W); Big Bad John, mine train (S); Twist n' Shout, wild mouse (S); Diamond Mine Run, kiddie (S).

In Crystal Falls, Crystal Cove is the 350,000-gallon wave pool, the High Sierra is a water slide complex, Grizzly Creek is an interactive family splash zone, and the Kodiak Canyon Adventure is an action river with rapids and waterfalls.

Both parks are included in the admission charge, under $30. Open May through September, the park runs daily from Memorial Day through mid-August.

CALIFORNIA

Adventure City

10120 South Beach Boulevard
Stanton, CA (714) 236–9300
www.adventurecity.com

Kids have quite a place to call their own here! The owners have done a great job building educational programs and disguising them as fun times. Even a spin on an amusement ride here is part of an overall lesson of some sort. It shows that learning can be fun. Great job.

Kids can pilot a barnstormer or take to the skies in the Balloon Race at the airport, pilot an emergency vehicle on the 911 Ride, see the city from the Crazy Bus, or take the train around town. There are 9 rides in all, including the Kid's Coaster and the circa 1946, 20-horse Allan Herschell carousel. Other attractions include face painting, live shows, a petting zoo, and the Thomas the Tank Engine play area.

 Roller coasters: Freeway Coaster, junior (S); Tree Top Racers, wild mouse (S).

The park is located down the street from Knott's Berry Farm and is open year-round, daily in the summer, and weekends and select days in winter and spring. Hours vary, so call first. A pay-one-price admission, including face painting, petting farm, live theater, and unlimited use of all rides, costs under $13.

 # TiM'S TRiViA

The amusement industry's leading trade magazine, Amusement Business, provides a free e-mail news service for late-breaking amusement park news. Whenever news happens you'll be among the first to know. Sign up at www.amusementbusiness.com and be notified immediately when something happens in the amusement park, theme park, and waterpark industries.

Anaheim Boomers

1041 North Shepard
Anaheim, CA (714) 630–7211
www.boomersparks.com

Located in the heart of southern California's theme park belt, Anaheim Boomers provides a good old-fashioned afternoon of fun. Visitors can play in the extensive game arcade, take a few swings in the batting cages, take a spin on the go-karts, or splash around on the bumper boats. The Big Top Family Fun Zone features 7 traditional amusement park rides including a Scrambler, a Yo-Yo, Red Baron, a Ferris wheel, and a merry-go-round. A full-service snack bar has a nice selection of items.

Attractions are on a pay-as-you-go basis and the park is open daily. Location is just off the Riverside Freeway.

Balboa Fun Zone

600 East Bay Avenue
Newport Beach, CA (949) 673–0408
www.thebalboafunzone.com

If you lose your hat as you spin around on the Ferris wheel here, chances are it will end up in the bay. That's how close you are to the water. In fact, the entire complex is along the bay walk on the Balboa Peninsula, mingled in with marinas, shops, restaurants, and the ferryboat landing.

Along with the Ferris wheel, bumper cars, carousel, tea cups, climbing wall, indoor miniature golf, and the Scary Dark Ride, there are other outdoorsy-type activities, including whale-watching cruises, parasailing, water bikes, and sightseeing cruises.

Dating back to 1936, the park was completely rebuilt by its current owners in 1986. Free admission, with all attractions on a pay-as-you-go basis. Open year-round. Hours vary, so call first.

Belmont Park

3190 Mission Boulevard
San Diego, CA (858) 488–1549
www.giantdipper.com

The original Belmont Park was closed in 1976, but through the efforts of many, the park's popular Giant Dipper wooden roller coaster was saved from the bulldozers and today is one of the great coaster classics of the West Coast.

A new, smaller version of the old park has sprung up around the coaster and today the complex offers 9 rides including the coaster. Among the rides are the Vertical Plunge, a kid's free fall; bumper cars; Tilt-A-Whirl; and a Crazy Submarine family ride. Pirate's Cove is a fun family center with a great kid's soft-play area.

 Roller coaster: Giant Dipper (W).

The Giant Dipper was completely renovated in 1990 and is now a National Historic Landmark. Built in 1925 by Prior & Church, the woodie is one of only two remaining California seaside coasters from the 1920s.

A new leaseholder for the complex plans to open Wave House, a sports park with surfing machines and skate bowls, as early as 2004 on the site next to the rides. He also plans on building a fun-house attraction, with many of the traditional fun-house elements.

Located next to Mission Beach in Mission Bay, the rides open at 11:00 A.M., with closing at either 10:00 or 11:00 P.M. Open daily during peak season, with operations cut back during the winter months. Free admission with rides on a pay-as-you-go basis, or an all-day ride pass is available, under $15.

Bonfante Gardens Theme Park

**3050 Hecker Pass (Scenic Highway 152 W)
Gilroy, CA (408) 842–2121
www.bonfantegardens.com**

As one of the unique parks on planet Earth, this horticulture-themed playland hybrid is a most welcome addition to North America's theme park lineup and is about as eco-friendly as an entertainment complex can be. The 28-acre site is situated among 600 acres of rural countryside and features 22 rides and more than 20 gardens, greenhouses, and other horticultural attractions. The mysterious and whimsical Circus Trees are an attraction in themselves.

The design team has done a fabulous job mixing Mother Nature's beauty with high-tech thrill and fun machines. One gets a sense that the trees grew up naturally around the rides instead of the rides being installed among the trees. The magnificent Monarch Gardens greenhouse is not only full of luscious foliage, but it also has the train, the monorail, and a river passing through it!

The 22 rides include a restored 1927 Illions Supreme Carousel. Themed rides with some great names include the Mushroom Swing, Strawberry Sundae, Artichoke Dip, and, since Gilroy is the garlic capital of the world, you'll also find the Garlic Twirl.

The feel of the park is mid-twentieth-century Santa Clara Valley before silicon chips took over. The 25 one-of-a-kind Circus Trees must be seen to be believed. They are full-grown trees that were moved here in 1985 and grown in unique shapes. They are coiled, scalloped, and spiral-shaped sycamore, ash, oak, and maple trees that began their lives 50 miles away.

The big thriller here is the Quicksilver Mine Coaster. The 2 lifts take riders through 576 full-grown mature trees, with a surprise around every corner. There's an authentic steam train ride, and Coyote Lake features paddleboat rides.

Paramount Parks, operators of nearby Paramount's Great America, took over management of this non-profit park in 2003.

To get there, take the Highway 152 W exit off Highway 101 between San Jose and Monterey. The park is on Highway 152, 3 miles west of Gilroy.

 Roller coasters: Quicksilver Mine Coaster, mine train, family (S); Timber Twister, family (S).

Castle Amusement Park

3500 Polk Street
Riverside, CA (909) 785-3000
www.castlepark.com

The lush vegetation and tree-lined paths make visitors forget they are actually in the desert when they are in Castle Park. Aimed at the family and with 32 rides, this place has something for everyone, from veteran thrill-seeker to first-time rider. The park is split into two parts.

The first is the amusement park, which has many traditional park favorites like Merlin's Revenge, a junior roller coaster, and a beautiful 1907 Dentzel carousel that is housed in its own million-dollar pavilion, complete with lions standing guard at the door to protect the rare ride. Don't miss the Dragon's Tower, an exciting shot and drop free-fall tower. The laid-back atmosphere is a nice change from the hustle and bustle of the state's megaparks.

The other half of the park has 4 of the most beautiful miniature golf courses you'll find, with palm trees, well-manicured landscaping, waterfalls, and miniature towns. Next door to the golf courses are 2 go-kart tracks and an arcade with hundreds of games and Ghost Blasters, an interactive dark-ride where guests shoot at animatronic ghosts for points.

 Extras: A train ride, along which you'll see a plethora of antiques, including wagons, mining equipment, and tools. A one-ton replica of the Liberty Bell is also on display.

 Season: Year-round.

 Operating hours: Rides open at 10:00 A.M. daily during the week and at noon on weekends and close at 10:00 P.M. or midnight. Golf courses and arcade are open 10:00 A.M. to 10:00 P.M. daily, midnight on Friday and Saturday. Rides are open daily during the summer and open only on weekends and holidays in winter.

 Admission policy: Free admission to the park. Rides are on a pay-as-you-go basis. Pay-one-price for all rides and unlimited golf also available, under $20. Parking charge.

 Top rides: Pepsi Challenge, a swing ride; Sea Dragon; The Log Ride, a flume ride; antique cars; a circa 1907 Dentzel carousel with 52 animals; Ghost Blasters, interactive dark ride; free fall.

 Roller coasters: Tornado, family (S); Merlin's Revenge, family (S).

 Plan to stay: 4 to 6 hours if you plan to play arcade games and/or golf.

 Directions: Located at 3500 Polk Street, off Riverside Expressway between the La Sierra and Tyler Street exits.

The Disneyland Resort

**1313 Harbor Boulevard
Anaheim, CA (714) 781-7290
www.disneyland.com**

There will never be another Disneyland. Sure, there are hundreds of other parks in the country and most of them offer great fun, but this is the original, the only theme park that was thought up by Walt Disney and some of the greatest pioneering minds in entertainment history. Of the 10 in operation, this is the only Disney park in which Walt Disney ever walked. It's hard to explain the magic that this original still possesses.

 TiM'S TRiViA

The Haunted Mansion darkrides at Disney parks are considered the best, most advanced rides of their kind in the world. Want to know more about these amazing rides? Check out www.doombuggies.com.

Disneyland was joined in 2001 by a new theme park, a new hotel, and a new retail entertainment area known as Downtown Disney. The entire complex is now known jointly as The Disneyland Resort.

A pedestrian esplanade runs from the hotels, through Downtown Disney, past the new Grand Californian Hotel to a plaza area with the entrance to the new Disney's California Adventure on your right, and the entrance to the original Disneyland on your left.

For explanation purposes, I am presenting first a specific look at each element of The Disneyland Resort. That information is followed by general data pertaining to the entire complex.

Disneyland

Few theme parks hold the imaginations of both children and adults like Disneyland. From a ride through space on a roller coaster to life in the Old West to being put into a cartoon, visitors experience a variety of things when they spend a day here. A Disneyland day is built around rides and attractions the entire family can enjoy together.

After passing through Main Street USA at the front of the park, visitors are invited to journey into one of 6 themed areas.

"Tea Cups," Disneyland Resort, Anaheim, California
Photo by Adam Sandy

The best 3 attractions to visit first are Space Mountain, a dark roller-coaster ride through the universe; the Indiana Jones Adventure, a high-speed jaunt with Indy through his adventures; and Splash Mountain, a Song of the South–themed log flume that shares the adventures of Brer Rabbit. These lines will stay long almost every day of the year.

The park has many rides still around from the park's first few seasons. Dumbo the Flying Elephant, Mr. Toad's Wild Ride, Snow White's Scary Adventures, and the Jungle Cruise are just some of the fun family rides that offer experiences unique to Disneyland. Don't miss the Haunted Mansion, considered by many as the finest haunted ride-through attraction in the world. Another park favorite is the King Arthur Carousel, which is a mixed machine that features horses from Dentzel, Looff, and Stein & Goldstein.

One thing the park does especially well is ensure that the rides fit both the children and mom and dad comfortably, so you will hardly ever have to squeeze into a seat.

You will want to familiarize yourself with Disney's Fast Pass system. The most popular attractions are set up with virtual queues that allow guests to pick up a ticket for a specific time later in the day. Come back at that time, and you won't have to wait in line. And, the service is available for no extra cost. If you want to ride the major attractions several times, Fast Pass makes the day at Disneyland much more manageable. Be sure to check out the park's Web site for more information on how the system works.

THE AMUSEMENT PARK GUIDE

No visit to Disneyland is complete without watching the first-class parades and getting to have a magical meeting with Mickey and all of his friends. Check the show schedule or ask the well-informed cast members (that's what employees are called at Disney) where the meet-and-greets take place. The most impressive show at Disneyland is Fantasmic. Held on the Rivers of America, guests start lining up as early as 6:00 P.M. for the 9:00 and 10:30 shows each night. A combination of pyrotechnics, lasers, and special effects in which Mickey battles the "forces of evil," it is sure to be a hit with everyone in the family.

 Roller coasters: Big Thunder Mountain Railroad, family mine train (S); Space Mountain, indoor family (S); Matterhorn Bobsleds, family (S); Gadget's Go-Coaster, kiddie (S).

Disney's California Adventure

Opened in 2001 as the nation's newest Disney product, this 57-acre park tells the story of the California adventure. And boy, is it a cool adventure. There are 4 lands—Golden Gate, Paradise Pier, Hollywood Pictures Backlot, and the newest, A Bug's Land, which opened in late 2002. The park has 17 rides and myriad shows and unique attractions.

Just across the esplanade from Disneyland's Main Street Railroad Station is the Golden Gateway entrance plaza of the new park. You can't miss it! Eleven-and-a-half-foot-tall letters spell out C A L I F O R N I A and you can walk through them if you please. Just beyond you'll see the monorail cross over a Golden Gate Bridge. Your visit to the Disneyfied version of California has begun!

 # TiM'S TRiViA

Disneyland has a grand heritage of unique rides and through the years it has added many new rides and attractions to its lineup of fantasy. Sometimes, however, an old ride or attraction must be taken out to make room for the new. There's a Web site that will fill you in on the history of the old rides and attractions: www.yesterland.com.

Golden State has six themed areas. Condor Flats, a celebration of aviation, features the park's most innovative, can't miss attraction, Soarin' Over California. Guests sit below glider wings, their feet dangling beneath them as they are

Disney's California Adventure, Anaheim, California
Photo by Tim O'Brien

swung into the middle of a huge dome-shaped movie screen. From that perch, you'll be taken on a "flight" from the Golden Gate Bridge to the San Diego Bay. You'll smell the orange groves and the freshness of the pine forests.

Also in Golden State are the Grizzly River Run rapids ride, the Redwood Creek Challenge Trail play and climbing complex, and the *It's Tough to Be a Bug* 3-D movie.

In the Hollywood Pictures Backlot, Disney celebrates the glitter and glamour of Hollywood with plenty of atmosphere entertainment and sound stages. Here you'll find *Jim Henson's Muppet*Vision* 3-D attraction and the Twilight Zone Tower of Terror, set to open in 2004.

Paradise Pier is a salute to the state's beachfront amusement piers of the past and it's here you'll find a great line-up of traditional amusement park rides with a magical Disney touch. California Screamin' is a 6,000-foot-long launch coaster; the Sun Wheel is a new version of the Wonder Wheel, which slides the gondolas toward the center of the wheel as it rotates; and on King Triton's Carousel you can ride on one of 56 of California's most popular sea critters. The Maliboomers is a 180-foot-tall 3-tower free-fall ride and the Golden Zephyr is an updated version of the ever-popular rocket ship swing ride.

Several family rides, a large boardwalk games area, and some great crazy roadside architecture can also be discovered in Paradise Pier.

A Bug's Land is the newest "land" at the park and is dedicated to children. The theming here features colorful, enormously oversized plants, fruits, and flowers, making visitors feel as tiny as insects! One of the areas in the new land is Flik's Fun Fair, where you'll find 5 kiddie rides, including Flik's Hi Flyers, whirling baskets similar to Disney's classic Dumbo ride; Tuck and Roll's Drive 'em Buggies, two-seater bumper cars; and Heimlich's Choo Choo train.

 Roller coasters: California Screamin', 1- loop (S); Mulholland Madness, Wild Mouse (S).

Throughout the park are themed restaurants, fast-food walk-ups, and amazing architecture. It looks like the park was designed from someone's California postcard collection. I can only imagine how proud Californians are of this unique salute to their state.

Downtown Disney

Downtown Disney is a 20-acre eclectic mix of shopping, dining, and entertainment experiences. Among the shopping opportunities is the 40,000-square-foot World of Disney, one of the biggest Disney character stores on the planet.

Other tenants along the beautifully landscaped pedestrian esplanade include the ESPN Zone restaurant and sports bar; House of Blues restaurant and nightclub; Ralph Brennan's Jazz Kitchen, a New Orleans–themed restaurant and live music venue; Hook's Point, a family restaurant with a mesquite grill; Naples Ristorante e Pizzeria; Rainforest Cafe; Granville's Steakhouse; and the La Brea Bakery cafe.

The Complex

 Season: Year-round.

 Operating hours: During peak summer and holiday hours, 9:00 A.M. to midnight or 1:00 A.M. During most winter months, park opens at 10:00 A.M. and closes at varying times.

 Admission policy: Pay-one-price, under $50. Parking charge. Special 2-day passes are available.

 Plan to stay: At least one day for each park.

Best way to avoid crowds: Come in the traditional slow periods, during the winter months when families are not traveling on vacations. Avoid the week between Christmas and New Year, if possible! During all periods, the busiest part of the day is at opening and right after lunch; the crowds tend to rush to the major rides first.

 Directions: Take the Disneyland exit off I–5 (Santa Ana Freeway), turn south, and follow signs to specific Disney destinations, including the large parking garage. If coming from the south, take the Katella Avenue exit off I–5. Turn left onto Katella, and then take a right onto Harbor Boulevard. Follow signs to various parking garages, parks, and resort hotels.

Escondido Boomers

830 Dan Way
Escondido, CA (760) 741–1326
www.boomersparks.com

Here's another quality Boomers attraction, complete with 3 miniature golf courses, batting cages, go-karts, bumper boats, and an arcade full of high-tech video and redemption games. Kid's County Fair features several kiddie rides, including a little roller coaster, train, swings, and airplanes.

Open daily year-round, including holidays, at 11:00 A.M. on weekdays and 10:00 A.M. on weekends. Closing times vary with the season. Several bonus passes and special promotional tickets available.

Fountain Valley Boomers

16800 Magnolia Street
Fountain Valley, CA (714) 842–1111
www.boomersparks.com

There are now nearly 30 Boomers fun centers in the United States, with each offering the same genre of fun and quality, but each varying a bit in its exact lineup of attractions.

Here you'll find one of the most diverse centers of them all. There are go-karts, batting cages, bumper boats, a motion-simulator ride, a redemption and video arcade, miniature golf, and the famous Cafe Boomers eatery. Among the ride offerings are kiddie balloons, a Ferris wheel, a kiddie roller coaster, bumper boats, and a kids' soft-play area, Kidopolis.

THE AMUSEMENT PARK GUIDE

Open daily year-round at 10:00 or 11:00 A.M., with closing between 10:00 P.M. and midnight. Pay-as-you-go admission.

Funderland

In William Land Park
1465 Sutterville Road
Sacramento, CA (916) 456-0115
www.funderlandpark.com

Serving the kids of the neighborhood since 1948, this cozy traditional park is located in a spacious city park, across the river from the Sacramento Zoo and adjacent to Fairytale Town, a storybook village.

Outside the gate is a large picnic area, and nearby is a pony-ride concession. Rides include a 1948 Allan Herschell carousel that has been in this location since its beginning, a train, Dragon Coaster, boats, planes, tea cups, and Oscar the Fish. In all there are 9 rides. A snack bar offers a full line of snack items, including popcorn, pink popcorn, ice cream, soft drinks, and candy.

Open daily from 10:00 A.M. to 6:00 P.M. during the summer and only on weekends from February through May and from Labor Day through November. Closed December and January. Free admission, with rides on a pay-as-you-go basis; pay-one-price available only on Fridays.

 Roller coaster: Flying Dragon, family (S).

Funderwoods

In Micke Grove County Park
11793 Micke Grove Road
Lodi, CA (209) 369-5437

The 258-acre, heavily wooded Micke Grove County Park serves as the backdrop to Funderwoods, an 11-ride traditional family amusement park. It's located right next to the Micke Grove Zoo.

The Tilt-A-Whirl, carousel, train, Tubs-O-Fun, Octopus, Scrambler, antique cars, Red Baron airplanes, and a small kiddie coaster are among the ride offerings. There's a small snack bar in the park that serves up fun food, including cotton candy and the rare but tasty pink popcorn, a park specialty. For more substantial food, there's a cafe at the zoo.

Open daily from 11:00 A.M. to 6:00 P.M. during the summer and only on weekends from February through May and from September through November. Admission to the amusement park is free, with rides priced on a pay-as-you-go basis; pay-one-price available, under $13. The county charges a parking fee for all who enter the county park.

 Roller coaster: Coaster, family (S).

 # TiM'S TRiViA

The first vertical loop of the modern steel roller coaster era was on the Revolution at Six Flags Magic Mountain, Valencia, California. The coaster opened on May 8, 1976, was designed by Anton Schwarzkopf and Werner Stengel, and is still thrilling riders today.

Knott's Berry Farm

8039 Beach Boulevard
Buena Park, CA (714) 220–5200
www.knotts.com

The story of how this place got started has to be one of the most unusual of any park anywhere. About 70 years ago, the Knott family decided to open a chicken restaurant to draw people out to their 20-acre farm in Buena Park to buy boysenberries. The eatery became so popular that the family added a handful of attractions to entertain guests while they waited for a table. Today the park has grown to 160 acres and is divided into 6 themed areas offering 45 rides. Oh, and by the way, the chicken restaurant is still operating and is as busy as ever!

Ghost Town is the original area and remains the heart and soul of the park. It contains many authentic buildings, some more than 100 years old, that were moved from ghost towns in California and Arizona and rebuilt at Knott's. The 6-acre Camp Snoopy, reminiscent of the California High Sierra, centers on Snoopy and all the Peanuts gang and features 30 kid-tested rides.

THE AMUSEMENT PARK GUIDE

For thrill-seekers, there's the Xcelerator, a launch coaster that blasts riders from 0 to 80 mph in 2.3 seconds through a 205-foot ascent and an immediate 20-story descent at 90 degrees! WOW!

 TiM'S TRiViA

Knott's Berry Farm is home to America's only exact brick-by-brick replica of Independence Hall, and when the real Hall in Philadelphia was being restored in 1996, the reconstruction committee asked to borrow the park's plans to the replica because the landmark's original blueprints couldn't be found.

 Extras: The Mystery Lodge is a multimedia, multisensory experience.

 Special events: The park becomes "Knott's Scary Farm" each Halloween season; "Knott's Merry Farm," Thanksgiving through Christmas; Camp Spooky, a non-scary Halloween celebration for the kids, is open weekends in October.

 Season: Year-round. Closed Christmas Day.

 Operating hours: 9:00 A.M. to 10:00 P.M. or midnight during peak season and 10:00 A.M. to 6:00 P.M. during winter months, open later on weekends.

 Admission policy: Pay-one-price, under $43; come in after 4:00 P.M., under $20. Parking charge.

 Top rides: El Revolution, Revolution; Joe Cool's GR8 SK8, Sky Skater; Supreme Scream, a 254-foot free fall; Kingdom of the Dinosaurs, an indoor ride through the days of the dinosaurs; Timber Mountain Log Ride, one of the first flume rides in the country; Calico Mine Ride, a narrated ride through a gold mine; Stagecoach, involving a ride around the park in a vintage stagecoach during which your party is attacked by bad guys; a 1902 Dentzel carousel; and the full-scale, narrow-gauge Ghost Town and Calico Railroad.

 Roller coasters: Xcelerator, 1950s-themed hydraulically lauched (S); Ghost Rider (W); Jaguar!, family (S); Boomerang (S); Montezooma's Revenge, shuttle loop (S); Timberline Twister, junior (S).

Plan to stay: 8 hours.

 Best way to avoid crowds: Come during off-season or on a weekday morning during season.

 Directions: Located 30 miles south of downtown Los Angeles. Take the Beach Boulevard exit off I–5 and go south 2 miles to Knott's.

Knott's Soak City U.S.A.

(Three locations)
Buena Park, CA (714) 220–5200
Chula Vista, CA (619) 661–7373
Palm Springs, CA (760) 327–0499
www.soakcityusa.com

The 1950s southern California era of surf woodies and long-boards is the theme at all three Knott's Soak City U.S.A. locations.

The Orange County facility is located adjacent to Knott's Berry Farm in Buena Park and requires a separate fee. This 13-acre park features 21 water rides including 16 body, tube, and speed slides, the 750,000-gallon Tidal Wave Bay wave pool, a lazy river, and a children's area known as Gremmie Lagoon.

The Chula Vista location is 5 miles east of San Diego, next to the Coors Amphitheater. Formerly known as White Water Canyon, the park was purchased by Knott's, who reopened it as Soak City U.S.A. in 2000. It's a 32-acre park with 22 water attractions, including 13 tube and body slides and 4 speed slides. The wave pool is known as Balboa Bay and the children's area here is also known as Gremmie Lagoon.

In case you're not familiar with California culture, allow me to offer this small piece of advice: Muscle Beach is the men's changing room, and Bikini Beach is the changing room for the ladies.

The Palm Springs park (formerly Oasis Water Park) enjoys a wonderful tropical atmosphere that's natural to its location, with colorful landscaping and hundreds of native palm trees dotting the facility. It has 17 water attractions, including the new Kahuna's Beach House, a 4-story interactive playground with 6 slides. The Rip Tide Reef is an 800,000-gallon wave pool, and Sunset River is a popular meandering lazy river. There are 8 adult slides, including 5 that are 7 stories high, and 5 kiddie slides. Most of them start on the man-made mountain in the center of the park.

The Buena Park and Chula Vista parks are open May through September, weekends only in May and September. The Palm Springs facility is open daily, mid-March through Labor Day, weekends in September and October. Admission is $22 at each, which includes all activities. Come in after 3:00 P.M., and save $8. Parking fee at all locations.

Legoland California
One Lego Drive
Carlsbad, CA (760) 918-5379
www.legolandca.com

You simply won't believe the incredible incarnations of real people, animals, places, and things that have been created out of Lego bricks at this 128-acre park! More than 30 million of the tiny blocks have been pieced together to form more than 5,000 models placed throughout the park, and more than 50 rides and attractions allow the young ones to get in on the action.

Targeted to families with children ages 3 to 12, Legoland is designed such that kids can push, pull, steer, pedal, squirt, build, crawl, climb, stomp, program, or build their way through the park. If you're looking for a fun family adventure, this is the place. If you're looking for thrill rides for your teenagers, go to Knott's Berry Farm or Six Flags Magic Mountain.

Clustered about a 1.73-acre lake are six major themed areas, or "blocks" in Legoland language. Most rides and attractions appear to have been built with large Lego bricks, and learning through Lego is the major theme here.

At the heart of the park is perhaps its most stunning exhibition, a Lilliputian landscape called Miniland that will be enjoyed as much by adults as kids. Here, five different regions of the United States—California, New England, New Orleans at Mardi Gras, New York City, and Washington, D.C.—are depicted in splendid detail. It took

Master Lego builders nearly three years and 20 million Lego bricks to create these exquisite scenes, with details as elaborate as the twinkling lanterns of Chinatown and the blazing neon signs of Times Square. There are several other notable Lego brick creations in the park as well, including Mount Rushmore, the Sydney Opera House, and a giant T-Rex.

While most won't notice, the designers have created a thoughtful balance between active areas and quiet time. Guests will move from one bustling interactive area to another through a peaceful, shady, winding path, which encourages a brief change of gears. Nice touch!

 Extras: Don't miss the 15½-foot-tall face of Albert Einstein; it contains 1.12 million Lego bricks. It took 2 million Lego bricks to build the red dinosaur and his two helpers that you'll find near the entrance.

 Season: Year-round.

 Operating hours: 10:00 A.M. to 9:00 P.M., June through Labor Day; 10:00 A.M. to dusk the rest of the year.

 Admission policy: Pay-one-price for adults, under $40; pay-one-price for children 3–16, under $34. Parking charge.

 Top rides: Lego Racers 4D, a multidimensional movie; Aquazone, personal watercrafts; Royal Joust, horse race around a track; Sky Cycle, a monorail with pedal cars; Kid Power Tower, kids self-propel their seats to the top of a 35-foot-tall tower for a free-fall ride; Driving School, learn to drive, get a license; Fairy Tale Brook, boat ride through fairy tales; Coast Cruise, a boat tour of Lego animated models.

 Roller coasters: The Dragon, family (S); Spellbreaker, dual-suspended, family (S); Lego Technic Coaster, wild mouse (S).

 Plan to stay: 8 to 10 hours.

 Directions: Located in Carlsbad, 30 minutes north of downtown San Diego, one hour south of Disneyland. Take I–5 to the Cannon Road exit, head east to Legoland Drive.

Pacific Park

**On Santa Monica Pier
Santa Monica, CA (310) 260–8744
www.pacpark.com**

Back in the golden years, amusement piers of all lengths, shapes, and sizes, were scattered along the California coast. Sadly, nearly all have been lost with time. Family-oriented Pacific Park at the end of the Santa Monica Pier is the only pier park now in the state. The star ride in the park is the Pacific Wheel, an open-gondola Ferris wheel and the only solar-powered wheel in the world. The wheel provides riders a magnificent view of the beach and ocean, all from more than a hundred feet above the water.

 TIM'S TRIVIA

Being near Hollywood means you'll have a good chance of running into some well-known celebrities while visiting Pacific Park on Santa Monica Pier. Among the stars that have been "sighted" there recently are Tim Allen, Nicolas Cage, George Carlin, Jerry Seinfeld, John Travolta, Shaquille O'Neal, and Jason Priestley.

The other rides include the West Coaster, a family coaster that runs the length of the park; a spinning ride called the Sea Fury; a swing ride that takes riders through the salty ocean air; and lots of children's rides. The rides can either be enjoyed with a pay-one-price wristband or on a pay-as-you-go basis. Pacific Park has the usual combination of rides, games, and eateries including a Taco Bell and Pizza Hut. As you stroll around the pier don't be surprised to see a celebrity or two. Many local stars are known to bring their children for a few rides after work.

Before leaving be sure to visit the Looff Hippodrome, which sits at the foot of the pier. The structure was built in the Byzantine–Moorish California architectural style and is a National Historic Landmark. Today it houses Philadelphia Toboggan Company carousel #62. The carousel, which was assembled in 1922, is the third machine to run in the building, which dates from 1916. The ride is an independent concession owned by the city of Santa Monica since 1977.

Roller coaster: The West Coaster, family (S).

Open year-round, with summer opening hours at 10:00 A.M. and closing at 10:00 P.M. Sunday through Thursday, and midnight on Friday and Saturday. Winter operating hours depend on weather. There is limited parking on the pier, with additional parking in city lots along the beach.

Paramount's Great America

2401 Agnew Road
Santa Clara, CA (408) 988–1776
www.pgathrills.com

If you've got a kid who loves Jimmy Neutron or SpongeBob SquarePants, a visit to this park is definitely a must. Both characters, plus many more Nickelodeon stars, are hanging out in the new Nickelodeon Central area, and SpongeBob even has a ride named after him!

As do most of the Paramount Parks, this one relies heavily on characters and shows from Nickelodeon, the number one kids' network, to attract the young families. And it works because of the great theme area that has been created. This is one of the best places in northern California to bring the kids. The Hanna-Barbera characters, including Shaggy and Scooby-Doo, can also be found at the park, in KidZville, an area with an additional 20 kid and family rides.

 TiM'S TRIViA

Would you like fries with that? Guests at Paramount's Great America certainly do. On average, 170 tons of french fries are sold each year. That's more weight than 44 full-grown elephants.

But the park is much more than kid's play. With 52 rides, including 10 roller coasters and a couple of major white-knuckle thrillers, there's plenty to do for adrenaline junkies as well. The Drop Zone, a 224-foot-tall free fall, and the Delerium, a high-spinning pendulum ride, are but 2 of the newer, high-tech thrill rides.

Season: Mid-March through October.

 Operating hours: Opens at 10:00 A.M. daily and closes at varying times during the season.

 Admission policy: Pay-one-price, under $47. Kids under 6, half price. Parking charge.

 Top rides: Drop Zone; Meteor Attack, 3-D simulator; Stan Lee's 7th Portal, 3-D simulator; Deliruim, a Frisbee-style thriller; Rip Roaring Rapids, a raging-rapids ride; Rue Le Dodge, bumper cars; Whitewater Falls, a spill-water raft ride; Celebration Swings, wave swinger.

 Roller coasters: Psycho Mouse, wild mouse (S); Stealth, flying coaster (S); Invertigo, inverted boomerang (S); The Demon, corkscrew/loop (S); The Grizzly (W); The Rugrats Runaway Reptar, kiddie (S); Vortex, stand-up (S); Top Gun, inverted (S); Taxi Jam, junior (S).

 Plan to stay: 8 hours.

 Best way to avoid crowds: Arrive at opening hours on weekdays or Sunday morning.

 Directions: Located 5 miles north of downtown San Jose. Take the Great America Parkway exit off Highway 101; then go east to the park.

Pharaoh's Lost Kingdom

1101 California Street
Redlands, CA (909) 335–7275
www.pharoahslostkingdom.com

An amazing assortment of activities makes this a unique entertainment facility. It's a waterpark. It's an amusement park. It's bigger than a family fun center, but not a full-blown theme park with long lines and high ticket prices.

To enter the gold, glass pyramid in the middle of this Egyptian-themed park, you walk under a large sphinx.

Inside is where you'll find a huge video and redemption arcade, laser tag arena, soft-play area for the kids, and a restaurant.

 Roller coaster: Screaming Mummy, family (S).

Outside, a 16-ride amusement area includes a Ferris wheel, a Tilt-A-Whirl, bumper cars, a family roller coaster, and the Pharaoh's Fury swinging ship ride. There are 3 go-kart tracks, 4 miniature golf courses, a Skycoaster, and a 20-attraction waterpark that has a sand beach, wave pool, and a variety of slides and play areas. A 2,500-seat amphitheater is the site for live shows and concerts, including top-name regional bands.

Admission is free, with rides and activities on a pay-as-you-go-basis. An unlimited-use ticket is available, under $30. Unlimited use of either park by itself is under $20. Open daily, 10:00 A.M., year-round.

Pixieland Park

In Willow Pass Park
2740 East Olivera Road
Concord, CA (925) 689–8841
www.pixieland.com

You don't want to miss this inviting little family fun park nestled in the pleasant surroundings of a large community park. The gently rolling terrain and tree-lined walkways add to the attractiveness of this traditional park for the entire family.

A colorful family carousel, spinning tea cups, Red Baron airplanes, Frog Hopper, an antique car ride, a Flying Dragon roller coaster, and a train ride around Willow Pass Park's Duck pond are the 7 rides. A small snack bar serves typical amusement park fare, and a great many picnic areas are available.

The rides open daily at 10:00 A.M., with closing times varying depending on the season. Daily operation runs in July and August, with weekend operation during the rest of the year. Park is closed from mid-December until the first week of February. Free admission, with all rides on a pay-as-you-go basis. An all-you-can-ride wristband is available during the week only, under $13.

Raging Waters

**Off Tully Road
In Lake Cunningham Regional Park
San Jose, CA (408) 238–9900
www.ragingwaters.com**

The largest waterpark in the Bay area, the 23-acre Raging Waters offers more than 20 water rides and attractions for the entire family. An 80-degree water temperature is maintained in all attractions.

One of the park's signature attractions is Barracuda Blaster, a slide that takes up to four riders, all on one toboggan, through more than 500 feet of curves, dips, and drops.

Buccaneer Bay wave pool creates a series of different waves for action lovers. For those preferring a more tranquil setting, the Lazy River provides a gentle current on which to float. Pirate's Cove is an interactive family water play area, with a 40-foot mast topped by a water-spilling pirate's skull. If it's thrills you're looking for, try out the Shotgun speed slide. At the bottom, there's a 10-foot free fall into a deep water pool.

The park is open daily 10:00 A.M. to 6:00 or 7:00 P.M. from mid-June through August, and on weekends in May and September. Admission is under $27, and there is a city-charged parking fee in Lake Cunningham Regional Park.

Raging Waters

**111 Raging Waters Drive
San Dimas, CA (909) 802–2200
www.ragingwaters.com**

Situated within a 50-acre parklike setting of tropically wooded rolling hills, this is one of the five most popular (by visitor count) waterparks in the country. Remembering the offerings here is easy. "We have 50 acres, 50 million gallons of water, and 50-plus rides, attractions, and pools," says the owner.

In all, there are 51 slides (many attractions have more than one slide); Neptune's Fury, a multpassenger tube ride through the dark; the Wedge, a V-shaped slide; Typhoon Lagoon wave pool; the Dark Hole two-person tube ride in the dark; Raging Rivers, a man-made river slide, with several pools along the route; Thunder Rapids six-person raft ride; and the themed Amazon Adventure lazy river.

Additionally, the Vortex is a themed, enclosed slide with lights, fog, and sound effects, and the Volcano Fantasy children's attraction features steam, smoke, sound, and slides. Splash Island Adventure is a large interactive family play area.

Open May through mid-September, 10:00 A.M. to 8:00 P.M. during the peak season. Admission, under $30. If you arrive after 4:00 P.M., admission is under $17. A 2-day ticket costs $10 extra.

Rotary Storyland & Playland

890 West Belmont
Fresno, CA (559) 486-2124

You gotta hand it to the Rotary Club of Fresno. It has taken the small fun zone in the city-owned Roeding Park and made sure the two classic family parks, dating back to the 1960s, are well operated and well maintained.

The commercial entertainment area within the big park consists of Storyland, a magic garden where fairy tales are brought to life, and Playland, a ride park featuring 6 rides. Located next to Lake Washington, the Rotary also operates the rental motorboats, rowboats and paddleboats.

The miniature railroad and the kiddie roller coaster are among the more popular rides, and live entertainment is presented during the summer at the Pinocchio Theater.

 Roller coaster: Roller Coaster, junior (S).

The facility is operated by the local Rotary Club, and all profits are used for cultural and recreational activities. Free admission, with rides on a pay-as-you-play basis. The most costly ride in the park is $1.50. Open daily mid-March through mid-October at 10:00 A.M. Hours vary, so call ahead.

Santa Cruz Beach Boardwalk

400 Beach Street
Santa Cruz, CA (831) 426-7433
www.beachboardwalk.com

The mile-long boardwalk is nothing less than amazing! The 33 rides, including 12 for the kids, are a combination of nostalgic traditional family attractions and modern-day high-tech machines that turn you every which way but loose.

What makes this, the West Coast's largest remaining major seaside amusement park, so special is that unique blend of old and new. The owners, while constantly updating with new technology, have been careful not to lose the traditional feel that makes this park stand out from the rest.

 # TiM'S TRiViA

Santa Cruz Beach Boardwalk is the last of the major seaside amusement parks that once dotted the California coast.

The entire park is on the State Historic Landmark list, and 2 of its rides, the circa 1911 Looff carousel and the circa 1924 wooden coaster The Giant Dipper, are on the National Historic Landmark list. The carousel, one of the few in which you can still grab for the brass ring (steel rings are now used because people were walking off with the brass ones), has 73 hand-carved horses and a rare 342-pipe Ruth and Sohn band organ, made in 1894. The coaster was designed and built by local resident Arthur Looff, the son of Charles Looff, who created the carousel. The Cave Train, a darkride originally built in 1961, has been renovated, with many of the nostalgic elements updated by new technology. The 3-D fun house is a colorful modern attraction with plenty of high-tech gimmicks, and the Ghost Blasters is an interactive family darkride where riders shoot at targets for scores. In addition, there are miniature golf, laser tag, the Trampoline Thing, a rock-climbing wall, bowling, and 2 major arcades.

Visiting the park at night is especially nice. The smells, the lights, the laughter, the screams, and the music coming from the band organ on the carousel could all be part of a long-gone decade.

 Extras: Neptune's Kingdom is a massive indoor amusement center with a 2-story miniature golf course, a restaurant, and a wide array of new and vintage arcade games.

 Special events: Friday night concerts, all season; craft and gifts fair, November.

Season: Year-round; during winter months, weekends only on limited operations.

Operating hours: Opens at 11:00 A.M. Closing varies, depending on season, crowds, and weather.

Admission policy: Free admission to board-walk; rides on a per-ride basis. Pay-one-price also available.

Top rides: Rock and Roll, 1950s-themed spin-ning ride; Crazy Surf; Fireball; Space Race; bumper cars; Logger's Revenge, a log flume; Cliff Hanger; Tornado; Tsunami.

Roller coasters: The Giant Dipper (W); Hurricane (S); Orient Express (S); Sea Serpent, family (S).

Plan to stay: 6 hours.

Best way to avoid crowds: Come midweek during the day.

Directions: Take Highway 17 or Highway 1 into Santa Cruz; then follow the numerous signs to the boardwalk.

Scandia Fun Center

1155 South Wanamaker Avenue
Ontario, CA (909) 390–3092
www.scandiafun.com

Scandia Fun Center is a quirky little park that offers Swedish-themed fun in southern California. There is something for everyone here. It features 15 rides (5 for children), go-karts, batting cages, an arcade, 2 miniature golf courses, bumper boats, and several park staples like the Viking Ship, a swinging boat ride; the Swedish Scrambler, a scrambler spinning ride; and the Nordic Spaceship, a centrifuge ride.

The highlight of the park for thrill-seekers is the Scandia Screamer roller coaster. It stands 90 feet high and has a clever combination of turns and drops that seems to please everyone. There's an extra thrill; planes bound for the nearby Ontario Airport often fly low over the coaster as they land.

There is no admission price and visitors can choose between pay-as-you-go and pay-one-price. At $20, the best deal for park guests is the "Unlimited Pass." This allows a visitor unlimited fun on the thrill rides, go-karts, and miniature golf. The park opens year-round at 10:00 A.M. and closes between 10:00 P.M. and 1:00 A.M., depending on the time of year. It's located on I–15, between the 10 and 60 free-ways. Exit on Jurupa.

 Roller coasters: Scandia Screamer, family (S); Little Dipper, kiddie (S).

SeaWorld Adventure Park
1720 South Shores Road
San Diego, CA (619) 226–3901
www.seaworld.com

High on a bluff overlooking Mission Bay, this was the first SeaWorld created, and since 1964 it has continued to grow and expand and today is one of the most beautiful marine parks in the world.

Situated on 150 mature and colorful acres, the park's animal habitats, rides, and attractions blend in nicely with what Mother Nature and SeaWorld gardeners contribute. While it will always remain a marine park with marine conservation at the forefront, the park also has some great shows and attractions and is adding more.

R.L. Stine's Haunted Lighthouse, a 4-D, multisensory, motion-based film, opened in 2003, and the popular Cirque de la Mer, featuring music, dance, and acrobatics, continues to pack them in to a specially designed outdoor stadium. In 2004, Journey to Atlantis is set to debut. This attraction, half roller coaster, half water flume, will be an updated version of the popular attraction at SeaWorld Florida.

However, the big star here is definitely Shamu and each of the shows in Shamu Stadium is usually filled to the rafters, so if you want to see the intriguing killer whale presentation, make sure you get there early. The Manatee Rescue is a 200,000-gallon attraction featuring the gentle manatees, and the Penguin Encounter is a great way to see those little guys up close in a natural habitat.

Shamu's Happy Harbor is for the kids and features more than 20 interactive water and play elements. Also, for extra fun, let the kids sit down close to the tank at the Shamu show. They'll not only see better than they would up in the stands, but they'll get splashed and be part of the show as well.

  Season: Year-round.

 Operating hours: 9:00 A.M. to 9:00 P.M. or later in summer, and 10:00 A.M. to dusk in winter.

 Admission policy: Pay-one-price, under $45. The Southern California ValuePass gives you 14 consecutive days of unlimited admission to both SeaWorld and Universal Studios Hollywood, under $82. Parking charge.

 Top rides: Shipwreck Rapids, raft ride; Skytower, a 320-foot-tall rotating tower that provides fantastic views of the Mission Bay area, extra charge; Sky Ride, a gondola ride across Mission Bay and back, extra fee; Wild Arctic, a motion-based simulator ride that takes guests on a journey to the Arctic, where you'll come face to face with live polar bears and beluga whales.

 Plan to stay: 8 hours.

 Best way to avoid crowds: Come during off-season, or come midweek during peak summer months. Because the killer whale show is extremely popular, get to Shamu Stadium early and plan the rest of your stay around this show.

Directions: Take the SeaWorld Drive exit off I-5 and follow signs west to the park.

Six Flags Hurricane Harbor
26101 Magic Mountain Parkway
Valencia, CA (661) 255-4100
www.sixflags.com

The tropical-themed waterpark offers more than 40 different water activities and legend has it that we can thank Captain Red Eye the Pirate for this oasis right here in southern

California. Hurricane Harbor is part of the Six Flags California complex and is adjacent to Magic Mountain.

Among the attractions are the Forgotten Sea wave pool; Black Snake Summit, with 5 speed slides; River Cruise lazy river; 10 slides, including Taboo Tower; Shipwreck Shores, with dozens of different interactive activities for the entire family; the Lost Temple Rapids, family rafting down a 560-foot-long aqueduct; Lizard Lagoon, a 3.2-acre 3½-foot-deep teen and adult activity pool; volleyball; and the Reptile Ridge tower with 5 body slides. There is a beach shop, an arcade, and several eateries.

Admission to Hurricane Harbor is $22, with a 2-day combo ticket available to both parks, for $53. Open weekends in May and September, daily from Memorial Day to Labor Day. Entrance to the waterpark is to the right of the theme park ticket booths. Parking charge.

Six Flags Magic Mountain

26101 Magic Mountain Parkway
Valencia, CA (661) 255–4111
www.sixflags.com

Don't forget your sneakers! You'll be doing a lot of walking as you explore this hilly, 111-acre park. With a beautiful location and plenty of huge old shade trees and mature landscaping, this is one of the nicest parks on the West Coast.

It's also a popular park for roller-coaster and thrill-ride fans. Added in 2003, Scream!, a floorless coaster, is the park's sixteenth. X, which opened in 2002, is the world's one and only four-dimensional roller coaster. Riders on X are not only treated to a fast and high coaster ride, but each seat spins 360 degrees forward and backward during the journey over 3,600 feet of track at 76 mph.

There are 49 rides, including 16 for the kids in the 6-acre High Sierra Territory and Bugs Bunny World area. The major rides are almost hidden from one another by the heavy woods and steep terrain throughout, whereas the kiddie rides are located near the entrance on relatively flat land. As in the rest of the Six Flags parks, the Looney Tunes cartoon characters are the official residents here and can be found just about everywhere.

The 4-row circa 1912 Philadelphia Toboggan Company carousel, with 48 jumpers, 16 standers, and 2 chariots, is

"Revolution," Six Flags Magic Mountain, Valencia, California   Photo by Adam Sandy

still in operation, but most of the original horses have been replaced with fiberglass replicas.

 Extras: There is a kennel located in the parking lot. There is no rental fee and water is provided for the animals for free. Dive Devil, Go-Karts, Virtual Quest, and Turbo Bungy, extra fee.

 Special events: Fright Fest, weekends in October.

 Season: Year-round; during winter months, weekends only. The show schedule is cut back during winter.

 Operating hours: Opens at 10:00 A.M. daily. Most of the year, closing hours range from 6:00 P.M. to midnight.

 Admission policy: Pay-one-price, under $45. Parking charge.

The Amusement Park Guide

 Top rides: Superman the Escape, a 100 mph, 415-foot-tall free-fall thrill ride; Grand Carousel, a circa 1912 Philadelphia Toboggan Company carousel; Sandblaster bumper cars; Log Jammer, a log flume; Tidal Wave, shoot-the-chute; Roaring Rapids, raging-rapids ride; Jet Stream, a log flume–type boat ride.

 Roller coasters: Scream!, floorless (S); Goliath, hypercoaster (S); Canyon Blaster, family (S); Deja Vu, Super Boomerang (S); X, acrobatic coaster (S); Goliath Jr., family (S); The Riddler's Revenge, stand-up (S); Batman The Ride, inverted (S); Colossus, twin racing (W); Viper, multi-element (S); Flashback (S); Gold Rusher mine train (S); Ninja, suspended (S); Psyclone (W); Revolution, looping (S); Canyon Blaster, kiddie (S).

 Plan to stay: 8 hours.

 Best way to avoid crowds: Walk to the back of the park first, where you'll find Batman The Ride and The Riddler's Revenge. It takes a couple of hours for the backside of the park to fill up. So, you'll save time if you start at the back and work your way around toward the front. Take along a map and plot your day around the show schedules. The crowds are smaller during the week and during the off-season weekends.

 Directions: Take the Magic Mountain Parkway exit off I–5 in Valencia. Go west a couple of minutes and you'll be at the park. Located 30 miles north of Hollywood.

Six Flags Marine World

2001 Marine World Parkway
Vallejo, CA (707) 644–4000
www.sixflags.com

As the West Coast's only combination wildlife park, oceanarium, and theme park, Marine World has a strong and eclectic entertainment base. The park features 3,000 animals in 35 exhibits and shows, 35 rides, and 6 non-animal shows and attractions.

Six Flags has spent more than $100 million on rides and improvements since it took over in 1997 and started adding thrill rides to the marine park. Among those enhancements are ROAR!, a mighty wooden coaster, the Vertical Velocity steel coaster, the Medusa floorless coaster, and the Looney Tunes Seaport, a neat little themed area with family rides and attractions and the popular Looney Tunes characters.

 Extras: An underwater viewing area at the Bengal tiger swimming pool provides unusual views of the beautiful beast as it swims. For an additional fee, you can swim and interact with the dolphins. Reservations suggested.

 Special events: Festival Latinos, Labor Day Weekend; Fright Fest, weekends in October.

 Season: Mid-March through October.

 Operating hours: Opens daily at 10:00 A.M., Memorial Day through Labor Day. Open Fridays, Saturdays, and Sundays in spring and fall. Closing hours vary.

 Admission policy: Pay-one-price, under $45; Parking charge.

 Top rides: Voodoo, Top Spin; White Water Safari, rapids ride; Monsoon Falls, shoot-the-chute.

 Roller coasters: Zonga, 4-looping (S); Medusa, floorless (S); Vertical Velocity, LIM inverted (S); ROAR! (W); Kong, inverted (S); Boomerang (S); Cobra, family (S); Road Runner Express, family (S).

 Plan to stay: 8 hours.

 Best way to avoid crowds: Arrive late or early, midday is most crowded. Ride the popular rides during the dolphin or waterski shows, which are very popular and take people away from the rides. Last waterski show of the day is usually the least crowded. Since the popular show plays to capacity crowds, show up 30 minutes early to make sure you find a seat.

 Directions: Located 25 miles from San Francisco, 50 miles from Sacramento. Take Highway 37 exit (Marine World Parkway/Napa) off I–80.

Six Flags Water World USA

1950 Waterworld Parkway
Concord, CA (925) 609–WAVE
www.sixflags.com

The Big Kahuna water-powered water coaster is the star here. Four-passenger tubes are swished up and down through a wide trough of speeding water. This is a thrill ride that the entire family can ride together. More than 20 other rides and attractions are located among the 20 acres here as well. The Honolulu Halfpipe, known as the sidewinder in many other parks, is truly a heart-stopping slide. It looks somewhat like a U and you slide down one side and up another.

Breaker Beach is the Bay area's largest wave pool, Kaanapali Kooler is the longest lazy river in northern California, and there are only 11 other rides in the world like Cliffhanger, a 7-story speed slide. Treasure Island is an interactive water playground with lots of pools, slides, and activities for the small ones, and Wild Water Kingdom is a multilevel activity pool with shotgun slides, cargo nets, a lily pad walk, and a toddler pool.

Open daily, May through Labor Day, from 10:30 A.M. to 6:00 or 8:00 P.M. Admission is under $26; parking is free. Early in the day and Mondays are the best times to avoid crowds.

Take the Willow Pass exit off Highway 680. Travel east to Waterworld Parkway and turn left into the park.

Six Flags Water World USA

1600 Exposition Boulevard
Sacramento, CA (916) 419–9227
www.sixflags.com

The grounds of the California Exposition Center offer much more than a great fair each year, they also offer up a bit of the cool and colorful tropics all summer long. Nestled in the corner of the property is Water World USA. That's where you'll find some fantastic water rides, with vacationing-sounding names such as Calypso Cooler and High Tide Bay Swimming Pool.

The 3-story-tall Hook's Lagoon is one of the most fun family interactive water play areas in this part of the country. The different levels offer a multitude of slides, geysers, shower bursts, and water cannons. The entire family will enjoy this attraction and everyone will get wet.

The Cobra is a challenging 6-story dual speed slide with interlocking corkscrewlike flumes. Breaker Beach is northern California's largest wave pool, featuring up to 3-foot waves. Among the other attractions, you'll find a lot of interactive play elements at High Tide Bay.

Open weekends in May and September and daily in June, July, and August, from 10:30 A.M. to 6:00 P.M. Hours vary during the California State Fair. Admission is under $22, and after 3:00 P.M. it's half-price. Parking charge is $6.

Take the Exposition Boulevard exit off the Capital City Freeway. Travel 1 block east to the Cal Expo main entrance.

Tahoe Family Zone Amusement Park

2401 Lake Tahoe Boulevard
South Lake Tahoe, CA (530) 541-1300

As the only amusement park in Lake Tahoe for at least the past 30 years, this little entertainment area has been THE place to bring the kids, or, for many local residents, the grandkids. The 10 rides are set in a large, peaceful grove of tall pine trees, and even on a hot day it's pleasant in the park.

Its most popular rides are the Giant Slide, Paratrooper, Tilt-A-Whirl, and carousel. There's a kiddie go-kart track and an adult track.

 Roller coaster: Kiddie Coaster, kiddie (S).

Open May to October; hours vary, so call first. Admission is free, with rides on a pay-as-you-go basis.

Universal Studios Hollywood

100 Universal City Plaza
Universal City, CA (818) 508-9600
www.universalstudioshollywood.com

You get a bit of cinematic history here along with the rides, shows, and attractions. Many of Universal's top stars, old and new, as well as traditional blockbuster films by

Universal are featured in various ways throughout the park.

The working studio has been here since 1915, and the public tour opened as the first studio tour attraction in the United States in 1964. Now one of the 10 most-visited theme parks in North America, it is still a working studio, and on any given day you might see a star or two in the back lot area as you take the tram tour.

You'll also get to interact with the movies. My favorite attraction here is Jurassic Park, The Ride. You climb into a boat, and take a leisurely, albeit a bit scary at times, journey past a bunch of dinosaurs before taking a big plunge over a waterfall. It's quite a fun ride.

In other attractions, you'll be able to feel the heat from Backdraft and ride to the Green Planet with E.T. You'll go face to face with King Kong, see the seas part, be able to watch Jaws attack a fisherman, be stranded in a subway during an earthquake, and be caught in the middle of a flash flood.

Shrek 4D is a fun 15-minute romp with the big fuzzy guy. You'll experience the fun 3-D visuals, as well as a multitude of other special effects within the theater. The park's other inter-active film is *T2-3D*. It combines 3-D film, live actors, and robots to provide a very cool multimedia experience. And speaking of high-tech, The Waterworld stunt show is one of the best of its genre ever created. You have lots of action, both on land and in the water, and there's plenty of fire and explosions.

If you liked Lucille Ball, you'll love The Lucy Tribute exhibition and museum. If you enjoy animals, make sure you catch the Animal Planet Live production, based on the popular programs of the Animal Planet television network. If you want some physical fun, the Nickelodeon Blast Zone is an interactive wet and dry play area for the entire family. The Special Effect Stages attraction is a 30-minute interactive, fun journey that shows how effects were done for top Universal films.

You'll enter at the top of the hill in the Entertainment Center, where you'll find a multitude of live-action shows, active movie sets, and fine restaurants and shops. To visit the Studio Plaza in the lower lot, adjacent to the soundstages, follow the signs to the Starway Escalator and ride it down a 200-foot vertical drop. There you'll find more shops and attractions. A separate, less magnificent escalator will take you to another level where you'll find the boarding area for the action-packed tram ride.

 Season: Year-round.

Operating hours: Open daily, except Thanksgiving and Christmas. Peak-season hours: 8:00 or 9:00 A.M. to 6:00, 9:00, or 10:00 P.M. Restaurants and shops stay open longer. Hours are shortened during off-season months.

 Admission policy: Pay-one-price, under $47. Parking charge.

 Top rides: Jurassic Park, The Ride, a dark boat ride past dinosaurs; E.T. Adventure—The Ride, join the alien on a bicycle for a trip to the Green Planet; Backdraft, experience an explosion up close; Back to the Future, a simulator ride with Doc Brown. The 45-minute tram ride is action packed, and will take you through the top attractions, including Earthquake—The Big One, Jaws, King Kong, the flash flood, and the collapsing bridge.

 Plan to stay: 8 hours.

 Best way to avoid crowds: Come early in the day during the week and during non-holiday times.

 Directions: Take the Universal Center or Lankershim Boulevard exit off the Hollywood Freeway (Highway 101). The studio is located between Hollywood and the San Fernando Valley.

Upland Boomers

1500 West 7th Street
Upland, CA (909) 981–5251
www.boomersparks.com

If you want to play miniature golf and it's raining, don't worry, come on over to Boomers. This location of the national chain of fun centers has 4 miniature golf courses, 2 indoors, 2 outdoors.

In addition, there are go-kart tracks, batting cages, a rock-climbing wall, and a redemption and video arcade. Rides include bumper boats, a Ferris wheel, kiddie airplanes, kiddie tea cups, and a kiddie bounce.

Open daily, year-round. Opens at 10:00 or 11:00 A.M. and closes between 10:00 P.M. and midnight.

COLORADO

Fun Junction

2878 North Avenue
Grand Junction, CO
(970) 243-1522

Indeed, a proper name for a place to have a good time with your family. The locals have been coming here for their summertime fun for quite some time. In all, there are 11 rides, including 5 just for the little ones. In addition, there are bumper boats and miniature golf. The adult and teen rides lineup has a Rotor, Tilt-A-Whirl, Spider, Ferris wheel, Scrambler, and Rock-O-Plane.

Located in beautiful western Colorado, the park is open daily during the summer starting at 6:30 P.M. on weekdays and 1:00 P.M. on weekends. Closing times vary. Admission is 50 cents, with rides on a pay-as-you-go basis. Open May and September on weekends only.

Funtastic Fun

3085 South Broadway
Englewood, CO (303) 761-8700
www.funtasticfun.com

When it snows and blows here in Colorado, parents don't worry about the kids getting cabin fever, they just take them over to Funtastic Fun, a 20,000-square-foot indoor amusement park designed for kids 10 and under. The 7 rides include a train, carousel, tea cups, air bounce, and Whip. In addition, there's a huge teddy bear that's great for fun photos and a lineup of distortion mirrors that are always fun.

Open daily, 10:00 A.M. to 9:00 P.M.; an all-you-can-ride pass is $9 for the kids, with a special $6 price on Tuesdays and Wednesdays. Adults can't ride most of the stuff, so they get in for $3. Located 4 blocks north of the Cinderella City Mall, at Broadway and Dartmouth.

Heritage Square

18301 West Colfax
Golden, CO (303) 277-0040

Here's a fun mix of entertainment, shopping, and amusement rides, all situated in the foothills of the Rocky Mountains. There are 2 restaurants, a dinner theater/music hall, a Victorian House Events Center, miniature golf, water slides, a bungee jump, and 12 rides.

You take a chairlift to the top of a 500-foot-tall foothill and ride an Alpine slide down. The water slides are on the same foothill, but only about a third of the way up. Rides include a Ferris wheel, a narrow-gauge train ride, and a zipline challenge called Jungle Quest.

A fishing pond features trout fishing. You can rent your poles here and they'll even clean the fish for you to take home. You pay by the pound. Each October, one of the highest-rated haunted parties in the Denver area takes place here. It's called The Spider Mansion, and it's quite a production.

The rides and slides and miniature golf are all seasonal, but the shops and restaurants and other indoor activities are all open year-round. Located at Highways 40 and 93.

Hyland Hills Water World

1800 West 89th Avenue
Denver, CO (303) 427-SURF
www.waterworldcolorado.com

Thanks to the hilly terrain, many of the rides and slides here come off the tops of hills, not off big cumbersome and sometimes ugly towers. This not only makes the park look a bit more natural, but it also eliminates many of the steep steps found in other parks.

Located in the Denver suburb of Federal Heights, this 64-acre facility has a total of 41 attractions, including 3 river rides and 2 wave pools, and, to top it off, the water is heated!

The Zoomerang attraction is a futuristic U-shaped slide that gives tubers a unique ride experience. The Lost River of the Pharaohs and the Voyage to the Center of the Earth are family river-raft rides that take you through highly themed indoor thrill experiences, something like you'd find at a major theme park. High-tech robotics and intricate scenery and effects make both rides unique for a waterpark!

The Raging Colorado was the park's first river-raft ride. The Wave is a double Flow Rider surfing experience, The Screamin' Mimi is one of the most popular slides, Calypso Cove is the family interactive play area, and Wally World provides water activities for the wee ones.

A gondola skylift helps transport guests to the top of the hill and at the same time provides a great view of the nearby airport.

Open 10:00 A.M. to 6:00 P.M. daily, Memorial Day through Labor Day. There are plenty of shaded picnic areas, and you're allowed to bring in your own food. Admission is under $25. Free parking.

Lakeside Park

4601 Sheridan Boulevard
Denver, CO (303) 477–1621
www.lakesideamusementpark.com

If you're looking for a historic and nostalgic amusement park with classic adult and kiddie rides, a true old-time feeling, and inexpensive good times, this is the place to go. As the last true traditional park in the state, the park has a great blend of old and new rides, including a classic 1940s wooden coaster and a circa 1908 antique carousel, one of the rides that was in operation when the park opened on May 30, 1908.

There are 40 rides, including 15 for the little kids off in a kiddie playland of their own. Included among the rides is a coal-burning steam train that ran in the 1904 World's Fair in St. Louis. The steam locomotive runs on the weekend, while during the week a diesel locomotive pulls the passenger cars around the lake.

Open weekends in May, daily operation starts in early June and runs through Labor Day. Kiddie rides open daily at noon or 1:00 P.M. and operate until 10:00 P.M. Adult rides open at 6:00 P.M. during the week and 1:00 P.M. on weekends and run to 11:00 P.M.

 Roller coasters: Cyclone (W); Wild Chipmunk, wild mouse (S); Dragon, family (S).

General admission to the park is $1.50 and once inside you can buy individual ride tickets or an unlimited ride pass for under $12 during the week, under $16 on weekends. Kiddie rides are always 50 cents each.

Take the Sheridan Boulevard exit off I–70 and go south 2 blocks. The park is on the right.

Santa's Workshop

Highway 24
North Pole, CO (719) 684–9432
www.santas-colo.com

Mr. Claus and his favorite llamas, Leonard and Lucky, have called this mountainside holiday park their home since 1956. Located at the foot of Pike's Peak, the 27-acre park is full of Santa's magic and Christmas cheer. You'll leave here humming Christmas tunes and definitely believing in the big bearded guy!

There are 25 rides and attractions, including some great classic kiddie rides and several teen and adult rides. The neat thing about the rides here is that they all offer great views of the mountains! Among the adult and family attractions are a Ferris wheel, a Sky Ride, antique cars, a scrambler, tea cups, a train ride, and a neat circular red and white slide known as the Peppermint Slide.

 Roller coaster: Candy Cane Coaster, family (S).

One unique ride allows the kids to ride ornaments around a tall Christmas tree and a circa 1920 Herschell/Spillman carousel features a nice menagerie of animals including reindeer. A 1919 Wurlitzer military band organ is not attached to the carousel but provides some great atmosphere. Christmas music is everywhere.

The real stars here, however, are Santa and Mrs. Claus. They are here every day to meet and greet their fans in the cozy little Santa's House. In the middle of the park, across from Santa's House, is the North Pole, an ice pole that stays frozen year-round.

The Alpine Village area offers some great shopping and there are several areas where a snack can be purchased. Several shows, including a fun magic presentation, take place each day and are announced over the park's sound system, 10 minutes prior to show time.

The park is open May through December with daily operation in June, July, and August. It is closed Wednesdays and Thursdays in May, and September through December. Admission is pay-one-price, under $15. If you come in after 3:00 P.M., the next day is free.

Located 10 miles west of Colorado Springs. To get here, take exit 141 off I–25 and go west on Highway 24.

Six Flags Elitch Gardens Island Kingdom

**2000 Elitch Circle
Denver, CO (303) 595–4386
www.sixflags.com**

Without a doubt, this is Colorado's coaster and thrill ride capital, with 45 rides, shows, and attractions. There are 5 coasters, including the country's first Zamperla Flying Coaster, a unique ride that provides riders with a sense of flight.

Located in the Central Platte Valley in downtown Denver, the park features Bugs Bunny and all the Looney Tunes characters as well as the DC Comics superheroes, including Batman. Island Kingdom is included in the park admission and has a lush tropical theme that offers quite an environmental contrast here in the middle of the Rockies. Among its attractions are a lazy river, a wave pool, a great interactive kids' area, and a bevy of slides.

 Extras: The Gotham City Carnival of Chaos, a high-tech stunt show, is included in admission. Don't miss the beautiful antique carousel. Created by the Philadelphia Toboggan Company (#51), it was at the original Elitch Gardens from 1928 to 1995 and has been here in the new park since 1995.

 Season: Late April through October.

 Operating hours: Opens at 10:00 A.M. daily. Closes at 10:00 P.M. weekdays, 11:00 P.M. Fridays and Saturdays during peak season.

 Admission policy: Pay-one-price, under $34; Parking charge.

Top rides: Shipwreck Falls, shoot-the-chute; Tower of Doom, a 220-foot-tall free fall; Disaster Canyon rapids ride; Top Spin; Big Wheel, a 100-foot wheel offering a great view of downtown Denver.

 Roller coasters: Boomerang (S); Flying Coaster, family flying coaster (S); Mind Eraser, inverted (S); Twister II (W); Sidewinder, shuttle loop (S); The Great Chase, kiddie (S).

 Plan to stay: 6 hours.

 Best way to avoid crowds: Arrive early during the week.

 Directions: Take Speer Boulevard South (exit 212A) off I–25.

CONNECTICUT

Lake Compounce

822 Lake Avenue
Bristol, CT (860) 583–3300
www.lakecompounce.com

America's oldest continuously operated amusement park has never looked or sounded better than it does today. With more than 50 rides, shows, and attractions, a waterpark, some great mountainside rides, and one of the coolest kiddielands around, this place rocks!

 # TiM'S TRiViA

Magician Harry Houdini and a juggler named Orson Welles both played the stages of Lake Compounce during their careers. Back then, front-row seats cost 10 cents.

Founded in 1846 at the foot of Compounce Mountain, the park retains much of its old charm. The circa 1890 Starlite Ballroom is still in use as a restaurant and entertainment venue, the old arcade is now a bathhouse at Splash Harbor waterpark, and the circa 1893 antique carousel the park brought here in 1911 is still spinning. The rare machine has 49 horses, 2 chariots, and 1 goat and was carved by top craftsmen: Carmel, Looff, Stein & Goldstein, and Murphy.

TiM'S TRiViA

The Carousel Museum of New England, located at 95 Riverside Avenue in Bristol, Connecticut, is open year-round with a great selection of horses, memorabilia, and written information about the golden age of carousels. The museum operates and cares for the Bushnell Park Carousel in downtown Hartford as well. Located in the oldest public park in the country, the circa 1914 Stein & Goldstein carousel is open May through mid-October, Tuesday through Sunday. Rides are 50 cents each. The museum can be reached at (860) 585-5411 or on-line at www.thecarouselmuseum.com.

The Boulder Dash wooden roller coaster, built into the side of the mountain, is a work of art in itself. It hugs the side of the mountain while dashing around and very close to huge boulders. It's one of the country's unique and great coaster rides. A sky ride to the top of the mountain is a peaceful 25-minute round trip that provides a wonderful vista.

The water elements here are quite fun, including the wave pool, Clipper Cove play area, the slides, and the swimming in Lake Compounce. Characters Garfield and Odie hang out each summer at the Circus World, where you'll find the park's 11 themed kiddie rides. For an extra fee, you can enjoy miniature golf, go for a paddleboat ride on the lake, or take a plunge on the Skycoaster.

 Special events: Haunted Graveyard, weekends in October.

 Season: Memorial Day through October. Open daily from mid-June through late August.

 Operating hours: Opens at 11:00 A.M.; closes at 8:00 or 10:00 P.M., depending on season.

 Admission policy: Pay-one-price including all rides, slides, and beach, under $30.

Top rides: Ghost Hunt, an interactive family dark-ride with a haunted house theme; Giant Wheel; Log Flume; Flying Scooters; Trolley, ride on full-size antique trolley; Musik Express; Thunder Rapids, rapids ride.

 Roller coasters: Boulder Dash Mountain Coaster (W); Wildcat, circa 1927 (W); Zoomerang, boomerang (S); Kiddie Coaster, kiddie (S).

 Plan to stay: 6 to 8 hours if water elements and beach are used.

 Best way to avoid crowds: Crowds aren't usually a problem here except when the park hosts large corporate picnics. Even then lines are rarely longer than a 20-minute wait.

 Directions: Located on Route 229N, about 2 miles north of exit 31 off I–84, west of Hartford.

Quassy Amusement Park

**Route 64 at Lake Quassapaug
Middlebury, CT
(203) 758–2913/(800) FOR–PARK
www.quassy.com**

Located on the south shore of Lake Quassapaug, the park has 24 rides that the family can enjoy together. Activities range from a roller coaster to a relaxing train ride around the park to a swim in the lake.

If you're hungry, the restaurant provides a nice view overlooking the lake. There's a large video and redemption arcade, and the funky little *Quassy Queen* provides rides around the lake for a small extra fee.

Quassy is known as a picnic park and since 1908 the locals have been coming here with family and friends for the entertainment, the nice sandy beach, and the beautiful spring-fed lake.

 Season: April through mid-October.

 Operating hours: Rides open at 10:00 or 11:00 A.M. and close at 8:00 or 10:00 P.M. Beach and arcade open daily at 11:00 A.M.

THE AMUSEMENT PARK GUIDE

 Admission policy: Free admission, with rides and attractions on a pay-as-you-play basis. Pay-one-price also available, under $15 for all day, $5.50 after 5:00 P.M. Every Friday night after 5:00, all rides, hot dogs, colas, snow cones, and cotton candy are 25 cents each. Beach is free with any pay-one-price deal. Parking charge.

 Top rides: Frog Hopper; the Big Flush, wet and dry slide; train ride around park; Music Fest; bumper cars; Trabant.

 Roller coaster: Monster Mouse, wild mouse (S); Little Dipper, kiddie (S).

 Plan to stay: 6 hours, if you ride and swim.

 Best way to avoid crowds: The crowds are lightest during midweek.

 Directions: Take exit 17 (Route 64) off I–84. Go west about 4 miles; the park is on the right.

DELAWARE

Funland

6 Delaware Avenue
Rehoboth Beach, DE (302) 227–1921
www.funlandrehoboth.com

As the state's only amusement park, Funland manages to combine the best of the old boardwalk-style parks with some of today's best contemporary rides for a park experience the entire family should enjoy. The park takes up a little more than an acre but packs a lot into that little space, including 18 rides. The marquee attractions include the Haunted Mansion, an in-house built ride-through darkride; the Chaos, a spinning, tilting ride; the Frog Hopper, a children's free-fall ride; and the Merry-Go Round, a 1959 Allan Herschell carousel with metal horses.

The park is one of the most affordable in the country. Tickets cost 25 cents each, $5 gets you 24 tickets, and

$10 buys 54 tickets. The rides require between 1 and 5 tickets.

Funland is open mid-May through early September. The arcade opens at 10:30 A.M., the rides open at 1:00 P.M., and the Haunted Mansion opens at 6:30 P.M. Closing time depends on a number of factors each day including the crowds and the weather. The rides are all pay-as-you-play. Although the park has no food facilities, there are many places that serve traditional boardwalk fare all around Funland.

FLORIDA

Adventure Island
McKinley at Bougainvillea Avenue
Tampa, FL (813) 987–5600
www.adventureisland.com

Owned by Busch Entertainment Corporation and located adjacent to Busch Gardens, this 25-acre tropical paradise has enough activities to keep you busy and cool for hours, including 20 water attractions, sand volleyball courts, sunbathing areas, and an outdoor cafe, all in a soothing and fun Key West atmosphere.

The park features 15 water slides, with such descriptive names as Runaway Rapids, Water Moccasin, Gulf Scream, and the Tampa Typhoon. Wahoo Run is a family raft ride for up to five riders. Passengers plunge at 15 feet per second over the 600-foot journey. Splash Attack is a water play area with 50 interactive water elements. Key West Rapids is a 5-story-tall tube slide featuring many surprises, including geysers, spurts, and showers. Fabian's Funport is a children's play area with an activity pool, a mini wave pool, and various other slides and activities. The Endless Surf is the wave pool, and the Rambling Bayou is a lazy river.

Open mid-February through October, 10:00 A.M. to 5:00 P.M. Hours are extended during the summer peak periods. Admission is under $28 for the waterpark, and a 2-day combo pass with Busch Gardens sells for under $56.

Adventure Landing
Shipwreck Island

1944 Beach Boulevard
Jacksonville, FL (904) 246–4386
www.adventurelanding.com

This combination waterpark/family entertainment center near the Intercoastal Waterway gives you the option of frolicking in the water for a while, then walking over to the other attractions and paying to play only what you want. But if you do leave to enjoy the dry side, be sure to get your hand stamped so you can re-enter the waterpark.

Jacksonville's only waterpark features 12 slides, including Hydro Half Pipe, which confronts single, double, or triple tube-riders with a near-vertical drop of 40 feet, then shoots them through a pool of water. There's also an uphill water coaster called The Rage and a lazy river. Admission is under $20.

The family entertainment center offers go-karts, laser tag, a large games arcade, miniature golf, and batting cages. The MaxFlight lets you create your own roller coaster design, then climb into a pod and ride it! All attractions are on a pay-as-you-play basis, with various family fun center/waterpark packages available.

The waterpark is open from late April through September, from 10:00 A.M. to 7:00 P.M. The entertainment center is open year-round from 10:00 A.M. to 11 P.M.

Big Kahuna's Waterpark

1007 Highway 98
Destin, FL (850) 837–8319
www.bigkahunas.com

There's plenty to do in Destin once you've tired of playing on the magnificent Gulf of Mexico beaches, and Big Kahuna's is a great place to start.

Among the 40 water attractions are 2 wave pools, 3 action rivers, speed slides, body flumes, and 4 kids' areas complete with pint-sized slides and attractions. There is also tropical miniature golf, 2 go-kart tracks, and 3 extreme thrill rides: a 130-foot-tall Skycoaster, a 140-foot-tall reverse bungee, and the Cyclone, on which passengers sit at the end of a 80-foot-long propeller and spin at high speeds.

The waterpark is open May through Labor Day and the rides and golf are open March through September.

Boomers
Dania Beach Hurricane

1801 NW First Street
Dania Beach, FL
(954) 921–1411 for Boomers;
(954) 921–RIDE for Dania Beach Hurricane
www.boomersparks.com

Boomers features 3 indoor virtual simulator rides, a Skycoaster, the Blender ride, new bumper cars, several kiddie rides, and a 1.5-mile-long go-kart track, the longest in south Florida. There are also 5 miniature golf courses, a climbing wall, laser tag, and an indoor arcade with 800 video and redemption games.

It is also home to south Floida's only wooden roller coaster, the Dania Beach Hurricane. The 100-foot-tall, 3,200-foot-long woodie opened in late 2000 and has proven to be a real winner. Being the only woodie in this part of the world has brought the crowds, and the press, out in droves. The ride is not owned by Boomers, but rests on land owned by the family entertainment center.

Boomers and the Dania Beach Hurricane operate year-round, with both opening at 10:00 A.M. daily. Monday through Thursday, the coaster closes around midnight and the park at 2:00 A.M. On Friday and Saturday, the coaster has varying extended hours and the park closes at 4:00 A.M.

Boomers offers various ride, golf, and go-kart all-you-can-ride specials. A single ride on the Hurricane will cost you $6.25.

Busch Gardens

3000 Busch Boulevard
Tampa, FL (813) 987–5082
www.buschgardens.com

Africa on the west coast of Florida!

Lions, tigers, roller coasters, live shows, 4-D films, a replica of King Tut's tomb, and a wild adventure in an out-of-control Land Rover all combine to make a trip here about as close as

THE AMUSEMENT PARK GUIDE

you can get to the real Africa without going there. Complete with areas representing Morocco, the Serengeti Plain, Egypt, and other regions of Africa, the park combines its 335 acres of tropical landscape with Florida's humid climate to create a realistic effect.

In addition to its 25 rides, the park offers up the Budweiser Clydesdales and more than 2,700 animals, making this one of the top zoological gardens in the country, as well as one of the 10 most-attended theme parks in the country.

R.L. Stine's Haunted Lighthouse is a multisensory, motion-based 4-D experience, based on the children's horror books of R.L. Stine. This fun family film stars Christopher Lloyd and Weird Al Yankovic, among others. Rhino Rally is a unique ride through the wilderness in a Land Rover that turns into a wild trip down a white-water river. Edge of Africa is a great place if you want to see some animals up close and personal. It's a 15-acre walk-through area with numerous naturalistic habitats.

 Extras: Included in park admission is a mono-rail, a sky ride, and a steam train ride through the 60-acre Serengeti Plains, where more than 500 large African animals live. Land of the Dragons is a fun kiddie area that includes a Ferris wheel, a dragon carousel, and a 3-story-tall tree house.

 Season: Year-round.

 Operating hours: 9:30 A.M. to 6:00 P.M. Extended closing times during peak summer season.

 Admission policy: Pay-one-price, under $55. Combo tickets are available with the Adventure Island waterpark, and with SeaWorld Orlando. Parking charge.

 Top rides: Akbar's Adventure Tour, a motion-based simulator ride starring Martin Short; Serengeti Express Railway; Tanganyiki Tidal Wave, a spill-water raft ride; Congo River Rapids, a rag-ing-rapids ride; Stanley Falls, a log flume.

 Roller coasters: Gwazi, dueling coaster (W); Kumba, multi-element (S); Montu, inverted (S); Python, corkscrew (S); Scorpion, looping (S).

 Plan to stay: 8 hours.

Best way to avoid crowds: Come during the fall, when the crowds are most scarce, or midafternoon during the peak season.

 Directions: Located at the corner of Busch Boulevard and 40th Street, 8 miles northeast of downtown Tampa. Take exit 33 (Busch Boulevard) off I–75 and go east 2 miles to the park. Or take exit 265 off I–75, go west 2 miles, and follow the signs.

Fun Spot Action Park

5551 Del Verde Way
Orlando, FL (407) 363–3867
www.fun-spot.com

Follow the colorful Giant Wheel and at its base you'll find a real fun spot. There are 4 go-kart tracks, 6 kiddie rides, 6 adult and thrill rides, and a 10,000-square-foot, air-conditioned arcade with more than 100 games including the latest interactive games.

Three of the four tracks are multilevel wood tracks built over a water retention pond. The Quad Helix track is 1,600 feet long with 4 corkscrews and 25-degree banked descending curves. Rides include the Revolution Ferris wheel, 1001 Nachts, bumper cars, bumper boats, and a Paratrooper.

Open daily, year-round, 10:00 A.M. to midnight during the peak season, and 2:00 to 11:00 P.M. or midnight during the week and 10:00 A.M. to midnight on Saturday and Sunday during the rest of the year. Attractions on a pay-as-you-play basis, with an all-day unlimited ride ticket for $30. Located between the Belz Mall and Wet 'n Wild near the intersection of International Drive and Kirkman Road. Take exit 75A off I–4 and look for the Giant Wheel.

Fun World at Flea World

Highway 17-92
Sanford, FL (407) 330–1792
www.fleaworld.com

If you get tired of riding the attractions at this enjoyable little family park, it offers you the wonderful option to hop next door and go shopping at Flea World, "America's

Largest Flea Market!" But don't leave before you've had the chance to sample its 21 rides, 2 go-kart tracks, miniature golf, and giant video arcade/game room with 350 games.

Among the rides are bumper cars, a vintage carousel, Himalaya, Tilt-A-Whirl, Loop-O-Plane, Round-Up, a giant slide, and 7 kiddie rides. Animal acts, magic shows, and family circus-style shows are scheduled year-round at the Fun World Pavilion stage, free to visitors.

Admission to Fun World (and Flea World, featuring more than 1,700 dealers) is free, with rides on a pay-as-you-play basis. Unlimited rides for the 8 kiddie rides in Kids World are available for under $6; unlimited rides for all rides in park, under $16.

Adult rides are open every Saturday and Sunday, 11:00 A.M. to 6:00 P.M. Kiddie rides are open every Saturday and Sunday, 10:00 A.M. to 6:00 P.M. Open year-round, free parking.

Miracle Strip Amusement Park

12000 West Highway 98A
Panama City, FL (850) 234-5810
www.miraclestrippark.com

Across the street from the beautiful white-sand beaches of the Gulf of Mexico, this park is a traditional, well-maintained, family-oriented attraction offering a good mix of rides, games, and excitement.

Along with its 31 rides, the park offers a wide selection of things to do. New in 2002 was the O2 Tower, a drop ride that offers spectacular views of the Florida Panhandle's coastline. But don't expect to enjoy the view for too long, because after a few seconds at the top, you'll be treated to a breathtaking 185-foot drop back down to the ground!

Though the park itself has no theme, many of the individual rides do. One such ride is Dante's Inferno, housed in a giant, devil-shaped building that you enter by walking across the devil's tongue. Another ride is set inside a huge igloo.

 Season: Mid-March through Labor Day.

 Operating hours: Open Sunday through Friday 6:00 to 11:00 P.M., Saturday 2:00 to 11:00 P.M.

Admission policy: General admission under $6, plus rides. Pay-one-price also available, under $18. A 2-day combo, pay-one-price unlimited-use ticket for this park and its sister park, Shipwreck Island, located across the street, is available, under $33. Free parking.

 Top rides: O2 Tower, drop ride; a log flume; Haunted Castle, a darkride; The Dungeon, an enclosed Tilt-A-Whirl; a Ferris wheel that offers a great view of the park; Matterhorn; Musik Express; Shockwave, a 360-degree swinging ship.

 Roller coaster: Starliner (W).

 Plan to stay: 3½ hours.

 Best ways to avoid crowds: Avoid Saturdays. Best times to visit are weekday nights or anytime during the last two weeks in August, when the resort community begins to thin out.

 Directions: Take Route 231 south from I–10. Turn right on Highway 98 and go 10 miles. The park is on the right.

Old Town

**5770 West Irlo Bronson Highway (Route 192 West), Kissimmee, FL
(800) 843–4202
www.old-town.com**

Enjoy a stroll back in history when you enter this re-creation of a Florida community at the turn of the twentieth century, located on 192 West about 2½ miles from Walt Disney World. Open year-round, it features more than 78 shops, 8 restaurants, and 18 amusement rides and attractions, all situated around a tree-lined pedestrian boulevard.

The classic "oldies" music from the 1950s and 1960s is broadcast on Old Town's own AM radio station, WOTS, and can be heard throughout the complex. To add to that nostalgic flavor, between 200 and 600 classic cars show up each Friday and Saturday for Cruise Night. Remember when cruising was in? Remember the music? Remember the fun?

The rides include the 1955 Eli Bridge prototype Scrambler, a roller coaster, bumper cars, a Ferris wheel, go-karts, and a spring-powered Ejection Seat called The Slingshot, the largest of its kind in the world. A kiddie Frog Hopper and Pharaoh's Fury were recently added, and the world's tallest Skycoaster is situated next door. The adult rides are up front along Route 192, while the kiddie rides are in the back, and a first-class haunted house and a laser tag attraction are located amid the boulevard shops.

Free admission, with everything on a pay-as-you-go basis. Rides and attractions are open from noon until midnight, or, as the owner says, "until everyone goes home."

 Roller coasters: Windstorm (S); Dragon Wagon, family (S).

SeaWorld Adventure Park

7007 SeaWorld Drive
Orlando, FL (407) 351–3600
www.seaworld.com

Deep in the heart of central Florida, the charm of some of your favorite seaside dreams comes alive. The Key West area evokes a bit of the Keys, the entrance plaza a bit of New England, and in 2003 the Mediterranean area came to life in a new shopping and restaurant district along the shores of the lake.

The focus of this lushly landscaped 135-acre marine park is on the ocean, not only on the critters that live there. Even the mythological sea is represented, with the Kraken floorless roller coaster being themed after a mythological beast, and the Journey to Atlantis is a half roller coaster, half water flume attraction set in a realistic Greek fishing village.

The Pacific Point Preserve is one of the best animal habitats ever created. In it, California sea lions and harbor seals splash and live along the rugged northern Pacific coast. In the Manatees: The Last Generation? exhibit, the magnificent creatures can be seen swimming along as visitors hear about the plight of these behemoths.

Don't miss The Shamu Adventure Show, the landmark event at any SeaWorld park. For a very funny performance, catch the Clyde and Seamore show. They are the funniest otter and sea lion you'll ever meet! The 3-acre Shamu's

"Journey to Atlantis," SeaWorld, Orlando, Florida   Photo by Tim O'Brien

Happy Harbor area is full of all sorts of activities for the kids. The Penguin Encounter lets you see a variety of penguins in a natural-like environment.

 Season: Year-round.

 Operating hours: 9:00 A.M. to 7:00 P.M. Extended hours during the peak summer season and on holidays.

 Admission policy: Pay-one-price, under $55. There are numerous ways to save, including purchasing 5-Park FlexTicket for under $210, which gives you 14 consecutive days of unlimited admission to SeaWorld, Wet 'n Wild, Universal Studios, Universal's Islands of Adventure, and Busch Gardens in Tampa. Buy on-line before leaving and save 10% to 20%. Parking charge.

Top rides: Journey to Atlantis, a water ride/roller coaster combo; Wild Arctic, ride simulator; a 400-foot-tall sky tower that rises over the lake in the center of the park, extra charge.

 Roller coaster: Kraken, floorless (S).

 Plan to stay: 8 hours.

 Best way to avoid crowds: Come during off-season, in late afternoon; few of the locals visit the park from May through Labor Day or on holidays. During the season, come early and take in the major shows first; then wander through the exhibits at your own pace.

 Directions: Located at the intersection of I–4 and the Bee Line Expressway, 10 minutes from downtown Orlando.

Shipwreck Island

12000 West Highway 98A
Panama City, FL (850) 234–0368
www.shipwreckisland.com

It's quite a choice you'll have to make if you're vacationing here for awhile and want to have some fun in the water. The nicely themed and very inviting tropical waterpark lies directly across from some of the most beautiful white-sand beaches on the Gulf Coast. But this place has fresh water, plenty of shade, and lots of ride and slide action, just a few of the things Mother Nature's huge waterpark across the street can't offer.

As a sister park to the adjacent Miracle Strip Amusement Park, it opens in mid-April and runs through Labor Day weekend. Open 10:30 A.M. to 5:30 P.M. daily, the park offers 20 slides and flumes, including the White Knuckle Ride, a family raft ride; Tree Top Drop, a 3-story-high speed slide; Pirate's Plunge, 6-story speed slides; Ocean Motion, the wave pool; the Raging Rapids, a not-so-lazy river; Tadpole Hole children's area; a lazy river; food service; and a beach shop.

Admission is separate from the amusement park, but a 2-day Double-Parked combination pass that allows unlimited use of both parks is available, under $33. Admission to the waterpark only, under $24. The days do not have to be consecutive.

Universal Orlando Resort

1000 Universal Studios Plaza
Orlando, FL
(407) 363-8000/(888) 331-9108
www.universalorlando.com

In 2002, with the completion of its third hotel, the framework of the Universal Orlando theme park resort was completed, a process that started in the late 1980s.

All the major elements are now there, but the fine-tuning will surely continue as new rides, shows, attractions, restaurants, and shops are added to the mix and as the older attractions are updated and replaced.

Universal Studios Florida opened in 1990 as a 110-acre theme park with 13 attractions. Today, Universal Florida is a 550-acre resort destination with four distinct areas: the original Universal Studios theme park; the Islands of Adventure theme park; CityWalk, a 30-acre entertainment complex that serves as a hub for the two theme parks; and the hotel district, with the Portofino Bay, Hard Rock, and Royal Pacific Resort, all Loews hotels.

Universal Studios

This is the park that started it all for Universal in Florida in 1990.

In 2003 two of the original attractions were replaced with fresh new family-oriented attractions. The FUNtastic World of Hanna-Barbera has been replaced with the whimsical world of Nickelodeon. The motion-based ride is now known as Jimmy Neutron's Nicktoon Blast. SpongeBob SquarePants and a couple of the Rugrats characters join Neutron in this adventurous romp.

The Alfred Hitchcock 3-D attraction has been replaced by a new 4-D presentation starring the big green hairy guy, Shrek. The 15-minute animated film features 3-D visual effects as well as multiple special effects within the theater that are heard, felt, and smelled. Officials say it was filmed in all-new Ogrevision.

Now missing from the Universal landscape is Kongfrontation, another original attraction. A new, high-tech rollercoaster ride, based on *The Mummy* films, is set to debut in its place in early 2004.

TiM'S TRiViA

While you enjoy a cheeseburger in paradise at Jimmy Buffett's Margaritaville restaurant at Universal's CityWalk, keep an eye on the scenery behind the Volcano Bar. An active volcano erupts lava-like Margarita mix whenever the blender needs replenishing. Where you gonna go when the volcano blow?

This is one of the most cohesively themed parks in the world. You walk among movie sets whose facades range from the streets of New York City to the architecture and lagoons of Amity Harbor to the San Francisco wharf area. The major rides and attractions are located in the various themed areas and all but one, Jaws, is located indoors. That means they are also air-conditioned and that's good news in Florida, especially in the summer.

With the park's overall theme that this is where one can "Ride the Movies," there are several movie rides. Men in Black Alien Attack is a darkride adventure where you shoot at the aliens; on the E.T. Adventure attraction, you get to help the little guy get back to the Green Planet while you take a trip on a flying bicycle; Earthquake—The Big One lets you experience an earthquake while riding in a subway car; you journey with Doc Brown in Back to the Future, as you travel to another time; and in Jaws, you take a ride on a pontoon boat and get attacked by the big fish itself.

The Woody Woodpecker's Kid Zone features the Nuthouse Coaster and the Curious George Goes to Town play area. The Twister attraction is a must-see! Based on the movie, you'll experience a "real" tornado inside the building, complete with a flying cow! In the *T2-3D* interactive film adventure, film and live actors combine for one of the best multimedia shows on the planet.

Roller coaster: Woody Woodpecker's Nuthouse Coaster, family (S).

Islands of Adventure

Orlando's first true "ride park" opened in 1999 and in doing so provided guests with a bevy of traditional amusement park rides themed in a true Universal way. This is the park where the worlds of myths, legends, and superheroes from the greatest stories of all time come alive.

Unlike major theme parks of the past, including its sister park, Universal Studios, Islands is not a world of unfamiliar prototypical rides. There are roller coasters, there are water rides, and there's a carousel. What they've done here is to take the rides we already know and love and create a heavily themed, well-known experience around each. Who hasn't heard of Popeye, of Dr. Seuss, of Jurassic Park, of Dudley Do-Right? They all come alive here.

 TiM'S TRiViA

SpongeBob SquarePants and Jimmy Neutron are now starring in their own attraction at Universal Studios Orlando. They are joined by a couple of Rugrat characters in the fun new Jimmy Neutron's Nicktoon Blast, a motion-based movie ride.

There are five themed islands in the park: Seuss Landing, Toon Lagoon, Marvel Super Hero Island, the Lost Continent, and Jurassic Park. You'll find The Cat in The Hat Ride, the Caro-Suess-el, and the Green Eggs and Ham Cafe in Seuss Landing. Everyone's favorite cartoon characters (150 of them to be exact) live in Toon Lagoon, where Dudley Do-Right's Ripsaw Falls ride drops riders 75 feet downward beneath the surface of the water. On Marvel Super Hero Island, the Spider-Man Adventure combines moving vehicles with filmed 3-D action and live action. The Incredible Hulk Coaster blasts riders out of Dr. Bruce Banner's lab, reaching 40 mph in two seconds. Doctor Doom's FearFall is a twin-tower, 200-foot-tall free fall.

The Jurassic Park River Adventure provides an up-close three-dimensional world of Jurassic Park, where one can also climb aboard Pteranodon Flyers and soar high above the island. On Lost Continent, the Dueling Dragons roller coaster features two intertwined tracks that wind over and around each other through the trees of a medieval forest and over Dragon Lake. The two "dragons" dive at each other at 60 mph three times during the three-minute ride.

THE AMUSEMENT PARK GUIDE

Roller coasters: Dueling Dragons, inverted racing (S); Incredible Hulk Coaster, 7 inversions (S); Pteranodon Flyers, family suspended (S); Flying Unicorn, family (S).

In addition to the rides, there are several high-tech shows and some great places to eat and shop.

Why stay at one of the hotels here? In addition to being great themed hotels with amazing amenities, guests who stay on-site get a one-of-a-kind special privilege. With an admission ticket to either park, resort guests get in early and never have to wait in line for a ride, show, or attraction. Plus, both parks are within a five-minute walk of the hotels. Great convenience!

CityWalk

All guests coming to or leaving the two theme parks will pass through CityWalk on the way to parking garages. The 30-acre entertainment complex is a 2-tiered promenade of live music clubs, dance clubs, restaurants, retail facilities, and 2 outdoor entertainment theaters. Admission is free, with some individual clubs charging a cover at the door.

Among the featured facilities: Hard Rock Cafe Orlando and Hard Rock Live performance venue; Jimmy Buffett's Margaritaville; the popular Pat O'Brien's watering hole, direct from New Orleans; Motown Cafe; Bob Marley's A Tribute to Freedom; Latin Quarter dance club; NASCAR Cafe; and the 20-screen, 5,000-seat Universal Cineplex.

The Complex

Season: Year-round.

Operating hours: Parks open at 9:00 A.M., close at varying times, depending on the season. CityWalk venues are the last to close.

Admission policy: Pay-one-price, under $55. Parking charge.

Plan to stay: At least 1 day in each park.

Best way to avoid crowds: Most shows and attractions have preshows that help cut the anticipated waits. Don't be fooled by the short lines you see outside: Most of the lines here are inside air-conditioned buildings. All resort hotel guests have a "no line, no wait" admission policy.

 Directions: Main entrance is ½ mile north of I–4, off exit 30B (Kirkman Road/Highway 435). Another entrance is off Turkey Lake Road: Take exit 29 (Sand Lake) off I–4 and turn right onto Turkey Lake Road within ½ mile of the interstate.

Walt Disney World Resort
Routes 4 and 192
Lake Buena Vista, FL (407) 824–4321
www.disneyworld.com

The world's largest family resort complex evokes images of Mickey Mouse, Cinderella Castle, and droves of children (and adults!) wearing Mouse Ears emblazoned with their first names.

But Walt Disney World Resort is more—so much more.

In fact, it takes more than 54,000 "cast members" (Disney parlance for employees) to make the "magic" for the millions who trek to see Mickey and his pals each year. But when you have the creativity and imagination of Disney behind you, making magic is not a job—it's a mission. After all, what would you expect from a company that has an entire creative division called "Imagineering"?

In the mid-1960s, when Walt Disney scouted the site he dubbed the "Florida Project," few probably thought his creation would grow into what the world knows today as the 47-square-mile Walt Disney World Resort. From the miles of undeveloped land, cypress swamps, and lake-studded grovelands sprang the world's most beloved entertainment resort.

Today, the Orlando-area Vacation Kingdom boasts four theme parks: the Magic Kingdom (which opened in 1971), Epcot (1982), Disney–MGM Studios (1989), and Disney's Animal Kingdom (1998). In addition, the House of Mouse is home to two major waterparks, nighttime entertainment districts, more than 300 restaurants, nearly 20 Disney-owned and -operated resort hotels, an international sports complex, recreation of every sort, and countless special events throughout the year.

Open 365 days a year (one of the reasons Walt chose the site was for the warm climate), Walt Disney World Resort is a living legacy to the man who started it all. True to his original vision, the complex is constantly evolving with new themed attractions and resorts.

To get you on your way to the Wonderful World of Disney, I'll offer some highlights from each park, the waterparks, and a few of my favorites from the massive resort.

The Magic Kingdom

With more than 30 years and countless smiles on its lengthy resumé, the Magic Kingdom is the park most guests associate with the name "Walt Disney World." Here you'll find the hallmark Disney attractions—many based on famous fairy tales—in a world of happily-ever-after fantasy and futuristic wonder.

The 107-acre site is divided into seven lands: Main Street USA, Liberty Square, Frontierland, Adventureland, Fantasyland, Tomorrowland, and Mickey's Toontown Fair. More than 40 major attractions, designed for adults and children to enjoy together, make the Magic Kingdom the most-visited theme park in the United States, and the second most-visited, behind only Tokyo Disneyland, in the world.

 # TiM'S TRiViA

Walt Disney World is a golfer's paradise, with 99 holes on nearly 800 acres. And yes, Mickey's presence is even found on the golf course. On the sixth hole of Disney's Magnolia course, there is a sand trap in the shape of Mickey's head. Not surprisingly, it's called "The Mouse Trap."

Once inside this theme park marvel, you'll find Disney's famous attention to detail around every corner. Here, it's hard to tell reality from fantasy, and it's fun trying to decide what's real and what's not. For instance, the Barber Shop on Main Street USA appears as merely a turn-of-the-century facade. Not so! As horse-drawn trolleys and antique fire engines outside roll by the candy-cane barber pole, real barbers inside are hard at work cutting and styling hair for walk-in customers. I hear "first haircuts" for children are a specialty for Disney's tonsorial artists.

Shows and entertainment: The Magic Kingdom is home to Disney's most popular daily parade, so stake your claim along Main Street USA. for a front-row view. Or, for a great photograph of the parade action, line up early and position yourself near the park's famous Cinderella

Castle—the 190-foot icon serves as a dramatic backdrop for any parade photo.

In mid-2003, Walt Disney World's fifth 3-D film experience was set to open. *Mickey's PhilHarmagic* is a *Fantasia*-like musical romp through both the old and new Disney film classics. If you like Donald Duck, you'll love this attraction!

To get up-close and personal with Mickey and his friends, head to Mickey's Toontown Fair. A host of characters (including "The Big Cheese" himself) appear at various times throughout the day for photographs and autographs.

Attractions: Thrills for the young and young-at-heart can be found throughout the park. Space Mountain sends riders 44 inches and taller hurtling through the twisting, turning darkness on a wild, galactic ride, while The Many Adventures of Winnie the Pooh takes guests (in their very own Hunny Pot) through the fabled Hundred Acre Wood. A few favorites in the Magic Kingdom: The Haunted Mansion, the best of its kind worldwide, with some whiz-bang special effects that still amaze after all these years; Buzz Lightyear's Space Ranger Spin, a spinning, interactive, laser-enhanced attraction where guests take aim at toon-ish targets; and Splash Mountain, a towering log ride offering splashy thrills, a great soundtrack, and the longest flume chute in the world.

Disney-MGM Studios

"Hollywood East" brings charm to this 154-acre working television, film, radio, and animation studio and theme park combination. Silver screen animation production (*Mulan* and *Lilo and Stitch* were created here) allows guests to peek in on the "action" inside animation studios and soundstages. The park has grown by leaps and bounds since its grand opening in 1989, with its best thrill offerings—Star Tours, The Twilight Zone Tower of Terror, and Rock 'n' Roller Coaster Starring Aerosmith—all added to the park since opening day.

Shows and entertainment: Predictably, many of the live entertainment shows at the Disney-MGM Studios are based on famous Disney films and television shows: *Voyage of the Little Mermaid* and *Beauty and the Beast— Live on Stage* are two of the best. *Voyage of the Little Mermaid* combines the film's famous music with puppets, lasers, and other special effects to tell the story of the young mermaid as she lives "Under the Sea." The long-running

Beauty and the Beast—Live on Stage is performed in the giant Theater of the Stars and delights guests with its fairy-tale magic and Broadway-style staging.

The world-famous Muppets star in a laugh-a-minute 3-D film, *Jim Henson's Muppet*Vision 3-D*, inside a specially constructed theater that transforms as quickly as the action on-screen. Cornpone humor combines with spectacular 3-D effects, costumed characters, and some spectacular Disney Audio-Animatronics to bring Kermit and his pals to life. He makes being green seem easy.

Hands down, the best show in the park is *Fantasmic!* Presented in a waterside amphitheater, the 26-minute show features stunning water, laser, and pyrotechnic effects combined with live Disney characters and puppets. The production brings to life Mickey's dream-turned-nightmare when Disney villains invade his imagination. In true Disney fashion, good ultimately triumphs over evil and the audience celebrates with a boatload of Disney characters under a burst of celebratory fireworks. The show is presented every evening (sometimes twice, depending on the season). The theater fills fast, so be sure to line up early.

 TiM'S TRiViA

Disney–MGM Studios acquired a new icon in 2001: a 12-story-tall Sorcerer Hat that Mickey made famous in the classic film Fantasia *now serves as the backdrop for guests taking family photos as they enter the park. Special lighting effects make the hat come to life when the sun goes down.*

Attractions: The park's Sunset Boulevard area is home to two of the best thrills anywhere at Disney—The Twilight Zone Tower of Terror and Rock 'n' Roller Coaster Starring Aerosmith. The Tower of Terror sends guests on a 13-story trip through a darkened (and haunted) hotel maintenance elevator, ending with more than a few surprises that send occupants hurtling up and down the shaft at top speeds. Rock 'n' Roller Coaster, located next door to the Tower of Terror, delivers one of the best themed coaster experiences anywhere in the world. Entering the fictional studios of "G-Force Records" (get it?), riders discover rock legends Aerosmith in the rehearsal hall. The band invites the crowd to its sold-out Los Angeles concert and orders a "super-stretch" car for their cross-town ride. The fin-tailed coaster train, modeled after a classic limousine, takes off at top speed, hitting 60 mph in less than three seconds, while synchronized Aerosmith songs thunder from 120 on-board speakers.

Other attraction highlights include: Star Tours, the simulator attraction based on the *Star Wars* films, and "Who Wants to Be a Millionaire–Play It," which re-creates the popular game show.

Epcot

Walt Disney once said, "In the discovery of knowledge, there is great entertainment." Walt's dream of an Experimental Prototype Community of Tomorrow became reality in 1982 with the opening of Epcot, a combination of education and entertainment. The 300-acre theme park is divided into two sections: Future World and World Showcase. Designed as an ever-changing center of discovery and culture, Epcot features one of the most-recognized theme park icons anywhere—Spaceship Earth, the brightly shining geosphere at the park entrance. Epcot is also home to two of Disney's most popular annual festivals: the Epcot International Food & Wine Festival and the Epcot International Flower & Garden Festival. The festivals are presented for multi-week engagements each year and are included in regular park admission.

Shows and entertainment: The best 3-D film at Walt Disney World is found at Epcot: *Honey, I Shrunk the Audience*, based on the hit Disney comedies *Honey, I Shrunk the Kids, Honey, I Blew Up the Kid*, and *Honey, We Shrunk Ourselves*. It's a definite "E-Ticket" attraction. The action doesn't just happen on-screen—it spills into the audience. I won't ruin the surprises but will say that guests with certain phobias (especially those afraid of certain creepy-crawly critters) should consider bypassing this attraction.

Mission: SPACE, a multi-million-dollar family attraction, was set to open in mid- to late- 2003. It's an immersive interactive experience, with everyone taking a role during each visit. The preshows are amazing and Disney officials say the ride itself, which simulates space flight, is the first of its kind on this planet.

Live entertainment at Epcot is brilliantly themed from country to country in World Showcase: a Beatles-esque foursome performs in the United Kingdom; street theater is performed in Italy; drummers and percussionists make some serious noise in Japan; and acrobats amaze guests in China. But Epcot saves the best for last: IllumiNations: Reflections of Earth is the park's "kiss goodnight," with fireworks, lasers, fire torches, synchronized music, water cannons, and pyro barges coming together in World Showcase Lagoon for the 12½-minute show.

Disney's Animal Kingdom

The largest theme park at Walt Disney World (topping 500 acres), Disney's Animal Kingdom is also its newest. Disney Imagineers spent years re-creating African and Asian lands, dinosaur dig sites, wildlife reserves, and lush jungles. The result is nothing short of amazing. Animals of every sort, thrill rides, carnival-like attractions, and live entertainment combine to make this theme park much more than a zoo.

Shows and entertainment: My choice for best live entertainment presentation at all of Walt Disney World takes "pride" in thrilling guests every day in Disney's Animal Kingdom. *The Festival of the Lion King* is a brilliant adaptation of the animated film. Influences from the Great White Way can be seen in the interpretive costuming, songs, and staging for this "in-the-round" performance. If you plan to see it, get there early—most shows are filled to capacity.

Attractions: Living up to the park's name, several top-notch attractions focus on animals. The first stop for anyone should be the Kilimanjaro Safaris, a ride through Disney's African wildlife reserve. Giraffes, zebras, gazelles, rhinos, hippos, cheetahs, warthogs, lions, and more can be seen from your safari vehicle. With no fences in sight, many of the animals wander throughout the savanna, giving guests a close look at them in a natural setting. Be sure to take your camera, and load up the zoom lens for a closer look.

The other top choice for the park is *It's Tough to Be a Bug*, a rollicking 3-D adventure starring Flik and his pals from the hit film *A Bug's Life*. Similar to *Honey, I Shrunk the Audience* at Epcot, this film is very interactive, with surprises built into theater seats and the ceiling. While the animals at Disney's Animal Kingdom take center stage, there are also a number of attractions that offer

Disney's Animal Kingdom at Walt Disney World Resort, Lake Buena Vista, Florida Photo by Tim O'Brien

old-fashioned thrills and family fun: Dinosaur! is a wild (and bumpy!) simulator-hybrid ride through a prehistoric jungle and Chester and Hester's Dino-Rama is a new "mini-land" that re-creates a campy roadside carnival. While there, be sure to take a spin on Primeval Whirl, a spinning family coaster. It's definitely a blast from the past.

Downtown Disney

Once known only as a place to shop for Disney merchandise, Downtown Disney is now a 120-acre, lakeside entertainment district that includes three areas: the Marketplace, a shopping paradise; Pleasure Island, billed as a "nightclub theme park," and West Side, an eclectic mix of shops, restaurants, and theaters.

Downtown Disney Marketplace: One of the best places to shop at Disney, the waterside village features more than 25 unique shops and restaurants.

Downtown Disney Pleasure Island: When the sun goes down, the night lights up at Pleasure Island, a collection of nightspots with live music, dancing, and a Disney touch of theming.

Downtown Disney West Side: The newest area of Downtown Disney (opened in 1998) brought more big-name entertainment to Walt Disney World: House of Blues, Cirque du Soleil, celebrity chef Wolfgang Puck, and singers Gloria and Emilio Estefan all call West Side "home," with entertainment venues and restaurants. Also in this hot corner of the "world" are DisneyQuest, a 5-story, indoor theme park with cutting-edge games and interactive experiences, a Virgin Megastore, and a 24-screen AMC movie theater complex.

Water Parks

Walt Disney World turns into Walt Disney "Wild" at two of the most-attended water parks in the world.

Disney's Blizzard Beach: If you have the need for speed—on water, that is—this is the place for you. The park's best-known attraction, the 120-foot-tall Summit Plummet, is a free-fall water slide, with brave guests plunging down the slope at nearly 60 mph. Those in the mood for a little racing competition can head to the Downhill Double Dipper, a side-by-side inner-tube run, or to Toboggan Racer, where guests in 8 lanes zip down a 250-foot slide. Other highlights: Slush Gusher, a 250-foot slide; Teamboat Springs, a 1,400-foot, twisting, turning family raft ride (designed for up to six passengers); and Tike's Peak, a pint-sized waterpark designed for children ages four and under.

Disney's Typhoon Lagoon: A storm-ravaged, tropical surf lagoon sets the stage for Typhoon Lagoon. When it opened in 1989, Disney Imagineers set a new standard for water adventure parks. Nearly 3 million gallons of water create giant waves in the main pool, many of which reach the 6-foot mark as they come crashing into the beach area. The rolling waves are so large that guests can body surf on the swells. (For those who want to do some real surfing, Disney even offers "learn to surf" classes for an additional fee.) Shark Reef is a saltwater environment where guests can snorkel with sharks and other tropical marine life. Gear is provided. Other park highlights: Humunga Kowabunga, a combination of 3 speed slides with 50-foot drops; Gangplank Falls, a family raft ride; Ketchakiddie Creek, the children's waterpark; and my favorite, Castaway Creek, a 2,200-foot "lazy river" on which guests drift at a leisurely pace through tunnels, caverns, grottoes, and even a rain forest. It can take up to 45 minutes to make one trip around the park, and tubes are supplied.

Viable Information for All Disney Attractions:

 Food service: There are more than 300 locations across Walt Disney World, ranging from counter service to buffeterias to full-menu, table-service restaurants. Yes, you can still have a chili dog at the Magic Kingdom, but how about a Grand Marnier soufflé as you dine on Royal Doulton china, and Sambonet silver and order from personalized menus at Victoria & Albert's inside Disney's Grand Floridian Resort & Spa?

Beer, wine, and spirits are available at all table-service restaurants except those in the Magic Kingdom. Calling ahead for "Priority Seating" is suggested for most table-service locations. Some of the most popular Disney dining spots are character meals, where Mickey and his pals join the fun and roam from table to table. It's a great way to give your kids some one-on-one time with their favorite characters. Each experience features a different set of characters, so be sure to ask when you call to make your Priority Seating request. Disney also features several dinner show experiences. Two of the most popular are the long-running *Hoop-Dee-Doo Musical Review* at Disney's Fort Wilderness Resort & Campground and the *Polynesian Luau* at Disney's Polynesian Resort

 Extras: Disney's BoardWalk, a 1920s-era boardwalk featuring restaurants, clubs, live entertainment, dancing, and shopping, is a great place to stroll in the evening. Recreation and sports of every sort are offered across Walt Disney World: boating, guided bass fishing, parasailing, water-skiing, horseback riding, surfing, and scuba diving are available for those who want to walk on Disney's wild side. You can even take a spin in a real stock car around Disney's 1-mile speedway in the Richard Petty Driving Experience.

 Season: Everything is open every day of every year.

 Operating hours: Hours vary according to theme park and season. Also, parade times and fireworks schedules are seasonal. Be sure to call ahead.

 Admission policy: Pay-one-price, with single theme park admission under $55. "Park Hopper" and "Park Hopper Plus" tickets are also available and range in price between $200 to $260, with entitlements to multiple theme parks and other Disney attractions.

 Best way to avoid crowds: Parks are busiest during holidays and peak vacation seasons, like summer and spring break. A basic rule of thumb

is that when children are out of school, many of them are at Walt Disney World with their families. Utilize FAST-PASS whenever you can—you'll save time and be able to enjoy other attractions and shows. The middle of the day is the most crowded in the theme parks. Many seasoned Disney guests staying at an on-property hotel will hit the theme parks early in the day, take a midday break, lounge by the pool, then head back in the evening to enjoy the parks until closing time.

 # TIM'S TRIVIA

Walt Disney World knows its wine—the resort has more than 200 certified sommeliers, the most of any company in the world. All of the Disney wine experts have been certified by the Court of Master Sommeliers.

Wet 'n Wild

**6200 International Drive
Orlando, FL (407) 351–1800
www.wetnwild.com**

The granddaddy of all the world's waterparks is alive, well, and still the third most-visited waterpark in North America, hosting more than a million thrill-seekers a year. And the park has never looked better or been more fun.

As the first waterpark in the world, there's a great combination of unique rides, including older rides and the latest high-tech rides and slides. Among the newest is The Storm, twin bowl slides where you go down a water slide, drop into a bowl, and go round and round until you drop through a hole at the bottom, like a funnel!

Other thrill slides include the Bomb Bay, which in itself is the ultimate free-fall slide. You climb into a bomb-shaped compartment, and you don't know when the floor will drop out, sending you down a 76-foot-high, nearly vertical slide. There are many other single- and multi-person slides and rides including a mile-long Lazy River and a newly renovated kids' area that offers miniature versions of the adult rides, including a wave pool with 12-inch-tall waves.

Unique here is Knee Ski. You crawl onto a kneeboard and hang on as a cable mechanism pulls you on a half-mile course around the lake. Great fun, and it's included in the cost of admission.

The park is open year-round, with the water being heated in cooler months. Open between 9:00 and 10:00 A.M., closing between 5:00 and 11:00 P.M., depending on season.

Admission is under $32. A special 5-day, money-saving pass allows unlimited visits to this park, Universal Studios, Islands of Adventure, Busch Gardens, and SeaWorld Adventure Park. Special hotel rates are also part of the package. The park is now owned by Universal Studios.

Wild Waters

5656 East Silver Springs Boulevard
Silver Springs, FL (352) 236–2043
www.wildwaterspark.com

Located adjacent to its sister park, Silver Springs, this watery playground has thrills for all ages. Among the attractions for the more daring at this 10-acre waterpark is the Hurricane, a 400-foot-long twin flume that douses riders with an 80-gallon "turbocharge" blast midway through the ride; the Tornado, an enclosed flume with a 40-foot drop culminating in a splash pool below; and the Thunderbolt, a free-fall speed slide. The Silver Bullet is a 220-foot-long racing flume and the Twin Twister slides drop from a 6-story-tall platform.

The water in the Wave Pool ranges in depth from 3 inches to 8 feet, with waves on for 10 minutes, off for 10. Over in the Tad Pool wading area, little tots get to play in shallow water as their older brothers and sisters play in an interactive area known as Cool Kids' Cove. The Caribbean Spray Ground is a cooling play area.

There's a miniature golf course, 4 eateries, and a beach shop. Open March through Labor Day, 10:00 A.M. to 5:00 P.M., with closing times extended to 7:00 p.m. during peak season. Admission is under $24, with half-price tickets available after 3:00 P.M. A combination pass may be purchased for the waterpark and Silver Springs.

GEORGIA

Alpine Amusement Park

Edelweiss Drive
Helen, GA (706) 878–2306

The employees here don't dress in period costume and the attractions aren't themed, but the Germanic influence of the town where this park is located is apparent. Helen, nestled in the foothills of the Great Smoky Mountains, has strict building and operating codes to ensure that Bavarian theming remains constant throughout the community.

There are 10 rides, including a Ferris wheel, a Tilt-A-Whirl, bumper boats, a Roll-O-Plane, 5 kiddie rides, Water Wars, remote-controlled boats, miniature golf, and an arcade, and gold panning and gem grubbing have recently been added. The park also boasts the largest go-kart facility in northern Georgia.

Open daily during summer and on weekends through the fall and spring seasons, weather permitting. The park is closed December through February. Rides open at 1:00 P.M., with the park closing at different times, depending on weather and the season. Admission is free, rides on a pay-as-you-go basis.

American Adventures

250 North Cobb Parkway
Marietta, GA (770) 424–9283
www.whitewaterpark.com

If you're looking for thrill rides, you won't find them here, even though this is a Six Flags–owned property. If you want coaster thrills, you need to go down the road a few miles to Six Flags Over Georgia. If you want water thrills, you'll only have to walk a few steps to White Water waterpark, another Six Flags property, which is directly adjacent to this neat little family entertainment center.

With a turn-of-the-twentieth-century ambience, the park offers Victorian-style architecture and a comfortable, shaded setting for families with kids up to age 14 or 15.

Outside, there are 14 rides including a family roller coaster, swinging ship, a Tilt-A-Whirl, bumper cars, and a train. The center of fun here is indoors, however. That's where you'll find the 3-story Foam Factory. It's a 40,000-square-foot kids' participatory playhouse featuring 50,000 foam balls that can be shot out of 80 different types of launchers at other players or at targets. Great fun!

 Roller coaster: Buffalo Coaster, family (S).

You'll also find miniature golf and go-karts. Open March through November; an all-day pass for unlimited use of everything is available, under $17. If you're an adult, and you bring a kid with you, you get to play all day for $5! Call for hours.

Located just north of Atlanta at exit 265 off I–75.

Lake Lanier Island Resort

On Lake Sidney Lanier
Lake Lanier Islands, GA (770) 932–7200
www.lakelanierislands.com

Set around the beautiful 38,000-acre Lake Lanier, this amazing all-in-one resort offers everything from a state-of-the-art waterpark to horseback riding to water-skiing and hiking.

The waterpark features a surfing pool; Wild Waves, the state's largest wave pool; FunDunker, an interactive aquatic playground with more than 100 ways to get wet; and several other attractions, including Kiddie Lagoon and WiggleWaves. Plus, there's a 1.5-mile-long sandy beach, supervised lake swimming, and free canoe and paddleboat use. There are also a miniature golf course and climbing wall.

Other resort amenities include the newly renovated, 216-room Emerald Point Resort and Conference Center, 30 luxury lakeside house rentals, campgrounds, hiking trails, boat rentals, jet ski rentals, golf, hiking, and biking.

The magical Nights of Lights is a 6.5-mile drive-through animated holiday light show, billed as the world's largest, and runs from mid-November through December.

The resort is open year-round, but the beach and water-park are seasonal, open daily Memorial Day through Labor Day, with weekend operation only during spring and fall. Located north of Atlanta. Take I–85 to 985 North, then proceed to exit 8 and follow the signs.

Lake Winnepesaukah

Lakeview Drive
Rossville, GA
(706) 866–5681/(877) LAKEWIN
www.lakewinnie.com

Known locally as Lake Winnie, this little gem, just a few miles from Chattanooga, is one of the South's most-loved traditional amusement parks. Getting its name from the lake it surrounds, the park is a great place to enjoy a laid-back day filled with fun, colorful rides.

The park's unique attraction is the 1926 Boat Chute. It is the only remaining old mill left in the United States that ends with a significant drop. The park has several other antique rides including a Bill Tracey darkride called the Castle. The circa 1916 Philadelphia Toboggan Company carousel has been in the park since 1965 and features 4 rows of 68 horses and 2 chariots, 1 of which has a cupid and swan design to it. It was the seventeenth carousel that famous company completed.

These classics are combined with newer thrill rides such as the Wild Lightnin', a wild mouse roller coaster, and the Orbiter, a spinning flat ride.

Lake Winnie has thrilled visitors since 1925 and still has that old style of Southern charm combined with classic rides to make for a fun day out.

 Extras: Miniature golf and paddleboats are available for an additional charge. Top-name entertainers perform most Sunday afternoons in Jukebox Junction, no additional charge.

 Season: April through September.

 Operating hours: Opens at 10:00 A.M. on Thursday and Saturday, and noon on Friday and Sunday. Closes at 10:00 or 11:00 P.M. Closed Monday (except holiday Mondays), Tuesday, and Wednesday.

Admission policy: Small gate admission charged, with rides and attractions on a pay-as-you-go basis. Pay-one-price also available, under $18. Admission includes access to the park and to all entertainment. Free parking.

 Top rides: Frog Hopper, kiddie free fall; Pirate Ship, a swinging ride; Boat Chute, a circa 1926, tunnel-of-love-type spill-water attraction; Matterhorn; Alpine Way, an aerial ride taking you over the lake and back; Tilt-A-Whirl; Pipeline Plunge, a raft ride down a 72-foot water slide.

 Roller coasters: The Cannon Ball (W); Wacky Worm, kiddie (S); Wild Lightnin', wild mouse (S).

 Plan to stay: 4 hours.

 Best way to avoid crowds: Go to the Boat Chute first. It's a quick walk from the front gate. It's a low-capacity and very popular ride and the line stays long most of the day. Do the Castle darkride next and then head over to the other side of the lake and work your way back to the entrance.

 Directions: Take the Route 41 exit off I–75. Take Ringold Road 2 miles to McBrien Road, turn left, and the park is about 2 miles at the end of McBrien Road on Lakeview Drive.

Six Flags Over Georgia
I–20 and Six Flags Parkway
Atlanta, GA (770) 948–9290
www.sixflags.com

Superman, Batman, and Bugs Bunny all live together harmoniously here in one of the world's most beautiful amusement parks. High-tech thrill rides combine with magnificent trees and well-landscaped hilly terrain to make this 331-acre park a true jewel in the Six Flags crown.

The park was built in 1967 as the second Six Flags property. In 2002 it introduced Superman–Ultimate Flight flying roller coaster to rave reviews, and the year before it opened the Acrophobia drop tower and the Deja Vu, Super Boomerang coaster. There are now 36 rides, including 9 coasters, spread throughout the park's nine themed areas. In true Six Flags fashion, there is a viable mix of thrill rides and family and kiddie attractions.

 Extras: The Riverview Carousel dates back to 1908 and was ridden by President Warren Harding and Al Capone at its former location in Chicago's Riverview Park. Daredevil Dive skycoaster, additional fee.

 Special events: Fright Fest, October.

 Season: Mid-March through October. March, April, May, September, and October, weekends only.

 Operating hours: Opens 10:00 A.M. Closing varies throughout season.

 Admission policy: Pay-one-price, under $41; Parking charge.

 Top rides: Acrophobia, rotating 200-foot-tall tower drop; Thunder River, a raging-rapids ride; The Great Gasp, a 20-story-tall parachute drop; Six Flags Air Racer, a 90-foot-tall airplane ride; Looping Starship, a 360-degree shuttle ride; Monster Plantation, a boat ride through a flooded antebellum mansion; Splashwater Falls, shoot-the-chute; Log Jamboree, log flume.

 Roller coasters: Superman–Ultimate Flight, flying (S); Deja Vu, Super Boomerang (S); Georgia Scorcher, stand-up (S); Batman The Ride, inverted (S); Dahlonega Mine Train (S); Georgia Cyclone (W); Ninja, multi-element (S); Great American Scream Machine (W); Mindbender, 2-loop (S).

 Plan to stay: 8 hours.

 Best way to avoid crowds: Come early in the week, and see everything in one area the first time you visit it. Doubling back at a park this size is very time-consuming.

 Directions: 12 miles west of Atlanta on I-20. Take exit 47 and the park is 1 block south on Six Flags Road.

Six Flags White Water

250 North Cobb Parkway
Marietta, GA (770) 424-9283
www.whitewaterpark.com

Waterpark fans consistently rank this beautiful facility among the best in the world. Its location on a heavily wooded hillside makes it a scenic visit as well as a cool and refreshing one. Owned by Six Flags theme parks, which also owns the adjacent American Adventure park, everything here is top-notch and well kept.

There are a total of 45 rides, slides, and water activities, including the 90-foot-high Cliffhanger free fall; Run-A-Way River enclosed raft ride; the Little Hooch lazy river; the Atlanta Ocean wave pool; the Tree House Island, a 3-story-tall interactive play area for the kids; and the Bahama Bobslide, a 6-person raft ride.

Open May through Labor Day, 10:00 A.M. to 8:00 P.M. Admission is under $31.

Summer Waves

On Jekyll Island
Jekyll Island, GA (912) 635-2074
www.summerwaves.com

This 11-acre waterpark is a major draw to state-owned Jekyll Island, located 6 miles off the Georgia coast and nicknamed "Georgia's Coastal Family Playground." Thirty-three of the original buildings are still standing from the era of 1886 to 1942, when this was an exclusive recreational retreat for America's wealthiest families. These buildings can still be visited in the historic district.

Quite a popular attraction in this part of the state, the waterpark area of the island features Pirates Passage, a 5-story-tall, totally enclosed tube ride; the Force Three tube and body slides; the Slow Motion Ocean lazy river; and the Frantic Atlantic wave pool. There's also a large children's water activity pool.

Hungry? McDonald's has three locations in the park. The surf shop at the entrance gate sells everything from sunscreen to the latest in swimwear.

In addition to the waterpark, you'll find 10 miles of beaches, the state's largest public golf resort, horseback riding, miniature golf, and 20 miles of scenic bicycling paths.

Open daily at 10:00 A.M.; closes at 6:00 P.M. during the week, 8:00 P.M. on Saturdays. Admission, under $16, includes the use of tubes and mats. Special "Night Splash" rates after 4:00 P.M.

Wild Adventures

Old Clyattville Road
Valdosta, GA
(229) 559–1330
www.wildadventures.net

With five parks in one, this is about as close to a one-stop amusement spot as you can get! There's a theme park, zoo, concert park, family entertainment center, and waterpark.

If there was a record for one person building a small amusement park and growing it in attendance and number of attractions in the shortest time, this park would hold that record. In a grass-roots approach to theme park development, Kent Buescher started adding rides to his small ani-

"Boomerang Coaster," Wild Adventures, Valdosta, Georgia
Photo by Tim O'Brien

mal and horse farm in 1997 and today has more than 55 rides, including 7 roller coasters.

He has also developed his small zoo into a collection of more than 500 animals, including lions, tigers, bears, and giraffes. The Safari Train ride takes visitors around the park and through several animal areas where those walking are not permitted to tread.

In 2002 Buescher added Adventure Quest, a family entertainment center with go-karts, miniature golf, and an arcade, and in 2003 opened Splash Island, a full-size waterpark with a wave pool, lazy river, slides, and several water play areas.

In 2003, two more family coasters were added: Fiesta Express and the unique Swamp Thing.

Open year-round, a major concert series takes place, with the cost being a part of admission. In 2002 there were more than 45 top-name concerts, including such acts as Vince Gill, Styx, Lynyrd Skynyrd, and Steven Curtis Chapman.

The Bugsville family and children's area is an innovative whimsical section with rides, shows, and games and has several "trainer" roller coasters for the kids to practice on before heading to the big coasters in the back of the park.

 Season: Year-round.

 Operating hours: Opens most days at 10:00 A.M.; various closing times, depending on season. During peak season, open until 10:00 P.M. During fall, winter, and spring, open Thursday through Sunday only, weather permitting.

 Admission policy: Pay-one-price includes zoo, theme park, Safari Train ride, shows, and concerts, under $29. Adventure Quest is a pay-as-you-go park, and Splash Island's fees were not determined as of press time. A special 2-day pass is available for a few dollars more, and a combination waterpark/theme park pass is available.

Top rides: Double Shot tower drop; Geronimo Skycoaster, extra fee; Tasmanian River Rapids; Frog Hopper, kiddie free fall; Blackfoot Falls, shoot-the-chute; Frontier Flume, log ride; Time Warp; Inverter; Century Ferris wheel; Chaos; Turbo Theater, motion simulator.

Roller coasters: Fiesta Express, family (S); Swamp Thing, junior inverted (S); Hangman, inverted (S); Boomerang (S); Gold Rush Coaster, family (S); Bug Out, wild mouse (S); Ant Farm Express, family (S); Cheetah (W).

Plan to stay: 4 to 5 hours.

Best way to avoid crowds: Large crowds aren't an issue in this local park. It hosts many school groups, however, so if you want to avoid the groups, call first.

Directions: Take exit 13A off I-75, south of Valdosta. Turn south on Old Clyattville Road. Park is 4 miles on right.

iDAHO

Roaring Springs Waterpark

400 West Overland Road
Meridian, ID
(208) 884-8842
www.roaringsprings.com

The big and bold Avalanche slide beckons as you drive by on the interstate, calling you into this 17-acre watery oasis in a suburb of Boise.

The most popular rides here are the Avalanche, a Sidewinder slide; the Mammoth Canyon, a four-person raft ride; Racing Ridge, 4-lane head-first mat slides; and White Water Bay, the wave pool. In all, there are 14 adult slides, a lazy river, an interactive kiddie area, and an action pool.

Open mid-May through mid-September, weekends only in May and September. Admission is $22, with the PM Plunge ticket costing you only $15 if you come in after 3:00 P.M.

TiM'S TRiViA

Beat the lunch rush by eating before noon or after 2:30 P.M. Don't waste your time in food lines. If you eat during non-prime times, you'll be able to ride the rides while everyone else stands in food lines.

Silverwood Theme Park
Boulder Beach

North 26225 Highway 95
Athol, ID (208) 683–3400
www.silverwood4fun.com

Although there are quite a few parks that you can visit by boat, this may very well be the only amusement park in the country that you can visit by flying your own plane to it. Originally solely an airstrip, the facility now has 26 rides and some beautiful turn-of-the-twentieth-century Victorian (reproduction) architecture.

Upon entering the park, visitors walk down Victorian Main Street, where they are greeted with shops, eateries, and a colorful carousel. They then can go to Tinywood, Country Carnival, or Northwest Adventure areas of the park.

In the corner of the park is Coaster Alley, where the 2 world-class wooden coasters can be found. The larger of the two, the 3,000-foot-long Tremors, follows an amazing route through the park. It goes through 4 underground tunnels and through a glass tunnel through a gift shop, where all can watch!

Along the Victorian Main Street is the entrance to the new Boulder Beach waterpark, which was to open by mid-season in 2003. Unlike most waterparks, you won't find the tropics copied here. This is an authentic Northwest, timber, stone, and pine tree park. Elkhorn Creek is the lazy river, Big Moose Bay is the wave pool, and Polliwog Park is a fun interactive playground with more than 50 elements. In addition, a slide complex provides four different tube slides. By the way, all the water is heated. Not a bad idea up here in Idaho!

 Season: May through October.

 Operating hours: 11:00 A.M. to 10:00 P.M. weekends, 6:00 P.M. or 8:00 P.M. weekdays.

THE AMUSEMENT PARK GUIDE

 Admission policy: Pay-one-price, under $26. Parking charge.

 Top rides: Antique cars; a narrow-gauge steam train, taking you 3.5 miles into the wilderness, where you'll be robbed; Scrambler; Round-Up; carousel; Thunder Canyon, rapids ride; Roaring Creek, log flume.

 Roller coasters: Tremors (W); The Gravity Defying Corkscrew (S); Timber Terror (W); Tiny Toot, kiddie (S).

 Plan to stay: 6 hours.

 Best way to avoid crowds: Come during the week and avoid the holidays.

 Directions: 15 minutes north of I–90 and Coeur d'Alene, on Highway 95. Located 50 miles northeast of Spokane, Washington.

iLLiNoiS

Blackberry Historical Farm

Barnes Road
Aurora, IL (630) 892–1550

You'll take a step back in time when you enter the front gates of this 54-acre complex, whose theme is Midwest village life during 1840 to 1910. Numerous costumed guides and other old-time touches make this an educational as well as entertaining place to visit.

There are 4 rides, including a train and a carousel; in addition, there are pony and wagon rides, as well as a free petting zoo. Special events are scheduled most Sundays.

Pay-one-price, under $10. Open May to mid-October, 10:00 A.M. to 4:30 P.M.

Kiddieland

North and 1st Avenues
Melrose Park, IL (708) 343-8000
www.kiddieland.com

Originally opened in 1929 to serve only children, the 17-acre park today has rides for everyone in the family. Its unique character can be seen in little touches throughout the grounds like the neon sign that beckons visitors into the park and the 2 well-kept antique carousels, one a German children's machine and the other a circa 1925 Philadelphia Toboggan Company model, the seventy-second that company made.

The park offers 30 attractions, many of which are just for the children. Services like baby-bottle warming, changing stations, and stroller rental all help parents feel comfortable bringing along kids of all ages. Known for its large fireworks display every July 4th, the park also features guest appearances by nationally known characters for kids such as Clifford and the Veggie Tales gang.

 Season: April through October.

 Operating hours: Hours and days of operation vary greatly. During peak summer, daily, 11:00 A.M. to 10:00 P.M.

 Admission policy: Pay-one-price, under $19. Price includes parking, all rides, and unlimited Pepsi soft drinks.

 Top rides: Pipeline water-coaster slide; Log Jammer flume ride; Race-A-Bouts, antique cars; Ferris wheel; bumper cars; Galleon, a swinging pirate ship; Tilt-A-Whirl.

 Roller coaster: Little Dipper, junior (W).

 Plan to stay: 3 hours.

 Best way to avoid crowds: The area's day-camp groups come at opening and leave at 2:30 P.M. From that time to 7:00 P.M. is usually the slowest time of the day.

The Amusement Park Guide

Directions: Located between the Eisenhower and Kennedy Expressways, 15 miles from downtown Chicago. Take I–294 to the Eisenhower Expressway and go east to First Avenue. Go north on First until you reach the park, at the corner of North and First Avenues.

Knight's Action Park Caribbean Water Adventure

1700 Recreation Drive
Springfield, IL (217) 546–8881
www.knightsactionpark.com

The only problem you'll have when visiting this fun center is deciding which way to head first! The park has myriad attractions the entire family can enjoy. The dry side of the park features batting cages, laser tag, go-karts, 2 miniature golf courses, and a driving range. The Caribbean Water Adventure features a wave pool, bumper boats, water slides, Seal Bay children's play area, a lazy river, and pedal boats on a 7-acre lake. You can enjoy the afternoon sun in the waterpark and then spend the evening hours enjoying the action on the other side of the park.

The Action Park is pay-as-you-play while the Caribbean waterpark is pay-one-price, under $18, with a special of $4 off per person after 3:30 P.M.

Navy Pier

On Lake Michigan
Between Grand Avenue & Illinois Street
Chicago, IL (312) 595–5101
www.navypier.com

Built in 1916, Navy Pier today is a wonderful assortment of activities, events, and attractions that everyone in the family is sure to enjoy. Plus, it has the added aura of being located over the water.

Among the attractions on the pier is a 150-foot-tall Ferris wheel that provides a grand view of the Chicago shoreline, a Wave Swinger, and a carousel built to re-create the pier's golden age of the 1920s. Three specialty attractions add a uniqueness to the pier's fun lineup. Amazing Chicago is a

15-minute sensory experience that is a cross between a fun house and a virtual-reality ride. You have to navigate through a series of mirror mazes and special effects that are all Chicago-themed. Time Escape is Chicago's only 3-D ride. It's a multi-sensory, multi-element presentation that takes visitors from the year 85 million B.C. to the year 2333, all in Chicago. The Pier's IMAX 3-D Theatre presents the latest in IMAX films.

In addition, there is a miniature golf course, a 32,000-square-foot indoor botanical garden, the Chicago Children's Museum, an ice-skating rink in the winter, a beer garden, the Chicago Shakespeare Theatre, and a stained-glass window museum.

There are several specialty restuarants including the Bubba Gump Shrimp Co., as well as dozens of other eateries and shopping opportunities, and the pier is the debarkation point for many cruise and sightseeing boats.

The outdoor attractions are open spring through fall, and the indoor attractions are open year-round. The ferris wheel is open year-round, weather permitting. It would be advisable to call ahead. There is plenty of parking on the pier itself, at the end of Grand Avenue.

Santa's Village Amusement Park & Polar Dome Racing Rapids

Routes 25 & 72
Dundee, IL (847) 426–6751
www.santasvillageil.com

This is where Santa puts in his time during the summer. But there's a lot more here than a fat guy dressed up in a red outfit. In addition to providing Santa a place to meet his Chicagoland fans, the heavily wooded 55-acre park is loaded with fun family things in its three areas. Santa's Village is where the park started and is full of unique Christmas and candy architecture, Old McDonald's Farm is a petting zoo and animal attraction, and the Coney Island area features most of the 28 amusement rides.

The original frozen North Pole provides a fun meeting spot on a hot summer's day and the park's tree-lined groves provide a nice place to picnic during the season. The adjacent

THE AMUSEMENT PARK GUIDE

Racing Rapids, a 10-acre waterpark, features some great slides, a lazy river, bumper boats, and a neat children's play area, complete with an auto kid wash. You'll find the go-karts in the waterpark. You don't have to be dismayed when the rides and waterpark close down for the season, because that's when the Polar Dome opens. From September through April, the dome has public ice skating.

 Season: Mid-May through September.

 Operating hours: 10:00 A.M. to 6:00 P.M. or dusk.

 Admission policy: Pay-one-price, under $20. A combination ticket for both parks is available, under $30. Free parking.

 Top rides: Skyride; Balloon Race; Snowball, a cuddle-up ride with a winter theme; Great Wheel; and a Yo-Yo.

 Roller coasters: Typhoon, single looping (S); Dracor Dragon Coaster, family (S).

 Plan to stay: 5 hours.

 Best way to avoid crowds: Visit on weekdays and after Labor Day.

 Directions: Located 45 minutes from downtown Chicago among the tall timbers of the Fox River Valley area. Take the Route 25 exit off I–90 at Elgin; go north 2 miles to the intersection of Routes 25 and 72.

Six Flags Great America
I–94 & Route 132
Gurnee, IL (847) 249–1776
www.sixflags.com

Bugs Bunny and his Looney Tunes pals call this place their home, but they are more than happy to share their big and whimsical backyard with thousands of guests each year.

Opened in 1976, the park now features mature trees and landscaping along with its trademark arsenal of thrill rides

"Columbia Carousel," Six Flags Great America, Gurnee, Illinois
Photo by Adam Sandy

and shows. Among the thrillers are 12 roller coasters, 4 major (and drenching) water rides, several themed interactive children's areas, 10 daily shows, and a multitude of street performers. The shopping is great and if you're looking for a mug or a cap with a Looney Tunes character on it, this is the place!

TiM'S TRiViA

If you like the macabre, visit your local Six Flags park during October. That's when you'll find the popular Fright Fest in full operation. Held weekends during October, the parks present haunted houses, special foods, and frightening entertainment. The celebration takes place at most North American Six Flags and Six Flags–owned parks. See www.sixflags.com for more information.

The designs and themes of the park's seven areas highlight different aspects of Americana. The focal point as you enter the park through Carousel Plaza is Columbia, the fantastic 10-story-tall, double-deck carousel next to the reflecting pond. Hometown Square is 1920s rural America; the yearly celebration of the local fair comes alive in County Fair; Southwest Territory takes guests back to a frontier Western town; Yukon Territory is the rugged

THE AMUSEMENT PARK GUIDE

Klondike during the gold rush era; Yankee Harbor is a New England fishing village; and Orleans Place features the charm of New Orleans's French Quarter circa 1850.

 Special events: Fright Fest, weekends in October.

 Season: The end of April through October.

 Operating hours: 10:00 A.M. to 9:00 or 10:00 P.M.

 Admission policy: Pay-one-price, under $45; kids, half price. Parking charge.

"Vertical Velocity," Six Flags Great America, Gurnee, Illinois   Photo by Adam Sandy

Top rides: Giant Drop, free fall; IMAX theater featuring *To Fly: Space Shuttle America*, simulated lunar mission; Sky Trek Tower, a 330-foot-tall observation ride; Splashwater Falls, shoot-the-chute; Ameri-Go-Round, a circa 1910 Dentzel carousel; Roaring Rapids, a raging-rapids ride; Logger's Run, a log flume.

 Roller coasters: Superman–Ultimate Flight (S); Raging Bull, hyper twister (S); Batman The Ride, inverted (S); Demon, loop/corkscrew (S); American Eagle, twin racing (W); Iron Wolf, stand-up (S); Viper (W); Whizzer, speedracer (S); Spacely's Sprocket Rocket, kiddie (S); Vertical Velocity, LIM shuttle (S); Deja Vu, Super Boomerang, flying coaster (S).

 Plan to stay: 8 hours.

 Best way to avoid crowds: Come midmorning or midafternoon on Wednesday, Thursday, or Friday.

 Directions: Located between Chicago and Milwaukee on I–94 at Route 132 East (Grand Avenue).

INDIANA

Columbian Park
Scott and Main Streets
Lafayette, IN (765) 771–2220

Lafayette is a city giving back to its people. This small city park contains an amazing number of attractions, including a zoo, an amusement ride area, sports fields, a playground, a picnic area, and an aquatic center called Tropicanoe Cove. It features the Banana Peel, a family tube slide; Toucan Chute, an enclosed slide; Sunfish Bay, a kids' play area; Cattail Crik, a lazy river; and the Frog Pond wave pool.

Since 1949 the park's ride area has been entertaining the kids of the community. Today, it has 7 attractions, 4 of which are for children. Among its offerings are classic park staples like a Scrambler, a pint-sized Ferris wheel, a train, and a car ride with unique autos.

The rides are open from late May to September and closed weekdays when school is in session. The dry rides are pay-as-you-go and there is a separate entrance fee for the aquatic center of under $7 for adults and under $6 for children. Every Wednesday night is family night, with all rides discounted. Be sure to check out the custard stand that lies just outside the zoo entrance. YUM!

Fort Wayne Children's Zoo

3411 Sherman Boulevard
Fort Wayne, IN
(260) 427-6800

Part theme park, part zoo, and lots of fun, this facility is a leader in combining the best parts of family entertainment offerings to create a unique place to observe and interact with nature. It features themed areas like the African Veldt, the Australian Adventure, and the Indonesian Rain Forest along with some traditional zoo areas and exhibits.

The park's 1994 carousel is one of the few wooden machines to be carved in recent times. The Carousel Works of Ohio carved the ride, and instead of horses it features endangered species such as tapirs and spotted leopards; there is even a chariot carved in the shape of a peafowl. The Dugout Canoe, a log flume, takes visitors through the Australian section of the park and past many outback animals like dingoes and kangaroos.

The admission is under $8 and the rides cost an additional $1 or $2. The zoo is open every day from late April through mid-October from 9:00 A.M. to 5:00 P.M.

Fun Spot Amusement Park & Zoo

County Road 200W
Angola, IN (260) 833-2972/
(888) 534-8421 www.funspotpark.com

Looking around, it's easy to see that the people here are really enjoying themselves. From the kids in kiddieland to the thrill-seekers screaming from the coasters, there are smiles everywhere. The circa 1949 Allan Herschell 2-row carousel is one of the focal points. In addition, there are several traditional favorites like the Flying Skooters and the Bayern Kurve.

The 2 main thrill rides are the Zyklon and Afterburner roller coasters. The Zyklon is a standard twisting and diving ride, while the Afterburner launches riders forward and backward through a loop. The park also operates a coaster just for the little ones, the Safari Kiddie Coaster.

There are approximately 30 rides, a zoo, and an arcade to keep everyone in the family happy during your visit.

 Roller coasters: Zyklon, family (S); Afterburner, launch with loop (S); Safari Kiddie Coaster, kiddie (S).

 Operating hours: Open Memorial Day through Labor Day, 10:00 A.M. to 5:00 P.M.

 Admission policy: Pay-one-price, under $15.

 Directions: Located on County Road 200W, ¾ miles from I–69.

Holiday World and Splashin' Safari

Routes 162 & 245
Santa Claus, IN
(812) 937–4401/(800) GO–SANTA
www.holidayworld.com

No newcomer to this park could ever imagine that behind the cheerful gates lie 2 of the best wooden coasters on the planet, one of the cleanest parks in existence, and one of the best-valued amusement parks in the country.

The Raven and The Legend have garnered the park international fame, as people from all over the world come to ride the coasters. The Raven towers over the parking lot and flies through the woods next to Lake Rudolph, while The Legend, based on the tale of Sleepy Hollow, is set back in the woods so that little can be seen from the midway.

"ZoomBabwe," Holiday World and Splashin' Safari, Santa Claus, Indiana Photo by Adam Sandy

The park opened in 1946 and bills itself as the world's first theme park. It is divided into three main areas: Christmas, the Fourth of July, and Halloween. Nine of the 22 rides are kiddie rides, most of which are located in a children's area called Rudolph's Reindeer Ranch—where each of the rides are named after one of Santa's reindeer—at the front of the park and Holidog's Funtown at the rear. There is a lot for hungry visitors to eat; the pizza at Kringle's Kafe and the Mexican food at the Alamo are great and all guests can get unlimited free drinks all day long.

The adjacent Splashin' Safari waterpark is included with the admission price. It features tube slides of all sizes; a wave pool; Monsoon Lagoon, a children's play area; and ZoomBabwe, the world's largest enclosed water slide at over 10 stories tall and 900 feet long. In addition to the unlimited free soft drinks, the park offers free sunscreen and free use of tubes to everyone in the waterpark. Oh, by the way, the parking is free as well.

 Extras: A petting zoo, a wax museum, an antique toy collection, and an opportunity to meet Santa Claus, all for no additional charge.

 Season: May through October.

 Operating hours: Opens at 10:00 A.M. Closing times vary.

Admission policy: Pay-one-price, under $30. A second-day ticket is available for an additional $15. Free parking.

 Top rides: Liberty Launch, double shot freefall; HalloSwings, flying carousel; Raging Rapids, a raging-rapids ride with a Western theme; Frightful Falls, a log flume.

 Roller coasters: The Legend (W); Raven (W); The Howler, family (S).

 Plan to stay: 7 hours.

 Best way to avoid crowds: Most people visit the ride park in the morning, eat lunch, and then go to the waterpark. To avoid the crowds, do the opposite.

 Directions: Located in the southwestern part of the state about 7 miles off I–64. Take the U.S. 231 or Indiana 162 exit off the interstate and head south to the park entrance, where the two roads meet.

Indiana Beach

306 Indiana Beach Drive
Monticello, IN (219) 583–4141
www.indianabeach.com

Many say this place has the feel of an old Atlantic City boardwalk combined with a traditional Midwest amusement park. It features 26 adult rides, 9 kiddie rides, and a plethora of shops and eateries built over and under one another on a boardwalk that sits next to Lake Shafer. In addition to the ride park there is a waterpark with several slides, a lazy river, and a sand beach.

The managing family, who has owned the park since it opened in 1926, had to be creative when fitting everything in, and the result is that many ordinary rides become extraordinary experiences when shoehorned onto the pier. The best examples of this are the park's 2 wooden roller coasters, the Hoosier Hurricane and the Cornball Express. The Hurricane is an out-and-back ride that runs along the back of the boardwalk, over the miniature golf course, and over a part of the lake. The Cornball Express runs around the kiddie rides, the Tig'rr roller coaster, and several eating pavilions. The ride is enhanced in that the first drop plunges very close to the log flume, refreshing coaster riders with a fine, cooling mist on hot summer days.

There are several classic rides here including Frankenstein's Castle, an extra-charge attraction that many consider one of the country's best walk-through haunted houses, and the Den of Lost Thieves, a darkride where riders shoot at targets for points. Because of the park's unique location, the lake adds to the thrills of several rides. Classic attractions like the Paratrooper are built over the water and guests on the Water Swings actually fly out over the lake.

The park has traditional food staples like hot dogs and cotton candy, but tucked in above the rides and the rest of the action are 2 outstanding eateries. The first is the Roof Lounge, which is for those 21 and over. The second is the Skyroom, a full-service restaurant with a great menu selection.

 Extras: Miniature golf, Skycoaster, jet skis, boat tag, all at extra charge. Waterpark and beach, extra charge. Make sure you try the park's famous tacos. Olé!

 Season: May through Labor Day.

 Operating hours: Rides are open 11:00 A.M. to 11:00 P.M. daily. The beach opens at 9:00 A.M.; the waterpark at 10:00 A.M.

 Admission policy: General admission, plus rides, waterpark, and beach on a pay-as-you-go basis. A 7-hour, pay-one-price ticket also available, under $17. Free parking.

 Top rides: Den of Lost Thieves, interactive darkride; Double Shot, free fall; Frog Hopper, kids' free fall; Water Swings, swing ride over the lake; Shafer Queen, paddle-wheel excursion on Lake Shafer; Giant Gondola Wheel; sky ride, a ride over the pier and many of the attractions; Rocky Rapids Log Flume.

 Roller coasters: Cornball Express (W); Hoosier Hurricane (W); Lost Coaster of Superstition Mountain, a unique coaster inside a mountain (W); Tig'rr, family (S); Galaxy, family (S).

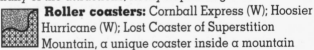 **Plan to stay:** 8 hours, if you use the waterpark.

Best way to avoid crowds: Come midweek or anytime in early June or late August.

 Directions: Take Route 24 to the 6th Street exit in Monticello. Go north through town to the lake; the park is on your right. Located 95 miles northwest of Indianapolis and 120 miles from Chicago.

Indianapolis Zoo
1200 West Washington
Indianapolis, IN (317) 630-2001
www.indianapoliszoo.com

Officials here like to joke that their Kombo roller coaster is the tallest, longest, and fastest roller coaster in a zoo in the United States. They're right, but it is the only zoo *with* a coaster in the United States. At 20 feet high and 18 mph, it won't set any national records, but it's a perfect family coaster for this sort of facility. The zoo also has a carousel, a train ride, and a safari-themed 4-D virtual-reality ride.

The Enchanted Mill area offers fun activities for the kids, including special water features that are especially welcome on the hot, humid days that often occur in this city. The zoo is a modern, well-kept facility with fabulous landscaping and gardens. It was the nation's first institution to be accredited in three disciplines: habitat botanical garden, zoological park, and aquarium.

The zoo is part of the impressive and expansive White River State Park, which also includes the zoo's sister facility, the White River Gardens. Other attractions located within this urban oasis are the Indiana State Museum, an IMAX theater, the NCAA Hall of Champions museum, and the Eitelborg Museum of American Indians and Western Art.

Located in downtown, the zoo is open every day of the year, weather permitting, with peak season hours of 9:00 A.M. to 6:00 P.M. There is an additional fee for the rides.

 Roller coaster: Kombo, family (S).

Admission to zoo, under $12. Rides are $2 each; three rides for $5; or seven rides for $10.

ALAMEDA FREE LIBRARY

River Fair Family Fun Park

Indoors at the River Falls Mall
I–65 & Route 131
Clarksville, IN (812) 284–3247

The Grand Carousel is the centerpiece of this indoor family fun center, which features 5 kiddie rides, a motion-simulator ride, a NASCAR Raceway simulator, a climbing wall, a kids' net-climb unit, and an 18-hole miniature golf course.

There are also remote-control boats and bumper cars. The train ride takes a trek around the rides, through the miniature golf course, across a small creek, through a tunnel, and around the adjacent food court. Among the rides are a Convoy and the Red Baron airplanes.

The center is located on the second floor of the mall, at the main entrance, and admission is free, with everything on a pay-as-you-play basis. A pay-one-price ticket is available for certain hour blocks and includes everything but golf and the simulators. Open daily at noon, closes with the mall at 9:00 or 10:00 P.M.

ioWA

Adventureland

I–80 & Highway 65
Des Moines, IA
(515) 266–2121/(800) 532–1286
www.adventureland-usa.com

Owned by the same family that founded the park in 1974, this is one of the largest independently owned theme parks in the country. The Main Street area, inspired by Disneyland, features buildings that are replicas of structures from across Iowa. Thousands of flowers and plants add a rainbow of color throughout the park, and the trees

ALAMEDA FREE LIBRARY

are so well respected here that instead of cutting one down to make room for the sky ride, the park designers cut a hole through the dense canopy of shade so the ride could fit through! With more than 100 rides, shows, and attractions, it is no surprise that this is one of Iowa's largest tourist draws and is a well-established family destination.

 Extras: A nice picnic area lies next to the parking lot, outside the gate. A hotel and RV camping facilities are also on the property. Don't miss the distorted mirrors, located at the exit of the Dragon roller coaster in the back of the park; as people get off the coaster, they look at the mirrors and are dismayed to see what the Dragon did to them.

 Season: May through September daily, late May through mid-August.

 Operating hours: Opens at 10:00 A.M.; closing times vary.

 Admission policy: Pay-one-price, under $26. Parking charge.

 Top rides: Saw Mill Splash, a 60-foot-tall splashdown ride; Inverter, 360-degree over-the-top thrill ride; Space Shot, a 200-foot-tall free fall; the Mixer, a rotating, spinning ride; Lady Luck, a roulette wheel–themed Trabant, a spinning platform ride; Silly Silo, a rotor inside a silo; Raging River, a raging-rapids ride; the Log Flume; Giant Gondola Wheel; Falling Star.

 Roller coasters: The Underground, indoor (W); Dragon, 2-loop (S); The Outlaw (W); Tornado (W).

 Plan to stay: 7 hours.

 Best way to avoid crowds: Tuesday is the least crowded day. Once you leave the Main Street area, go through the park in a clockwise fashion.

 Directions: Take exit 142A (Highway 65) off I–80, east of Des Moines. The park is at that intersection.

Arnolds Park

Highway 71 & Lake Street
Arnolds Park, IA (712) 332–2183
www.arnoldspark.com

Here's a great playland that's the epitome of parks of days gone by. It is located in the northwest corner of Iowa on the shores of a popular summer resort area surrounding Lake Okoboji.

Arnolds Park suffered some financial woes during the 1990s and it looked like the park might go the way of so many other traditional parks, but in 1999 investors stepped forward and saved it. For the 2002 season the Boji Falls log flume was added to the great mix of 22 rides, which includes the classic 1927 Legend roller coaster by legendary designer John Miller, a kiddie carousel from William F. Mangels, and a 63-foot-tall Ferris wheel that provides riders a great view of the lake and surrounding area.

The park is worth a stop if you are passing through the area, or your day can be combined with one of the many activities in town like concerts or a visit to the nearby waterpark.

To enter the parking lot, you drive under a sign mounted on the side of a section of reconstructed roller coaster, complete with two coaster trains climbing the hill. The sign proclaims that you're entering AN IOWA CLASSIC.

 Extras: Go-karts and miniature golf, available for extra charge. The Tipsy House and the Haunted House of Mirrors are unusual walk-through attractions that shouldn't be missed; both are included in the admission fee. Officials say the Pirate's Cove Sandbox is the world's largest; a Godfather's Pizza is located inside the park and now serves roasted chicken.

 Season: Mid-May through early September.

 Operating hours: Opens at 11:00 A.M. daily; closing times vary depending on season.

 Admission policy: Pay-one-price, under $17. Free car and boat parking. An "observer's ticket" is available for nonriders, $5.

Top rides: Gondola Ferris wheel providing a splendid view of the lake; bumper cars; toboggan; Paratrooper; Tilt-A-Whirl; the Bug House.

 Roller coasters: The Legend (W); Little Coaster, junior (S).

 Plan to stay: 4 hours.

 Best way to avoid crowds: This is a compact park, involving not too much walking, but during peak times, the midways can get crowded. Early June, before the resort cabins fill up, is a good time to visit; during the season, Wednesdays are usually less crowded.

 Directions: Take the Jackson Mountain exit off I–90 and go south on Route 71 to the park.

KANSAS

Joyland

2801 South Hillside
Wichita, KS (316) 684–0179
www.joylandwichita.com

Here can be found a trio of rides that any facility calling itself a traditional amusement park must offer: a wooden roller coaster, a classic darkride, and an antique carousel. The coaster dates from 1949 and is the last one in the United States to feature fixed-lap-bar trains from the Philadelphia Toboggan Company, the darkride is from legendary designer Bill Tracey, and the carousel is a 3-row machine with metal horses from the Allan Herschell Company.

The park has beautiful picnic groves and a well-rounded kids' section along with 13 rides for adults. There are several annual family events including an Easter Egg Hunt in April and fireworks every Fourth of July.

 Extras: Go-karts and Skycoaster, extra charge. Turn-of-the-twentieth-century restored Wurlitzer Band Organ, "played" daily by Louie the Clown.

THE AMUSEMENT PARK GUIDE

 Season: April through mid-October.

 Operating hours: 2:00 to 10:00 P.M. on weekends and holidays and 6:00 to 10:00 P.M. on weekdays. Closed Monday and Tuesday.

 Admission policy: General admission charge, with rides on a pay-as-you-go basis. Pay-one-price "Ride-a-Rama" ticket also available, under $15. Free parking.

 Top rides: Log Jam, a flume ride; Wacky Shack, a darkride; Paratrooper; Dodgems.

 Roller coaster: Roller Coaster (W).

 Plan to stay: 4 hours.

 Best way to avoid crowds: Come during the week.

 Directions: Take exit K15 off the Kansas Turnpike; go east on Route 15 to 31st Street. Then go east to Hillside Avenue and north 5 blocks to the park.

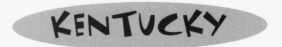

Beech Bend Raceway Park

Beech Bend Road
Bowling Green, KY (270) 781-7634
www.beechbend.com

Talk about a successful rebirth of a park! Originally opened on a bend in the river in a thicket of beech trees as a local picnic grove in the late 1880s, the park received its first rides in 1946 and was quite the place to be until it closed in the early 1980s. It reopened in 1997.

Today, thanks to its new owner, the park is once again a fun gathering place for the region. There are now 43 rides in operation, plus a new miniature golf course and a swimming pool. In addition, there is a stock car track, a drag strip, a large shaded campground next to the river, and great year-round party and banquet facilities.

TiM'S TRiViA

History, inventory, news, photos—just about everything you want to know about roller coasters, you'll find at www.ultimaterollercoaster.com.

Among the rides are the Whitewater Express log flume, the Power Surge, adult and kiddie bumper cars, a Ferris wheel, Tilt-A-Whirl, Star Ship 2000, a looping roller coaster, a carousel, and a classic Pretzel darkride that may be the only one in the United States that is air-conditioned. There are several original buildings still in use and many nostalgic rides mixed in with the new breed of thrill rides and new facilities. It's a great blend of family rides.

General admission is $5 and includes use of the swimming pool, with rides on a pay-as-you-go basis. An all-day armband is available for under $17 and includes everything but the go-karts.

Located 60 miles north of Nashville and 95 miles south of Louisville, the park is open daily Memorial Day through mid-August and on weekends in May and September. Take exit 28 off I–65 and follow signs to Bowling Green. Take a right at the fourth light, which is Riverview. Park is 2 miles from that light.

 Roller coasters: Flying Dragon, family (S); Looping Star, 1-loop (S).

Guntown Mountain

I–65 & Highway 70
Cave City, KY (270) 773–3530

Cowboys, goats, amusement rides, and great views are the order of the day here on Guntown Mountain. At the top of the mountain, there are plenty of shows and fun in the Old

West town, and at the base there are 12 rides and a traditional Funni-Frite walk-through fun house, one of the last of its kind in any U.S. amusement park.

Among the rides are an Eli Ferris wheel that provides great views of the valley, bumper cars, a Scrambler, a Twister, a carousel, and 5 kiddie rides including a classic Mangels Kiddie Whip. A train ride around the side of the mountain features a stop at a petting zoo, and under much of the mountain is Onyx Cave, with guided tours available each hour.

Smith's Country Store has been on the property since 1906 and offers up souvenirs and great country ham. An authorized trading post for the Cherokee Indians is next to the general store.

Open daily at 10:00 A.M. during the summer, weekends only in May, September, and October. Everything, including the ride up the mountain to the Western town on a chairlift, is on a pay-as-you-go basis, or you can purchase an all-day pass for everything but the cave tour for under $17.

The complex is located at exit 53 off I–65 at the Cave City exit, just minutes from Mammoth Cave National Park.

 TiM'S TRiViA

Looking for a great darkride? Check out the Web site created by the Darkride and Funhouse Enthusiasts group (www.dafe.com) and you'll find a state-by-state, park-by-park inventory, as well as a history of North America's darkest rides.

Kentucky Action Park
Jesse James Riding Stables
3057 Mammoth Cave Road/Highway 70 West, Cave City, KY (270) 773–2560
www.kentuckyactionpark.com

An Alpine slide down the forested mountainside is the star at this small but mighty fun center. You'll take a chairlift up the mountain and slide down to the bottom. That's where you'll climb back on the chairlift that will take you back to where you started. It's about a 20-minute adventure that the entire family can enjoy.

In addition to the quarter-mile slide, there are bumper boats, bumper cars, go-karts, and a fun, Western-themed miniature golf course. The riding stables feature a guided trail ride through the scenic countryside that Jesse James once frequented. There is a glass-blowing shop, an old-time photo parlor, and an air-conditioned snack bar.

Located a couple miles west of I–65 at exit 53, the park is 3 miles from Mammoth Cave. Open daily late May through mid-October.

 # TiM'S TRiViA

A fun diversion while you're in the Mammoth Cave area is Big Mike's Rock & Gift Shop, billed as having the state's largest collection of minerals and fossils. It also is home to Big Mike's Mystery House, part gravity tilt house, part fun house, and Big Mo, a 65-million-year-old fossilized mosasaur skull. The guided tour is a real hoot and it will cost you only a buck. This fun and funky place is located on Old Mammoth Cave Road in Cave City, 4 miles west of I–65, off exit 53. Open daily, year-round. (270) 773–5144.

Six Flags Kentucky Kingdom Hurricane Bay Water Park

Kentucky Fair and Exposition Center
Louisville, KY
(502) 366–2231/(800) SCREAMS
www.sixflags.com

Tucked into the corner of the state fairgrounds, the park is typical of the Six Flags brand. It has a bevy of thrill rides, fun architecture, a lot of roller coasters, and a lineup of live shows. There are more than 100 rides and attractions, including the cool and refreshing waterpark.

Among its stars are Chang, one of the world's tallest, fastest, and longest stand-up roller coasters, and Twisted Twins, the world's first dueling wooden coasters.

Included in its arsenal of rides are 7 roller coasters, most of which you can see looming over the rest of the fun as you approach the parking lot. Hurricane Bay Water Park features a wave pool, 4 adult water slides, a lazy river, and Hook's Lagoon, a towering water treehouse for kids with slides and splash activities.

TIM'S TRIVIA

Having built its first park in 1961, Six Flags now has 39 water and theme parks in 8 countries with a chain-wide attendance of nearly 50 million annually, second only to the Walt Disney Company park chain.

There are plenty of Looney Tunes characters hanging around Looney Tunes Movietown, a ride and show area especially for the kids. That's where you'll find the Road Runner Express, a themed family roller coaster, and the Pounce 'n' Bounce kiddie free fall.

 Extras: The Top Eliminator Dragsters allow you to drag race against five others in a full-size dragster. You'll race 400 feet, achieving speeds of 75 mph in 2.8 seconds. There is an extra fee. There are also additional fees for Thrill Karts go-karts, the Skycoaster, the Slingshot, and the climbing wall.

 Special events: Fright Fest, weekends in October.

 Season: Weekends April, May, September, October; daily in June, July, and through the third week in August.

 Operating hours: Opens daily at 10:00 or 11:00 A.M., closing hours vary. Waterpark opens daily at 11:30 A.M., and closes at 7:00 P.M., Memorial Day through Labor Day.

 Admission policy: Pay-one-price, under $37; Waterpark is included in park admission. Parking charge.

 Top rides: The Hellavator, a free fall with your feet dangling below your chair; Penguin's Blizzard River, rapids ride; Mile High Falls, shoot-the-chute; Giant Gondola Wheel; Thrill Park Theater, motion-based simulator.

 Roller coasters: Greezed Lightnin' (S); Chang, shuttle loop stand-up (S); T2, inverted (S); Thunder Run (W); Roller Skater, family (S); Twisted Twins, dueling (W); Road Runner Express, family (S).

 Plan to stay: 7 hours.

Best way to avoid crowds: Come early during the week. Go directly to the back of the park, and ride the big rides first and work your way to the front.

Directions: Located adjacent to the Kentucky Fair & Exposition Center. Take the Watterson Expressway (I–264) exit off I–65, south of downtown Louisville. Follow the signs to the Kingdom and enter through the fair's main gates.

LOUISIANA

Carousel Gardens

City Park, #1 Palm Drive
New Orleans, LA (504) 482–4888

Highlighted by 13 rides, including the beautifully restored 1905 Carmel/Looff antique carousel housed in a vintage carousel pavilion, this small family amusement park is tucked in behind the huge oak trees in a shaded corner of City Park. The park was restored in 1988 and today looks like a turn-of-the-twentieth-century facility, complete with brick sidewalks. A 20-minute train ride takes you out of the amusement park, around the large City Park, and across several of its bayous.

Adjacent to the amusement park is Storyland, a storybook park with puppet shows, roving entertainers, and costumed characters.

Gate admission fee, plus rides on a pay-as-you-go basis. Hours vary; call first.

Dixie Landin'
Blue Bayou Waterpark

18142 Perkins Road
Baton Rouge, LA (225) 756–4900
www.dixielandin.com

The state's largest waterpark and the state's newest theme park became one gated attraction in 2002 and in doing so became one of the best bargains in the bayou.

The parks are themed to resemble the towns and cities that lined the bayous and the rivers of 1920 Louisiana. The architecture, the food, and the landscaping all contribute to that Dixie feeling.

The theme park has 26 attractions and, in keeping with the theming, has some great ride names. There are the Gumbo Yo-Yo swings, the Cajun Collision bumper cars, the Ragin' Cajun coaster, and the Gilbeau's Galaxy coaster. The 11 slides and attractions on the water side have appropriate names as well. The Hurricane Bay Wave Pool is a favorite, as is the Atchafalaya Run Lazy River. The speed slides are known as Lafitte's Plunge, and the family interactive play area with 138 different activities is called Pirate's Cove. A separate 1-acre activity area contains a swimming pool and diving boards.

 Roller coasters: Ragin' Cajun, Boomerang (S); Gilbeau's Galaxy, family (S).

The waterpark is open June through Labor Day starting at 10:00 A.M. daily, and the ride park is open mid-March through October, daily from June through mid-August, also starting at 10:00 A.M. The waterpark usually closes around 6:00 P.M., while the rides go on to 10:00 P.M. during the summer. Admission to both parks is under $30.

The parks are located along I–10, 7 miles south of Baton Rouge. Take exit 166 off I–10, turn east on Highland Road, go under the pedestrian bridge, and turn left into the parking lot.

Six Flags New Orleans
Intersection of I–10 & I–510
New Orleans, LA (504) 253–8000
www.sixflags.com

Batman has found his way to New Orleans. He and Bugs Bunny and the other Looney Tunes and DC Comics characters now live about 20 minutes from the French Quarter at Six Flags New Orleans.

Six Flags took over the management of the bankrupt Jazzland in May 2002 and showed its true Six Flags power for the first time in 2003 when it rebranded the park, which included the name change; the addition of 6 new rides, including 2 new roller coasters; the introduction of the comic and cartoon characters; and the creation of two new areas within the park, Gotham City and a Looney Tunes–themed children's area.

The 140-acre park is divided into six distinct themed areas: Jazz Plaza, Cajun Country, Pontchartrain Beach, Gotham City, Mardi Gras, and the all-new Looney Tunes kids' area.

You'll enter this colorful ethnic experience through Jazz Plaza, where you'll need to stop by the Basin Street Bakery and pick up some amazing pastries. Pontchartrain Beach pays homage to the famed but now defunct park of the same name that closed nearby in 1983. It's Fat Tuesday every day in Mardi Gras, and the étouffée at the Creole Cafe in Cajun Country is always ready.

Gotham City, which has been created in several other Six Flags parks, seems most appropriate here in New Orleans. Batman The Ride, the amazing Batman Stunt Show, and several new rides can be found in this home to the eccentric Batman characters we've all grown to know.

The 38 rides include 6 roller coasters and a state-of-the-art interactive darkride called Jocco's Mardi Gras Madness.

 Extras: Skycoaster, extra fee.

 Season: March through early November.

 Operating hours: Weekends in spring and fall, daily during the summer months. Open 10:00 A.M. to 8:00 or 10:00 P.M.

 Admission policy: Pay-one-price, under $35. Parking charge.

 Top rides: Cat Woman's Whip, shake; Lex Luther's Invertitron, Windshear; Joker's Jukebox, Jukebox; Sonic Slam and Bayou Blaster, 2 free falls; Beach Bang-Up, bumper cars; Big Easy, 90-foot-tall gondola wheel; Voodoo Volcano, inverter; Spillway Splash-Out, shoot-the-chute; Mardi Gras Menagerie, carousel.

 Roller coasters: Batman The Ride, inverted (S); Jester, looping (S); Mega Zeph (W); Zydeco Scream, Boomerang (S); Muskrat Scrambler, wild mouse, family (S); Rex's Rail Runner, family (S).

 Plan to stay: 6 hours.

Best way to avoid crowds: Come during the week in late afternoon. As you leave the Jazz Plaza entrance area, turn left and start your journey through Cajun Country; work your way clockwise around the lake.

 Directions: 20 minutes from downtown and the French Quarter. Follow signs as you approach the convergence of I–10 and I–510.

MAINE

Funtown USA
Splashtown

774 Portland Road (U.S. Route 1)
Saco, ME
(207) 284–5139/(800) 878–2900
www.funtownsplashtownusa.com

Make sure you plan to spend enough time here to enjoy both the ride park and the waterpark. Both are top-notch. Home to Maine's only wooden roller coaster, this family-owned park offers a shaded, well-maintained facility with plenty to do for the entire family, both wet and dry.

Founded in 1969, the park has 21 adult rides and 11 family and kiddie attractions. Among the thrill rides is Thunder Falls, the longest and tallest flume ride in this part of the country. The waterpark has 6 slides, a family play area, and a swimming pool. There is no additional charge to play miniature golf.

 Extras: A large game arcade; Kartland go-karts and Grand Prix racers, extra charge.

 Season: May through mid-September.

 Operating hours: 10:00 A.M. to 10:00 P.M. during peak season

Admission policy: Pay-one-price, under $25 for Funtown USA; $16 for Splashtown. A combination pass for both parks is available for under $31. The combination pass also includes two rides each on the Grand Prix racers. General admission, with no rides, is $7. Free parking.

 Top rides: Dragon's Descent, a 200-foot-tall turbo drop; Frog Hopper, kiddie drop; Thunder Falls, a log flume; Astrosphere, an indoor Scrambler with a light show and music; Flying Trapeze, flying swings; Ferris wheel; tea cups; carousel.

 Roller coasters: Excalibur (W); Galaxi, family (S).

 Plan to stay: 4 hours.

 Best way to avoid crowds: The slowest days of the week are Monday, Tuesday, and Friday.

 Directions: Take I–95 to exit 5, which is a spur of the interstate. Take that to exit 2B (Highway 1) and go north about 1 mile.

Palace Playland

Old Orchard Street
Old Orchard Beach, ME (207) 934–2001
www.palaceplayland.com

Built up against the sandy beaches of the Atlantic Ocean just south of Portland, there's a lot to do at this little resort park, which rests at the foot of the Old Orchard Beach pier. The unique shops and eateries of this summertime get-away surround the park and its 25-plus attractions.

The somewhat short season (remember, we're in Maine here) lasts from Memorial Day through Labor Day. During daily operation from late June through August, the rides open at 11:00 A.M. or noon, with closing times varying depending on the day's weather and the crowds.

The Sun Wheel, a 75-foot-tall Ferris wheel, takes riders high above the beach and gives them a great view of the surrounding area. For those of you wanting to enjoy the park's thrills, be sure to ride the Galaxi coaster; the little ones can enjoy a spin on the Orient Express kiddie coaster and everyone will enjoy being whirled around on one of the few Crazy Dance rides in the country.

Admission is free and rides are on a pay-as-you-play basis. A pay-one-price pass is available for under $20 and paid parking is available at various city lots. The park is located in downtown Old Orchard Beach at the end of Old Orchard Street.

 Roller coasters: The Galaxi, family (S); Orient Express, junior (S).

York's Wild Kingdom Zoo and Amusement Park

Route 1
York Beach, ME (207) 363–4911
www.yorkzoo.com

A wild adventure awaits families who travel here. From exciting animals to thrilling rides, this 100-acre park has a wide variety of attractions to choose from. There are more than 15 rides to ride and many unique animals to learn about.

In addition to the rides, there are a miniature golf course, go-karts, paddleboats, and elephant and pony rides. The park opens Memorial Day weekend and the season runs through the end of September. The zoo has a longer season. Tickets can be bought for either the entire complex for under $16 or the zoo side only for under $13.

MARYLAND

The Baltimore Zoo

Druid Park Lake Drive
Baltimore, MD (410) 396–7102
www.baltimorezoo.org

The children's zoo at the Baltimore Zoo is rated as one of the best of its kind in the nation, due in part to its great diversity of activities. It offers a handful of rides as well as unique opportunities for children and animals to interact. The park has a carousel, a train ride, and a motion-based simulator.

Admission to the zoo is under $11 for adults, under $6 for children (ages 2 to 11); the rides cost extra. The zoo is open year-round from 10:00 A.M. through 4:00 P.M. and has extended hours from Memorial Day through Labor Day.

Jolly Roger Amusement Park Splash Mountain

30th Street & Coastal Highway
Ocean City, MD
(410) 289–3477
www.jollyrogerpark.com

Located on the beach in Ocean City, the park gives riders the chance to experience a bevy of fun-based amusements all within a few feet of the great Atlantic Ocean. The facility is divided into three areas: Jolly Roger Amusement Park, which has 36 rides including a rare tilt house/mystery shack called the Old Mine; Splash Mountain, a waterpark with 15 slides and play areas; and Speed World, a go-kart park with 16 tracks for drivers of all skill levels.

The waterpark has some unique attractions like the only Master Blaster water coaster in the Northeast, the Stealth Mark III half-pipe slide, a new wave pool, and a huge play activity pool for the family.

 Extras: 2 miniature golf courses: Jungle Golf and Treasure Hunt, extra charge. Skycoaster, extra fee.

 Operating hours: Noon to midnight.

 Admission policy: Rides and attractions on a pay-as-you-go basis. Pay-one-price for rides available, under $18. Combo ticket packages available for waterpark, go-karts, and rides. Free parking.

 Top rides: Giant Wheel; Jolly Roger Express, a vintage 1952 antique train. Water Flume, a log flume; Tilt-A-Whirl; bumper cars; Swing Ride, a wave swinger; Spider.

THE AMUSEMENT PARK GUIDE

 Roller coasters: Wild Mouse, family (S); Wacky Worm, kids (S).

 Plan to stay: 8 hours.

 Best way to avoid crowds: The least busy days are Friday and Saturday.

 Directions: Follow Route 50 across the bridge into Ocean City. When the highway ends, take Philadelphia Avenue north (it becomes the Coastal Highway) to 30th Street; the park is on the left.

Ocean City Pier Rides

401 South Boardwalk
Ocean City, MD (410) 289–3031
www.ocpierrides.com

This park has the wonderful flavor of many long-gone Atlantic pleasure piers. As you walk out the pier toward the ocean, you'll pass the midway games, then the amusement rides, and at the very end, you'll find an area set aside for fishing.

The pier has long been a part of the community. It opened shortly after the turn of the nineteenth century and has had rides for more than 70 years. Today guests can enjoy 11 rides, including the beautiful double-deck Venetian Carousel and the Looping Star roller coaster.

 Extras: The Ghost, a 2-level ride through a haunted house.

 Season: Easter through the third week of September.

 Operating hours: Rides open at 1:00 P.M., with closing times depending on crowds and weather.

 Admission policy: Free admission, rides on a pay-as-you-go basis. Pay-one-price available during the week, under $10.

Top rides: Hurricane, a Music Express with pictures of Ocean City storms of the past; Roc 'n Rapids, log flume; Giant Wheel, a Ferris wheel; 1001 Nights, a 360-degree platform ride; Venetian Carousel, an Italian double-deck carousel; Venturer, motion-based simulator; Crazy Dance, spinning ride.

 Roller coaster: Looping Star, 1-loop (S).

 Plan to stay: 4 hours.

 Best way to avoid crowds: Tuesdays and Wednesdays are the slowest days.

 Directions: Follow Route 50 across the bridge into Ocean City. When Route 50 ends, turn right onto Philadelphia Avenue and follow the signs to "Inlet Parking." Park is adjacent.

Six Flags America Paradise Island Waterpark

13710 Central Avenue
Largo, MD (301) 249-1500
www.sixflags.com

Ruled by two characters we all know, Bugs Bunny and Batman, this place is full of characters. Just about everywhere you look, you'll see Looney Tunes– and DC Comics–themed rides, attractions, gift shops, and, of course, the characters themselves.

Eight roller coasters and the tropical-themed Paradise Island waterpark with 15 of its own activities are among the 100-plus rides, shows, and attractions. Looney Tunes Movie Town is an area where the kids can meet the characters, watch them perform in a fun musical performance, and then expend some energy as they play in the multilevel soft-play area known as the Looney Tunes Prop Warehouse.

The Batwing roller coaster was one of the first "flying roller coasters" in the country. You ride it face down, horizontal with the ground, as you go headfirst through various loops and corkscrews. If you're looking for speed and height, the highly rated Superman Ride of Steel takes you up 200 feet and then back down at speeds up to 70 mph.

This park was originally opened as the Wildlife Preserve by naturalist Jim Fowler. Its name was changed to Wild World and it was purchased in 1991 by the company that is now known as Six Flags Theme Parks Inc. The name was changed to Adventure World in 1994, and then became a branded Six Flags product in 1999.

 Extras: Sonora Speedway go-karts, and rock climbing, both for an additional fee.

 Season: Mid-April through October.

 Operating hours: Opens 10:30 A.M. during peak season. Closing times vary.

 Admission policy: Pay-one-price, under $40. Parking fee.

 Top rides: Penguin's Blizzard River, spinning rapids ride; Tower of Doom, 140-foot-tall free fall; Iron Eagle, 82-foot-high spinning ride; High Seas, pirate ship; Typhoon Seacoaster, a reversing flume/river rapids ride; Flying Carousel, a swing ride; Renegade Rapids, river rapids; Shipwreck Falls, shoot-the-chute.

 Roller coasters: Batwing, flying coaster (S); Superman Ride of Steel, hypercoaster (S); Joker's Jinx, LIM, 4-loop (S); Two Face—The Flip Side, face-to-face boomerang (S); Mind Eraser, inverted (S); The Great Chase, family (S); Roar (W); Wild One (W).

 Plan to stay: 8 hours.

 Best way to avoid crowds: Monday is the slowest day. Most people enjoy the waterpark during midday when it's the hottest, and ride the rides in the morning and evening. To avoid lines, do the opposite.

 Directions: Take exit 15A off I–95; follow the signs to the park. Located 15 minutes from Washington, D.C., and 30 minutes from Baltimore.

Trimper's Rides and Amusements

South 1st Street & Boardwalk
Ocean City, MD (410) 289–8617
www.beach-net.com/trimpers

Time has been good to this prime piece of real estate, owned by the same family since 1890. But time has also brought changes, and today it looks little like the resort the Trimper family began more than 113 years ago. This ocean-side playground has a looming skyline of rides and roller coasters of all sizes that beckon from blocks away. The centerpiece is a 3-row menagerie Herschell/Spillman carousel that dates to the early 1900s.

The 37 rides are located in two areas. The children's rides are indoors, while the major attractions can be found outside. The Slingshot free-fall tower gives riders a great view of the beach. In addition, the Pirates Cove walk-through fun house was designed by Bill Tracey, and the Haunted House, with cars shaped as coffins, is a must-do.

 Extras: Miniature golf, extra charge. Also offered are an unusual mirror maze and an interesting walk-through called Pirates Cove, both included in pay-one-price admission.

 Season: Indoor rides run on weekends year-round. The entire park is open Easter Sunday through October, or as long as good weather holds out.

 Operating hours: Opens at 1:00 P.M. on weekdays and at noon on weekends; closes at midnight every night.

 Admission policy: Free admission, with rides and attractions on a pay-as-you-go basis. Pay-one-price also available, until 6:00 P.M., under $15. Parking at meters and paid lots nearby.

 Top rides: The Inverter; Wipe Out; Tilt-A-Whirl; tank tag; Frog Hopper, kids' free fall; Zipper. The 2-level Haunted House, which you ride through sitting in mini coffins made of wood, is located along the boardwalk.

 Roller coasters: Tidal Wave, boomerang (S); Toboggan, family (S); Kiddie Coaster, kiddie (S).

THE AMUSEMENT PARK GUIDE

 Plan to stay: 3 hours.

 Best way to avoid crowds: Mondays and Tuesdays are the slowest days.

 Directions: Follow Route 50 across the bridge into Ocean City. The highway ends at Philadelphia Avenue; turn right and go 5 blocks to Division Street. Then turn left and go 2 blocks to the boardwalk.

MASSACHUSETTS

Pirates Fun Park

Route 1A
Salisbury Beach, MA (978) 465–3731
www.piratesfunpark.com

If you're tired of the hustle and bustle of an urban-style seaside resort, Salisbury Beach could be what you're looking for. Located along a 4-mile beach, just south of the New Hampshire state line, the town offers a very family-oriented summer retreat. It's reminiscent of the seaside resorts you see on the old faded postcards.

The 18-ride park is located in the center of the town, just a short distance from the boardwalk, and is a popular playground not only for the locals but the tourists as well. Included in the ride lineup are a Tilt-A-Whirl, a merry-go-round, a super slide, a Ferris wheel, and 6 rides just for the kids. The Kastle Frankenstein is a fun darkride for the whole family.

 Roller coaster: Orient Express, family (S).

Admission is on a pay-as-you-go basis, with a pay-one-price, under $13, available only on Thursdays after 6:00 P.M. A kids' pay-one-price is available on Wednesday afternoon, under $8, and is good only for the kiddie rides. Located on the Atlantic seaboard, approximately 35 miles north of Boston.

Six Flags New England Hurricane Harbor

Route 159
Agawam, MA
(413) 786–9300/(877) 4–SIX FLAGS
www.sixflags.com

Although it's one of the newest members of the Six Flags family, this park is anything but new. We can all be thankful that Six Flags has helped maintain its traditional charm through millions of dollars of investment and new attractions. With plenty of mature landscaping and a great riverside location, the former Riverside Park is now New England's largest amusement park.

The park features more than 50 major rides, including 8 roller coasters. The signature coaster here is the 221-foot-tall Superman Ride of Steel, voted the number one roller coaster in 2000, 2001, and 2002! By the way, that's 71 feet taller than the Statue of Liberty, if you're looking for a point of comparison. The park also boasts the only floorless roller coaster in New England, Batman–The Dark Knight. It stands 117 feet and offers a smooth ride through 5 inversions.

The beautiful 1909 Mangels-Illions carousel, in the park since 1940, is still in operation and is now being enjoyed by its third generation. The big roundabout has 48 jumpers, 20 standers, 4 menagerie, and 2 chariots. Music is provided by a Wurlitzer 146-B band organ.

Looney Tunes Movie Town has 8 rides that families can enjoy together, and if you're looking to meet Bugs Bunny and a few of his friends, Movie Town is where you'll find them. The DC Comics area is where you'll find the Superman coaster and the Batman Thrill Spectacular stunt show featuring the Caped Crusader himself. Tiny Timber Town is the newest kids' area, with 5 rides, and Main Street in Rockville is a classic step back in time, featuring great '50s rock and roll and The Twister ride.

Hurricane Harbor was doubled in size in 2003 and has plenty of action, including a 500,000-gallon wave pool, plenty of action water slides, an interactive water play adventure land for the kids, and more.

THE AMUSEMENT PARK GUIDE

 Extras: Skycoaster, Euro bungee, virtual reality, and rock-climbing wall, additional charges. Musical events are staged periodically throughout the season.

 Special events: Fright Fest in October.

 Season: April through October; waterpark, Memorial Day through Labor Day.

 Operating hours: Opens at 10:00 A.M. Closing varies depending on season and weather.

 Admission policy: Pay-one-price, under $40. Late Gate admission, after 4:00 P.M., is under $25. Parking charge.

 Top rides: The Scream, a 20-story, 3-tower free-fall complex; Houdini, The Great Escape illusion house; Colossus, 150-foot-tall Ferris wheel; Shipwreck Falls, shoot-the-chute; Poland Springs Plunge, log flume; Blizzard River, white-water rafting ride.

 Roller coasters: Batman–The Dark Knight, floorless (S); Superman Ride of Steel, hypercoaster (S); Flashback, Boomerang (S); Poison Ivy's Twisted Train, family (S); Mind Eraser, inverted (S); Cyclone (W); Thunderbolt (W); The Great Chase Kiddie Coaster, kiddie (S).

 Plan to stay: 7 to 9 hours if you want to play in the waterpark.

 Best way to avoid crowds: Mondays through Thursdays are the slowest days.

 Directions: Take exit 3 off I–91, then follow Route 57 to Route 159 South (Main Street) and go south 3 miles.

 # TiM'S TRIViA

Take it easy on yourself! Pick up a guidebook, map, and entertainment schedule when you buy your ticket. Plan your day around the specific times of the shows you don't want to miss. Make a list of must-do rides and attractions and then plan your route so you won't be doing a lot of time-consuming and tiring backtracking.

MICHIGAN

Crossroads Village
Bray Road, South of Stanley
Flint, MI (810) 736-7100/(800) 648-PARK

This is one of the few historic villages in America that offers classic rides and attractions along with its historic structures. Along with its 32 re-created structures, including a blacksmith shop, a doctor's office, and a lumberyard, there is a circa 1912 carousel, a 1912 Ferris wheel, and the circa 1930 Venetian Swings.

The Huckleberry Railroad is a genuine Baldwin steam locomotive that takes passengers on 35-minute, 8-mile excursions, while the Genesee Belle paddle-wheel riverboat provides scenic 45-minute cruises on Mott Lake.

At the Lakeside Park amusement area, a beautiful 1912 C.W. Parker carousel stands out. It has 36 handcrafted wooden jumping horses, a dragon chariot, and 4 metal kiddie ponies with a mother's bench. A rare circa 1925 Artizan band organ provides the music for the carousel.

The 1912 Ferris wheel was also built by the C.W. Parker company in Leavenworth, Kansas, and is thought to be the only one of its kind still in operation. The Venetian Swings were built by the Allan Herschell Company in the 1930s in North Tonawanda, New York.

There are three different admission plans, each for under $15. Open daily, except non-holiday Mondays, late May through early September and selected weekends through the fall and early winter when special Harvest, Halloween, and Christmas festivals take place.

Dutch Village
12350 James Street
Off Route 31
Holland, MI (616) 396-1475

The first thing visitors notice about Dutch Village, which bills itself as "a bit of old Holland," is the abundance of vegetation throughout the park. Flowers are everywhere

THE AMUSEMENT PARK GUIDE

and people come from all over to see the Tulip Festival during the first week of May. The park has 3 rides: a swing ride, a wooden shoe slide, and a beautiful circa 1924 Herschell/Spillman carousel. The ride, called a *draaimolen* in Dutch, is a 3-row machine. Guests also relax and listen to the Gouden Engel (Golden Angel) organ, the second-largest Dutch organ ever built, which dates from 1882. The canals, buildings, and crafts all combine to make this a unique park experience for the family.

Pay-one-price, under $9. Open from the end of April through mid-October, 9:00 A.M. to 5:00 P.M.

Michigan's Adventure WildWater Adventure

4750 Whitehall Road
Muskegon, MI (231) 766–3377
www.miadventure.com

This 80-acre amusement park, which started life as a local deer park, was sold to park operator Cedar Fair for the 2002 season by the Jourden family, who had originally developed it into a ride park. It looks better than ever, as the new owners have been able to keep the spirit of the old park while adding many new attractions. The top thrill ride is one of the largest wooden roller coasters in the country, Shivering Timbers. At more than 5,000 feet long, the coaster is a series of nonstop hills and thrills.

The park has more than 33 rides, and at WildWater Adventure waterpark there are 14 different attractions, ranging from speed thrill slides and 2 wave pools to a tranquil family area and a lazy river.

 Season: May through mid-September.

 Operating hours: 10:00 A.M. to 7:00, 8:00, or 9:00 P.M.

 Admission policy: Pay-one-price, under $24. Parking charge.

 Top rides: Be-Bop Boulevard, 1950s-themed car ride; Frog Hopper, kiddie free fall; Adventure Falls, shoot-the-chute; Logger's Run, flume;

Falling Star, a 360-degree platform ride that keeps riders upright at all times; Sea Dragon, a swinging pirate ship; a 90-foot-tall gondola-type Ferris wheel; Grand Carousel.

 Roller coasters: Shivering Timbers (W); Corkscrew (S); Wolverine Wildcat (W); Zach's Zoomer, junior (W); Mad Mouse (S); Big Dipper, family (S).

 Plan to stay: 7 hours.

 Best way to avoid crowds: June is the slowest month of the season.

 Directions: Take the Russell Street exit off Route 31 and go north to Riley Thompson Road. Go west on Riley Thompson for about 2 miles; the park is on the right at Whitehall Road.

MINNESOTA

Camp Snoopy
Indoors, Mall of America
5000 Center Court
Bloomington, MN (952) 883–8600
www.campsnoopy.com

This is the largest and definitely the coolest indoor amusement park in the United States. It's located under 1.2 miles of clear glass skylights in the middle of the largest shopping mall in the country. The Peanuts cartoon gang, including Snoopy, lives here as costumed characters, and much of the theming and many of the ride names reflect their presence.

It's hard to believe you are indoors. The 100-foot-high glass ceiling allows natural light to flow into the park to help it achieve the grandeur of Minnesota's north woods. There are more than 400 trees standing from 10 to 35 feet high, and more than 30,000 plants. A 9-foot gradation in the rolling landscape gives the flowing streams and the banks of evergreens an even more natural appearance.

There are 20 rides, most of which the entire family can ride together. In addition to the rides, there are 2 full-service restaurants, a Taco Bell, Pizza Hut, Betty Crocker Kitchen, and Kemp's Ice Cream Parlor within Camp Snoopy. The Snoopy Boutique has the largest collection of Peanuts merchandise in the world.

 Extras: There's a rock-climbing wall; a petting zoo; and Kids Quest, a drop-off child care for kids up to 12 years, all for an extra fee.

 Season: Year-round.

 Operating hours: 10:00 A.M. to 9:30 or 10:00 P.M.

 Admission policy: Free admission, with rides and attractions on a pay-as-you-go basis. Pay-one-price available, under $25. Automated admission system permits you to buy various ticket packages from machines, without standing in lines.

 Top rides: Ghost Blasters, an interactive family darkride where riders shoot at the ghosts; Xcel Energy Log Chute, a log ride through a mountain of animated scenes; Mighty Axe, the only ride in the park that takes riders upside down; Mystery Mine Ride, a ride simulator; Skyscraper Ferris Wheel, 74 feet tall; Americana Carousel; bumper cars; and the Snoopy Bounce, a play bounce inside a huge, inflated Snoopy.

 Roller coasters: Ripsaw Roller Coaster, family (S); Lil' Shaver, junior (S).

 Plan to stay: 3 hours.

 Best way to avoid crowds: Crowds tend to grow as the mall becomes busier. Come early or during the week, and avoid the Christmas-shopping crowds.

 Directions: Inside Mall of America. Take 24th Avenue South exit off I–494.

TiM'S TRiViA

The $70 million Camp Snoopy opened on August 11, 1992, in the middle of the largest indoor mall in the United States, Mall of America. The 7-acre park, officials say, is an outdoor park that just happens to be indoors, with large pine trees, meandering rivers, and lush landscaping.

Como Park Amusement Park
Hamlin & Midway Parkway
in Como Park
St. Paul, MN (651) 335–4200

The family amusement facility that offers the best value in the Twin Cities is located in city-owned Como Park, between the beautiful Victorian greenhouse conservatory and the Como Park Zoo. The local city magazine says Como Park Amusement Park is the cleanest, most convenient, and least expensive place to enjoy family amusement rides in the region.

There's nothing pretentious about this place. No big fences, no fancy signs. You'll know you're there when you see the rides and the lone ticket booth that also serves as the snack bar. There are 15 rides on less than 2 acres, including a Tilt-A-Whirl, a Scrambler, a Round-Up, a carousel, a small family coaster, Dizzy Dragon, Windjammer, and several small rides for the wee ones.

 Roller coaster: Dragon Wagon, family (S).

Open daily from April through Labor Day, 10:30 A.M. to 8:00 P.M. No admission charge, with rides on a pay-as-you-go basis. A pay-one-price wristband is available Tuesday and Thursday nights, under $8.

A few hundred feet from the amusement park, near the conservatory, a circa 1914 Philadelphia Toboggan Company carousel (#33) has found a home in a new "million-dollar" pavilion. Operated at the nearby Minnesota State Fairgrounds from 1914 to 1989, the ride was purchased by a preservation committee, completely restored along with its Wurlitzer 153 band organ, and opened here in 2000. It is not a part of the O'Neil family–owned amusement park, but is within easy walking distance.

Paul Bunyan
Amusement Center

**Highways 210 & 371
Brainerd, MN (218) 829–6342
www.paulbunyancenter.com**

The legendary lumberjack Paul Bunyan, in the form of a funky 26-foot-high talking, moving statue, greets visitors to this fun and eclectic amusement center. Babe, his faithful blue ox, is also present in behemoth form. The park has been home to the north woods legend since 1950.

 Roller coaster: Roller Coaster, family (S).

Scattered throughout the 8-acre park are more than 40 attractions, including 17 amusement rides. Among the more popular attractions are the Ghost Mine, the Himalaya, a miniature train, Mine Shack tilt house/mystery shack, Space Probe, a climbing wall, Frog Hopper, miniature golf, picnic grounds, and lumbering exhibits.

Admission is under $12 for rides and attractions within the gates. There are separate charges for those outside. Open daily Memorial Day through Labor Day at 10:00 A.M.; closing times vary.

Valleyfair!
Whitewater Country

**1 Valleyfair Drive
Shakopee, MN
(952) 445–7600/(800) FUN–RIDE
www.valleyfair.com**

Anticipation grows as you walk through the front gates here. But don't be lulled into thinking the entire park is as laid-back and peaceful as the plaza area. The fountains and the archway, as well as the colorful flower baskets belie the true nature of your visit here.

Action-packed family fun and plenty of thrills greet you as you head out into the park. The new Steel Venom impulse roller coaster has a gut-wrenching 360-degree spiraling corkscrew at one end of the U-shaped track and offers a unique ride experience. Now with 7 coasters and 12 kiddie rides among its 37 rides, the park is by far the state's premier amusement playground. Berenstain Bear Country and Half-Pint Park are two fun areas for the smaller ones in your family.

The 3.5-acre Whitewater Country waterpark is included in the admission price and has all sorts of watery activities including the Ripple Rapids lazy river for adults and the Giggle Run lazy river for the kids. Panic Falls is a complex of 5 thrill slides and Hurricane Falls is a six-passenger family raft ride. Great fun!

Challenge Park, just outside the front gate, is where you'll find 2 miniature golf courses, go-karts, Can-Am–style go-karts, and bumper boats, all for separate fees.

 Season: May through September.

 Operating hours: Opens at 10:00 A.M. and closes at either 10:00 P.M. or midnight.

 Admission policy: Pay-one-price, under $31. Parking charge. Children under 48 inches tall, and visitors over 60 years of age get in for $6.95.

 Top rides: Power Tower, 3-tower, 250-foot-tall free fall; Frog Hopper; The Wave, shoot-the-chute; Hydroblaster, a dry ride down an enclosed water chute; Thunder Canyon, a raging-rapids ride; a circa 1915 Philadelphia Toboggan Company carousel; a log flume; a gondola-style Ferris wheel from which you can see the Minnesota River Valley.

 Roller coasters: Steel Venom, LIM, impulse (S); The Wild Thing (S); High Roller (W); Excalibur (S); Corkscrew (S); Mad Mouse, family (S); Mild Thing, kiddie (S).

 Plan to stay: 9 hours.

 Best way to avoid crowds: Come on weekdays, early in the day.

 Directions: Located southwest of Minneapolis on County Road 101, 9 miles west of the intersection of Highways 13 and 35W.

Mississippi

Fun Time USA

Highway 90 & Cowan Road
Gulfport, MS (228) 896–7315

Located on the beach, halfway between Gulfport and Biloxi, this small, clean park offers miniature golf, go-karts, a large arcade with video games, and Skee-Ball. It also has 9 rides, including bumper boats, a Tilt-A-Whirl, a C. P. Huntington train, a circa 1956 carousel, and 5 kiddie rides.

Admission is free, with rides on a pay-as-you-go basis. The park is open daily until midnight during the summer, with limited hours depending on the weather during the rest of the year.

 TiM'S TRIViA

Many parks are now offering special discount admission coupons and special deals on their Web sites, and most will let you download and print out the coupon at home. Check out the site of the park you're heading to. It could well be worth a few minutes of surfing!

Geyser Falls Water Theme Park

209 Black Jack Road
On the Mississippi Choctaw Reservation
Choctaw, MS (601) 389–3099
www.GeyserFalls.com

The state's largest waterpark opened in mid-2002 as part of the Pearl River Resort, a hotel/casino complex owned by the Mississippi Band of Choctaw Indians. The 15-acre, $20 million waterpark features 12 waterslides, including 3, 6-story speed slides, a large wave pool, a 1,200-foot-long continuous river, an interactive family play area known as Creaky Leaky Water Factory, and a water play area for the smaller members of the family.

Adjacent to the waterpark, a section of the 285-acre lake has been turned into a white-sand lagoon with a snorkeling trail and beach club. A big grizzly bear announces the start of the wave cycle at the wave pool with a loud roar. In addition to the waterpark, the resort has 2 casino hotels, an amphitheater, and a fitness and wellness center. Located 3 miles outside Philadelphia, 70 miles east of Jackson. Pay-one-price, under $20.

Magic Golf/Biloxi Beach Amusement Park
1785 Beach Boulevard
Biloxi, MS (228) 374-4338

This popular beachside facility has the extra benefit of having the magnificent Gulf of Mexico as its backdrop. Offerings here include 15 rides, with the Ferris wheel and bumper cars being the most ridden. In addition, there are go-karts, miniature golf, and a fun-filled games arcade. A small kiddieland features 6 rides for the wee ones.

There is no charge to get in, and everything is on a pay-as-you-go basis. Hours are 10:00 A.M. to 10:00 P.M. daily; longer hours on weekends and during the peak summer season.

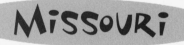

MISSOURI

Celebration City
Junction of Highways 76 & 376
Branson, MO (417) 338-2611
www.silverdollarcity.com

Set to open in the spring of 2003, Celebration City is being positioned as a nighttime theme park for the entire family by its owners, Herschend Family Entertainment Corporation, which also owns the nearby Silver Dollar City. So as not to compete with each other, the new park will open late each afternoon and stay open late into the evening while

Silver Dollar City theme park will continue to open each morning and close at dusk.

The new park's signature ride is the Ozark WildCat, a new $4 million classic twisting wood coaster that reaches speeds of 44 mph and has a drop of 80-plus feet. In all, there will be 3 roller coasters among the 20 rides and attractions.

 Roller coasters: Ozark WildCat (W); Thunderbolt, family (S); Jack Rabbit, family (S).

Other rides include The Accelerator, a double-shot free fall, and the Electric Star Wheel, a 95-foot-tall Ferris wheel. The Fireball is a turning, twisting thriller that takes riders 60 feet into the air.

The park has a twentieth-century theme, highlighting the various and colorful eras of the century, with a heavy emphasis on the 1950s, on historical Route 66, and on boardwalk parks and their unique atmosphere. There are 10 themed restaurants, including the '50s-style Last Chance Diner, and 10 themed shops, including a Route 66 memorabilia shop and an old-fashioned photo shop.

Each day will culminate with an outdoor laser production. The park will be open from April through October with daily operation during the summer months. Hours will be from 3:00 to 11:00 P.M. daily. Combination tickets for the theme parks, the waterparks, and other Silver Dollar City–owned properties are available. The park is located on the property that was once Branson USA Amusement Park. That facility was closed in 2001 when purchased by Silver Dollar City.

Oceans of Fun

4545 Worlds of Fun Avenue
Kansas City, MO (816) 454–4545
www.worldsoffun.com

Situated next to Worlds of Fun theme park, this 60-acre waterpark offers a full day of cool fun and adventure. There are 8 slides, the Surf City wave pool, the Caribbean Cooler lazy river, and Castaway Cove, an adults-only pool with a jacuzzi and a swim-up bar where alcoholic beverages are available.

Hurricane Falls is a 72-foot-high family raft ride that careens down a 14-foot-wide, 680-foot-long flume. Coconut

Cove is a children's play area with small slides and pools, and another kid's area, Crocodile Isle, offers a bevy of fun water activities for the little ones.

 TIM'S TRIVIA

Castaway Cove, an adults-only pool and sundeck in Oceans of Fun waterpark, is a wonderfully quiet and lush oasis from the rest of the park. No kids, no screaming. Take a book, buy a cold beer or a glass of wine, sit back, and enjoy the peace while your kids are off seeking watery thrills. If you want to stay in the water, try out the swim-up bar.

Park guests also have access to The Monsoon shoot-the-chute ride, located between the waterpark and the theme park. Open daily at 10:00 A.M., Memorial Day through Labor Day; closing times vary. Admission is under $25.

Silver Dollar City
Off Highway 76
Branson, MO (417) 338–2611/(800) 475–9370
www.silverdollarcity.com

A few miles and 100 years away from the glitter and glitz of nearby Branson, this hybrid of a park is truly a one-of-a-kind family attraction. What started out as a place offering tours of Marvel Cave has turned into a complex that offers 17 rides and attractions, 4 major festivals, 60 shops, and more than 50 live entertainment shows a day.

Huge trees, turn-of-the-twentieth-century architecture, friendly people, and a crafts colony of more than 100 artisans working at their art while interacting with the guests—that's what this park is all about.

Among all this quaintness and nostalgia, you'll find the rides, including the new Wild Fire steel, multilooping roller coaster.

 Extras: A 55-minute guided tour of Marvel Cave is free with admission to park. Geyser Gulch is a 2-acre participatory play area billed as "the world's largest tree house."

 Special events: World Fest, featuring international performers, April; Natonal Kid's Fest, June through August; Festival of American Music &

THE AMUSEMENT PARK GUIDE

Craftsmanship, September and October; Old Time Christmas, November through December.

 Season: Mid-April through December.

 Operating hours: 9:30 A.M. to 6:00 or 7:00 P.M. during peak season. Doesn't stay open after dark.

 Admission policy: Pay-one-price, under $39. Combination tickets with the company's other area attractions—Celebration City White Water waterpark, the *Branson Belle* showboat, and the Dixie Stampede dinner theater—are available. Free parking.

 Top rides: Frisco Silver Dollar Line, 20-minute train ride through the Ozark countryside; Great Shoot-Out, a ride-through shooting gallery; Lost River of the Ozarks, a raging-rapids ride; American Plunge, a log flume; Wilderness Waterboggan, an 8-story toboggan ride down a water chute; Fire in the Hole, an indoor, themed, dark action ride.

 Roller coasters: Wild Fire, multi-element (S); Buzz Saw Falls, part roller coaster, part water flume (S); Thunderation, mine train (S); Runaway Ore Cart, junior (S).

 Plan to stay: 7 hours.

 Best way to avoid crowds: The park is laid out in a circle; pick up a map and follow the circle without doubling back or crossing over. Weekdays, as well as spring and fall weekends, entail fewer people.

 Directions: Located off Highway 76, 9 miles west of Branson, 40 miles south of Springfield.

 # TIM'S TRIVIA

Six Flags Over Mid-America, which debuted on June 5, 1971, was the third and last Six Flags park built by company founder Angus Wynne. Six Flags Over Texas, near Dallas, was the first to open in 1961, and Six Flags Over Georgia, in Atlanta, opened in 1967. Six Flags Over Mid-America became Six Flags St. Louis in 1998.

Six Flags St. Louis Hurricane Harbor

Six Flags Outer Road
Eureka, MO (635) 938–4800
www.sixflags.com

Undulating hills with a plentiful supply of huge, mature shade trees and acres of lush and colorful landscaping form the palette for the family attractions and thrill rides here at the third Six Flags park to be built. Its maturity definitely contributes to both its beauty and its uniqueness.

The Looney Tunes characters and Scooby-Doo call the 200-acre facility home, and there are plenty of thrill rides and whimsically themed kiddie rides to make this a fun family outing. In the Brittannia section of the park, a beautifully restored circa 1915 Philadelphia Toboggan Company carousel is still in operation, and at the Scooby-Doo Ghostblasters darkride, passengers can help eliminate the ghost population of Scary Swamp while racking up points as they compete with the rest of the riders.

Spread out among the trees and the theming of the eight areas are 31 rides. In each area, the rides, architecture, and activities all carry out the theme of the area—1904 World's Fair, Gateway to the West, Warner Bros. Backlot, Chouteau's Market, Illinois, Brittania, DC Comics Plaza, and Looney Tunes Town.

The 12-acre waterpark is included in park admission and it features a huge wave pool, 3 high-speed slides, 4 tube slides, a lazy river, and a 5-story-tall interactive play structure.

 Special events: Fright Fest, October.

 Season: April through October.

 Operating hours: Opens at 10:00 A.M. daily during the peak season. Closing times vary from 6:00 to 10:00 P.M.

 Admission policy: Pay-one-price, under $43. Add $10 for the next day. Parking charge.

THE AMUSEMENT PARK GUIDE

 Top rides: Scooby-Doo Ghostblasters—The Mystery of Scary Swamp, interactive darkride; Thunder River, raging rapids; Tidal Wave, shoot-the-chute; Log Flume, a double-trough ride with great capacity; Colossus, a giant Ferris wheel; and the Grand Ole' Carousel.

 Roller coasters: The Boss (W); Mr. Freeze, LIM shuttle (S); Batman The Ride, inverted (S); River King Mine Ride (S); Ninja, multi-element (S); Screamin' Eagle (W); Acme Gravity Powered Roller Ride, kiddie (S).

 Plan to stay: 8 hours.

 Best way to avoid crowds: The least busy days are Tuesdays, Wednesdays, and Thursdays.

 Directions: Take Six Flags Road exit off I-44, 30 minutes southwest of St. Louis. The park is located there on the service road.

White Water

West Highway 76
Branson, MO (417)334-7487/(800)475-9370
www.silverdollarcity.com

Aloha. The tropical attitude is alive and well here at White Water, a 12-attraction waterpark in the midst of the Ozark Mountains. There are 6 slides and flumes, including the popular Paradise Plunge, a 207-foot-tall, triple-drop slide, and the Bermuda Triangle and the Typhoon Tunnel, both enclosed body flumes. RainTree Island is a family interactive area with more than 60 interactive activities, geysers, and slides.

Other activities and attractions include the Paradise River lazy river; Surf Quake wave pool; Splash Island kids' activity pool; live entertainment, including dive-in movies and beach dance parties; sand volleyball courts; food service; and a beach shop.

Located 5 miles from its sister park, Silver Dollar City, the park is along the "strip" in this busy tourist area, full of country music theaters, restaurants, and family activities.

Open May through Labor Day, daily from Memorial Day. Opens at 9:00 A.M., closes at 8:00 P.M. during peak season. Pay-one-price, under $27.

Worlds of Fun

**4545 Worlds of Fun Avenue
Kansas City, MO (816) 454–4545
www.worldsoffun.com**

Snoopy is king here and the kids love him! Wherever you see the costumed character, you'll find dozens of kids waiting in line and dozens of parents with cameras waiting to catch that special canine hug their kid is sure to get from the world-famous pooch.

That's only part of the family fun that's sure to occur at this laid-back, 175-acre, wooded Midwestern amusement park. It's clean, it's fun, and it's what a family park should be all about.

The park has 43 rides, including 13 for kids, and Kiddy Kingdom, a kids' play area. Camp Snoopy is a 1-acre family area where all the rides, shows, and attractions can be enjoyed by the entire family. Among the fun are the Woodstock Express train ride, and the Red Baron airplane adventure. Snoopy and all the Peanuts characters are here for fun meet-and-greets.

The rides and attractions are laid out in a big circle, making the park easy to get around in. You'll never be too far from anything.

 Extras: RipCord, Skycoaster, extra. Shaded picnic areas are located outside the park, adjacent to the parking lot. Oceans of Fun waterpark is adjacent, extra fee.

 Season: April through mid-October; daily mid-May through late August.

 Operating hours: Opens daily at 10:00 A.M., closing varies from 6:00 P.M. to midnight.

 Admission policy: Pay-one-price, under $35; big discount after 4:00 P.M. A combination pass with Oceans of Fun is available, under $60. Parking charge.

Top rides: Thunder Hawk, top spin; Detonator, twin 200-foot-high space shots; Fury of the Nile, a raging-rapids ride; Viking Voyager, a log flume; The Monsoon, shoot-the-chute.

 Roller coasters: Boomerang (S); Timber Wolf (W); Orient Express, multi-element (S); Wacky Worm, junior (S); Mamba (S).

 Plan to stay: 9 hours.

 Best way to avoid crowds: Come on weekdays during the peak season or on Sundays in spring and fall. Go to the farthest distance from the gate and work toward the front.

 Directions: Located on I–435 at exit 54, just north of the Missouri River.

NEBRASKA

Fun-Plex

7003 Q Street at 70th Street
Omaha, NE (402) 331–8426
www.fun-plex.com

It would be hard to not find something you want to do at this diversified entertainment complex. There's something around every corner, for every member of your family! You can choose from 2 go-kart tracks, bumper boats, 4 kiddie rides, a Tilt-A-Whirl, bumper cars, Spider, batting cages, miniature golf, a Billiard Center with 9 tables, 2 waterslides, the Motion Ocean wave pool, a kiddie pool, and a lazy river.

Opens at 11:00 A.M. daily, with weekday closing at 10:00 P.M.; weekends at 11:00 P.M. The complex is open year-round, with the waterpark in operation from Memorial Day through Labor Day; the rides run from late spring through fall as long as the weather holds out; and everything else operates year-round as weather permits.

NEVADA

In Nevada, many of the finest rides and attractions are not located in amusement parks, but in casino hotels instead. Following is a sampling of such facilities that have note-worthy rides and attractions.

The AdventureDome

**Circus Circus Hotel Casino
2880 South Las Vegas Boulevard
Las Vegas, NV (702) 794–3939
www.adventuredome.com**

Tired of the casino scene? Tired of the hot walk from one end of the Strip to the other just to find some non-gambling fun? On a hot day in the desert, there are few places better to visit than this 5-acre, climate-controlled, immaculately maintained oasis of indoor fun.

Located in its own big pink dome, behind the casino area, the park was designed to resemble a classic desert canyon with artificial rocks giving way to caverns, pinnacles, and steep cliffs. A stream flows gently through the landscape, finally cascading over a 68-foot-tall waterfall.

There are 13 rides, a children's soft-play area, an IMAX theater, and a laser tag arena. You'll also find rock climbing, bungee jumping, miniature golf, midway games, a virtual reality zone, and a video arcade. There are free clown shows daily. The Canyon Blaster is the only double-loop, double-corkscrew indoor roller coaster in the United States, and the Rim Runner shoot-the-chute takes riders on a scenic journey before dumping them over a 60-foot waterfall.

 Roller coaster: Canyon Blaster, loop/corkscrew (S); Miner Mike, kiddie (S).

Open year-round daily with gates opening on most days at 10:00 a.m.; closings vary with the season. Admission to the park is free, with all rides and attractions on a pay-as-you-play basis, or you may purchase an all-day ride pass, under $18.

Inside the Circus Circus Casino in the center stage area of the grand carnival midway, free circus acts begin performing daily at 11:00 A.M. From tightwire performers to the flying trapeze, several acts are booked each hour.

 TiM'S TRiViA

There are discounts available for just about every park in the country at just about anytime during the season. It's estimated that fewer than 20% of those paying to get into parks each year pay the full, posted price. Call your park and ask about its discounts before you go. Don't forget to ask for military, AARP, AAA, and even Sam's Club discounts. Also, check on soft-drink cans; parks love to offer discount coupons on them.

Buffalo Bill's

I–15 at the California border
Jean, NV (702) 679–7433
www.primadonna.com

Believe it or not, many people make the trek way out here just to enjoy the attractions and never even think about dropping any money into the myriad gambling devices!

The king of the attractions is the 209-foot-tall Desperado steel roller coaster. Outside, it looms over the complex, but don't look for the loading station out there. You'll pay and climb aboard the coaster inside the casino, then travel up through the roof as you ascend the first hill. You'll have a few seconds to enjoy the fantastic views before the real action starts!

The 180-foot-tall Turbo Drop free fall is located outside, as are 2 monorails that will take you to the other casinos on the property. Inside, there's a Frog Hopper for the kids, a MaxFlight cyber coaster, and the interactive Adventure Canyon log flume, where you'll be able to shoot at targets as you drift along.

The Vault is an amazing 3-D motion-based, state-of-the-art simulator ride that allows you to choose from one of the 10 available films. That means there are 10 different experiences you'll have to enjoy before you leave.

Each ride is priced individually, but a wristband is available that gives you unlimited use of the rides, a box of popcorn, a Coca-Cola soft drink, and admission to a full-length movie at the casino's theater, under $35.

 Roller coaster: Desperado, hypercoaster (S).

New York, New York Hotel and Casino

3155 West Harmon Avenue
Las Vegas, NV (702) 740-6969
www.nynyhotelcasino.com

The Big Apple, Las Vegas–style. An amazingly accurate, albeit smaller, version of the New York City skyline allows you to enjoy some of the flavor of the big city, while you shop, gamble, and play here on the Strip.

The only major ride here is the Manhattan Express, a 203-foot-tall coaster that loads and unloads in the casino. Once it goes out the roof, it works its way across and through the towers of the New York City skyline. The highly themed Coney Island Emporium fun center is located inside and has the feel of New York's venerable seaside amusement park. The emporium has laser tag, bumper cars, shooting gallery, midway games, and nearly 200 coin-operated video games.

 Roller coaster: Manhattan Express, multi-element (S).

Playland Park

In Idlewild City Park
1900 Cowon Drive
Reno, NV (775) 329-6008

The Reno Chief train is the star at this little amusement area along the Truckee River in Idlewild Park, just a mile from downtown Reno. The train celebrates its 40th year of operation in 2003, and remains the most ridden of the 13 rides in the park. The quarter-mile journey takes riders outside the amusement park and around a lake. Other rides include a Tilt-A-Whirl and a small steel family coaster.

 Roller coaster: Roller Coaster, junior (S).

Playland is open daily, Memorial Day through Labor Day; it's open weekends only in September and October and February through May, weather permitting. Usual operating hours are 11:00 A.M. to 6:00 P.M.

Admission is free, with rides on a pay-as-you-play basis.

Sahara Hotel and Casino NASCAR Cafe

2535 Las Vegas Boulevard South
Las Vegas, NV (702) 734-7223
www.nascarcafelasvegas.com

Speed, the West's first LIM launch roller coaster, begins its journey at the NASCAR Cafe, inside the Sahara Hotel and Casino. The ride blasts out of the building, and runs along the famous Las Vegas Strip, through a loop and through the world-famous Sahara neon sign! This is a great, smooth, coaster and well worth the $6 it takes to ride it. An all-day unlimited coaster pass costs $15.

Also inside the NASCAR Cafe is the Las Vegas Cyber Speedway. The 35,000-square-foot attraction has 24 model stock cars that provide a realistic racing experience, complete with sights and sounds of the track.

Both attractions are open during restaurant hours. Call for specifics.

Stratosphere Tower

2000 South Las Vegas Boulevard
Las Vegas, NV (702) 380-7777

High atop the tower are two ride experiences you won't find anywhere else in the world.

The High Roller, located near the top of the 1,149-foot-high structure, may not be the tallest coaster in the world, but it certainly is the highest, and it may not be the most

Speed," Sahara Hotel and Casino, NASCAR Cafe, Las Vegas, Nevada
Photo by Tim O'Brien

thrilling, but its location certainly makes you hold on tight. Starting at the 909-foot level, the coaster makes several laps around the top of the tower.

At the 921-foot level, the Space Shot free-fall ride propels riders approximately 160 feet straight up. (In case you missed it, that's 160 feet up from the loading platform, which is already located nearly 1,000 feet above the Las Vegas Strip far below . . . Yikes!)

The Strat-O-Fair is an indoor/outdoor 17,000-square-foot fun center down on the second level. It offers several rides including a Ferris wheel and the Frog Hopper free-fall ride for the kids. There's also a virtual reality bowling facility and a mechanical bull, a shooting gallery, and a huge selection of video arcade games.

Wild Island Family Adventure Park

250 Wild Island Court
Sparks, NV (775) 359-2927
www.wildisland.com

Here's another great example of a little park with a bit of something for everyone in the family. There's a waterpark with family slides, speed slides, an interactive area with a water dump bucket, a kids' play area, a half-pipe slide, a lazy river, and a wave pool.

In addition, there are a miniature golf course, go-karts, and the Wildcat, a family roller coaster. For the little kids, there's Frog City, an area with a Frog Hopper ride, a bounce, and a slide complex.

 Roller coaster: Wildcat, family (S).

Located at the Sparks Boulevard exit off I-80, the park is open year-round, with an all-day pass for the waterpark costing less than $20. Everything else is on a pay-as-you-go basis. Hours vary for the different attractions and the time of year.

Canobie Lake Park

North Policy Street
Salem, NH (603) 893-3506
www.canobie.com

Originally known for its flower gardens, promenades, and genteel attractions, this beautiful traditional park turned 100 years old in 2002 and it has never looked better! The trees are mature, the grass is green and lush, and the flowers are colorful and abundant.

One thing has changed, however. Most of the genteel attractions have given way to modern thrill rides and family attractions with a contemporary edge.

The tranquil lakeside setting forms the backdrop for 45 rides, including 14 for kids. The Old Canobie Village area of the park has a turn-of-the-twentieth-century theme and offers a rustic look at early New Hampshire. The big stone fountain was in operation when the park opened, as was the carousel building, just inside the main entrance.

 Extras: A swimming pool is included in park admission; The Old Man o' the Mountain, a climbing wall, requires an additional fee.

 Season: Mid-April through September.

 Operating hours: Noon to 10:00 P.M. during the peak season. Pool open daily, Memorial Day to Labor Day, 11:00 A.M. to 6:00 P.M.

 Admission policy: Pay-one-price, under $25. Discount after 5:00 P.M. Free parking.

 Top rides: Starblaster, double shot; Boston Tea Party, shoot-the-chute; The Timber Splash, wet and dry slide; Psycho-Drome, an indoor Scrambler with lights and sound effects; Mine of Lost Souls, darkride; Canobie Express, a steam train; an 85-foot-tall, gondola-style Ferris wheel with a computerized nighttime light show and a great view of Canobie Lake; a 1906 Looff/Dentzel antique carousel, with some horses dating back to the 1880s.

 Roller coasters: Canobie Corkscrew (S); Yankee Cannonball (W); Rockin' Rider, family (S); Dragon Coaster, family (S).

 Plan to stay: 7 hours.

 Best way to avoid crowds: Come early in the day or late afternoon during the week. The weekends are quite busy with commercial picnics and party groups.

 Directions: Take the Salem exit (exit 2) off Route 93. Follow Policy Street down about 1 mile to the park. Located 35 minutes from Boston.

THE AMUSEMENT PARK GUIDE

Clark's Trading Post

Route 3
North Woodstock, NH (603) 745-8913
www.clarkstradingpost.com

The owner of this place surely must have his tongue in his cheek! It's so much fun and the entire place is a step back into history. A roadside attraction since the 1920s, Clark's features several historical buildings, a couple of rides, a couple of fun houses, a steam train, and a trained-bear show.

Merlin's Mystical Mansion is a fun dark house with illusions, and Tuttle's Rustic House offers a fun-filled 15-minute guided tour through a tilt house. There are bumper boats, and the White Mountain Central Railroad is a 2.5-mile ride through the woods and across the scenic Pemigewasset River. One of only a few remaining wood-burning steam Climax locomotives pulls the train.

A fun time to visit is in mid-July during Wolfman Weekend. That's when a Wolfman look-alike and growling contest takes place, with all kinds of other offbeat fun being offered. Open weekends in early June and in September and October, daily mid-June through Labor Day, 9:30 A.M. to 6:00 P.M.

Santa's Village

Route 2
Jefferson, NH (603) 586-4445
www.santasvillage.com

Ever wonder how Santa gets ready for Christmas? A new 3-D film here in the Polar Theater follows Santa and his lead elf around as they prepare for the special holiday. *Christmas Chaos* is a fun animated film that leaves the entire family smiling!

It's important to note, though, that it's always Christmas here in the White Mountain. When you visit, you can talk with Santa, feed his reindeer, watch holiday shows, eat holiday food, and enjoy holiday-themed rides, from May through mid-October. The park reopens Thanksgiving weekend and operates weekends through mid-December.

In addition to all the fun shows and the colorful Christmas displays and decorations, there are 12 rides the

148

entire family can enjoy together. The favorites include the Yule Log Flume, the Reindeer Carousel, the Old Time Car Ride, the Jingle Bell Junction Train, Santa's Smackers bumper cars, Rudy's Rapid Transit roller coaster, and Santa's Skyway Sleigh monorail.

During the summer months, open 9:30 A.M. to 6:30 P.M. On fall weekends, open 9:30 A.M. to 5:00 P.M. Admission, under $20, includes all rides, shows, and activities.

 Roller coaster: Rudy's Rapid Transit, family (S).

Story Land
Route 16
Glen, NH (603) 383–4186
www.storylandnh.com

Few parks cater to the family as this one does. Fairy tales have been coming true since 1954 here in the New Hampshire woods in this magical, child-size world that kids love and in which parents can relax. Many of the 16 rides are scaled-down versions of standard amusement park attractions and everyone can ride most of them together.

One of the park's main attractions is the circa 1900 German-made carousel. It's a 3-row machine carved by renowned craftsman Friedrich Heyn. Packed with rides themed to traditional fairy tales, the park has a unique fantasy atmosphere. Hungry? Try the pizza from the Pixie Kitchen; it's something to come back for!

 Season: Memorial Day weekend through Columbus Day, daily mid-June through Labor Day.

 Operating hours: 9:00 A.M. to 6:00 P.M. during daily operation.

 Admission policy: Pay-one-price, under $20. Pay to enter after 2:00 P.M., next day admission free. Free parking.

 Top rides: Antique Car Ride; Dr. Geyser's Remarkable Raft Ride, a tamed-down version of the raging-rapids ride; Story Land Queen, a boat ride on the lake in a large swan; Bamboo Chutes, log flume; Pumpkin Coach Ride, taking passengers up to

Cinderella's Castle; Alice's Tea Cups; Oceans of Fun Sprayground, a water cool-down play area.

 Roller coaster: Polar Coaster, family (S).

 Plan to stay: 6 hours. A park official says the "park usually outlasts the kids."

 Best way to avoid crowds: The park is least busy on weekends, due to the travel patterns of this part of New England.

 Directions: Located in the White Mountain National Forest area, 6 miles north of North Conway, on Route 16, just north of the intersection of Routes 16 and 302.

NEW JERSEY

Boardwalk Parks

The following seven parks are grouped together because they all share one big attraction—the Atlantic Ocean. They are located on the boardwalk, along with many other attractions, restaurants, and activities. They are not theme parks, and most have no entertainment within the park itself. They are good, old-fashioned seafront parks. Go to each one and enjoy!

Casino Pier Waterworks

Boardwalk at Sherman Avenue
Seaside Heights, NJ (732) 793-6488
www.casinopier-waterworks.com

A fun, traditional day at the Jersey Shore is what you'll find here. A boardwalk lined with hundreds of games, miniature golf, food stands serving everything from fried seafood to saltwater taffy and caramel apples, and plenty of rides and attractions is what you'll have to choose from in, on, and around Casino Pier.

Today, there are 35 rides including more than a dozen for the tykes. Don't miss the wonderful circa 1910 Dentzel/Looff carousel, called the Dr. Floyd Moreland Carousel; some of its hand-carved animals date back to the 1890s. Other rides include the Nightmare Manor, a ride-through haunted house; the Poltergeist, an indoor Scrambler; Niagara Falls, a log flume; and Gravitron.

 Roller coasters: Wild Mouse (S); Wizard's Cavern, indoor (S); Star Jet, family (S).

Make sure you eat at Meatball City or play a round of miniature golf on the rooftop course. Waterworks, a waterpark owned by the same people, is located across the street and has more than 23 slides and attractions, including a 54-foot-tall speed slide and a quarter-mile lazy river.

Free admission, with rides and attractions on a pay-as-you-go basis. Pay-one-price available noon to 6:00 P.M. Wednesdays only, $12. Open from mid-April through September. Opens during the summer months at noon and closes at various times.

 # TiM'S TRiViA

If you're interested in the history and the preservation of amusement parks, you should consider membership in the National Amusement Park Historical Association (NAPHA). Membership includes two different publications dedicated to history and worldwide park functions. Check them out at www.napha.org.

Fun Town Pier

Boardwalk at Porter Avenue
Seaside Heights, NJ (732) 830–7437
www.funtownpier.com

For more than 75 years, this beachside fun spot has been entertaining summertime beach crowds. It's hard to miss; just follow the boardwalk to the Giant Wheel! The park features 35 rides, including 25 for children. The tallest ride in the park is the Tower of Fear, a 225-foot-tall free fall. Other popular adult rides include the bumper cars, the Chaos, and the Kamikaze. The stars of the kids' rides are the 20-foot-tall kiddie free fall, the kiddie log flume, and the *Bounty* pirate ship.

 Roller coaster: Roller Coast Loop, looping (S).

Opening for limited operation on Easter Sunday, the park remains in operation until the third week of September. Closing times vary, depending on weather and season, but rides crank up daily at noon. Admission is free, with rides and attractions on a pay-as-you-go basis. An unlimited-ride pass is available weekdays from 1:00 to 6:00 P.M., under $16.

Gillian's Island Waterpark

Boardwalk at Plymouth Place
Ocean City, NJ (609) 399-0483
www.gillians.com

The sister park of the Gillian family's Wonderland Pier, this park has 8 water slides, a lazy river, an activity pool, and a pirate-themed interactive children's play area called Li'l Buc's Bay. One of the nice things about this place is that you don't have to pay for an all-day ticket if you only want to play for a few hours! After all, the world's largest waterpark (the Atlantic Ocean) is just across the street. Gillian's Island Adventure Golf Course is adjacent to the waterpark.

There are three ticket options for the waterpark, a 2-hour pass, a 3-hour pass, or an all-day pass, ranging from $16 to $21. Opens daily during peak season at 9:30 A.M., closes at 6:30 P.M. Located 1 block south of Wonderland Pier, between 7th and 8th Streets.

Jenkinson's Beach Boardwalk & Aquarium

300 Ocean Avenue
Point Pleasant, NJ (732) 892-0600
www.jenkinsons.com

Stretched out along a mile-long boardwalk, this facility has 27 rides and a wide selection of just about anything you'd ever want while on a boardwalk, including 3 miniature golf courses, batting cages, 4 arcades, and many gift and souvenirs shops. There is also a modern, year-round aquarium.

There are 4 restaurants offering ocean views; a candy shop featuring fudge and caramel apples; a bar; and Jenk's Night Club, which is open year-round. Live musical entertainment occurs nightly, with a free concert on the beach every Wednesday night. Fireworks take place every Thursday. Events are scheduled year-round at the pavilion.

Among the more popular rides are the Himalaya, Spider, and 15 kiddie rides. The Funhouse features 4,000 square feet of gags and tricks, including "The Butt Room."

 Roller coaster: Flitzer, family (S).

The park is open April through October, and the games arcades are open every day of the year. There's no admission charge, with all rides and attractions on a pay-as-you-go basis. On Tuesdays, unlimited rides ticket, from noon to 6:00 P.M., for $10.

Morey's Piers
Raging Waters Waterparks
On the Boardwalk
Wildwood, NJ (609) 522–3900
www.moreyspiers.com

For those who don't live near the Jersey Shore or visit it very often, just the sight of amusement piers full of color and excitement jutting out toward England from the boardwalk is an amazing thing. It's something unique that I never tire of seeing. I want to start singing the song "Under the Boardwalk" every time I visit the shore.

Morey's Piers, Wildwood, New Jersey
Photo by Tim O'Brien

THE AMUSEMENT PARK GUIDE

Here in Wildwood, the Morey family has 3 ride piers packed with more than 100 rides and attractions, plus 2 full-size waterparks and several extreme rides. Remember, this is all on piers! A fourth pier, now under development by the family, contains several go-kart tracks and food stands until development plans are complete.

The 2 waterparks are located at the ocean end of 2 of the piers and between them have more than 2 million gallons of water and 50 rides, slides, and attractions. One has a surfboard-oriented, 1950s theme, while the other has more of a tropical feel to it.

Building more than 100 rides, including 7 roller coasters, and 2 full-size waterparks on those 3 piers was quite an engineering feat. As you approach, take note and admire how they go over, under, and through each other.

 Extras: Skycoaster, the Skyscraper, Spring Shot, miniature golf, climbing wall, Grand Prix go-karts, all priced separately.

 Season: Mid-April through mid-October. Ride park and waterparks operate daily, from Memorial Day through Labor Day.

 Operating hours: Rides open 12:30 P.M. to midnight, during daily operation; waterpark open 9:00 A.M. to 7:00 P.M. daily, weather permitting.

 Admission policy: Free admission, with rides on a ride-to-ride basis, or with pay-one-price ticket. Many ticket options: one day, all rides, $38 on weekends, $34 on weekdays. Multiple-day passes available, from $70 to $155. Family 4-packs and waterpark combination tickets available. Full-day waterpark tickets for both parks, under $26, with 2-hour, 3-hour, and early bird special tickets available. All unused days of multi-day passes can be used the following season.

 Top rides: Giant Wheel; Inverter; The Maelstrom; The Tornado; two-drop log flume; carousel; Skyride that goes out over the beach; giant slide; The Zoom Phloom.

 Roller coasters: Great White (W); RC-48, family (S); Great Nor'easter, inverted (S); DoWopper, family (S); Flitzer, family (S); Sea Serpent, boomerang (S); Rollie's Coaster, family (S).

Plan to stay: It will take two days if you want to enjoy all the coasters and waterparks, one day if you don't go to the waterparks or the beaches.

Best way to avoid crowds: Be there when the rides open at 12:30. During the week it's busiest in late afternoon and evenings. Fridays and Saturdays are the busiest.

 Directions: Take exit 4B off Garden State Parkway and follow signs to the Wildwoods Beaches. The parks are located on the boardwalk at 25th Avenue, Schellenger Avenue, and Spencer Avenue.

Playland Park

1020 Boardwalk at 10th Street
Ocean City, NJ (609) 399–4751
www.boardwalkfun.com

Originally opened in 1959, the park has grown through the years and today has more than 30 rides and attractions, including 15 just for the smaller members of the family. It has 2 miniature golf courses at 11th Street and Boardwalk and another miniature golf course and go-karts at 9th Street and Boardwalk.

Among the rides is the popular Double Shot, named by a local magazine as the best ride on the shore. It provides both a great view and a great thrill. Others in the ride lineup include the High Seas, a log flume; a Tilt-A-Whirl; a Ferris wheel; a C.P. Huntington train; adult and kiddie bumper cars; Typhoon; Sea Dragon; and the Whirlwind.

 Roller coasters: Wild Mouse, family (S); Flitzer, family (S); Sea Serpent, kiddie (S); Python, 1-loop (S).

Free admission, with rides and attractions on a pay-as-you-go basis. The arcade opens at 10:00 A.M., the rides at 1:00 P.M., and everything closes at midnight. Open mid-April through mid-October.

Wonderland Pier

Boardwalk at 6th Street
Ocean City, NJ (609) 399–7082
www.gillians.com

The 138-foot-tall Ferris wheel serves as a beacon for those searching for family fun, and it's especially beautiful at night with its colorful light patterns. The park is a mainstay in this seaside town and through the years has earned and maintained its reputation as a clean and safe gathering place for summertime family fun.

There are 38 rides, nearly 20 of them being suited for the little ones in the family. Park mascots Wonder and Landy are on hand to greet your kids.

Part of the complex is indoors, so don't let the bad weather keep you away from the boardwalk. The circa 1925 Philadelphia Toboggan Company carousel, in beautiful condition, is the focal point of the rest of the rides, which include a monorail; the Ferris wheel; the Music Express; Canyon Falls, a log flume; and the Raiders, a kids' participatory play unit.

 Roller coaster: City Jet, family (S).

The season runs from Easter to mid-October. Open noon to midnight daily from mid-June to Labor Day, weekends only in spring and fall. Admission is free, with rides and attractions on a pay-as-you-go basis (no pay-one-price available). The same family also owns Gillian's Island, a waterpark, 1 block south on the boardwalk.

New Jersey Parks

Here is the complete listing of New Jersey Parks. The parks found along the boardwalk are identified by page number only.

Bowcraft Amusement Park

Route 22
Scotch Plains, NJ (908) 233–0675
www.bowcraft.com

Following several years of rehabilitation, this park is better than it's ever been. Red brick walkways connect the stylish buildings and attractions, all of which cater to young families and kids from age 3 to midteen.

Among the 22 rides are favorites such as the Dragon roller coaster, the Crazy Submarine, the Turnpike, a Giant Slide, bumper cars, the Barnstormer, Swings, the Galleon, and a merry-go-round. The train ride encircles the entire park.

Other activities include a miniature golf course and Bowcraft's newest attraction, a water play area that, in keeping with the other attractions, offers scaled-down activities for kids.

Parking and admission are free, with rides and attractions available on both a pay-as-you-go and pay-one-price basis. Open weekends in March, April, May, September, and October and daily in June, July, and August. Opening times vary between 10:00 A.M. and noon, with closing times ranging from 6:00 to 10:00 P.M., depending on the time of the year.

Located just 15 miles from Newark; take exit 140 (Route 22) off the Garden State Parkway and go west 7 miles to the park.

 Roller coaster: Flying Dragon, family (S).

Casino Pier Waterworks, see page 150

Clementon Amusement Park SplashWorld Waterpark

Route 534, Berlin Road
Clementon, NJ (856) 783–0263
www.clementonpark.com

There's a nice blend of the old and the new here. Among the rides is the Jack Rabbit, the third-oldest operating wooden roller coaster in North America. Also among the rides are the Inverter and the Chaos, two high-tech rides. In all, there are 26 rides spread out across the 50-acre traditional park, founded in 1907.

 Extras: SplashWorld Waterpark has 4 large slides, a lazy river, and a children's activity pool. The *Clementon Belle* provides a leisurely trip around the 18-acre lake. Food baskets may be brought into the amusement park, but not the waterpark.

 Season: May through Labor Day.

 Operating hours: Noon to 10:00 P.M., Tuesday through Sunday; closed Monday. Open days are limited in May and June.

THE AMUSEMENT PARK GUIDE

 Admission policy: Pay-one-price for either park, under $22. Discount after 5:00 P.M. A combination ticket for unlimited use of both parks available, under $25. Free parking.

 Top rides: Inverter; Turtle Whirl; Kite Flyer; a 100-foot-tall Ferris wheel; Falling Star; Chaos; Whip; Neptune's Revenge, a log flume in the lake; Sea Dragon, a pirate ship; Ferris wheel; train ride around the lake.

 Roller coaster: Jack Rabbit, circa 1919 (W).

 Plan to stay: 5 hours.

 Best way to avoid crowds: Wednesdays are least crowded.

 Directions: Take exit 3 off the New Jersey Turnpike. Go south 4 miles on Route 168 to Route 534. Go east on 534 for 4 more miles; the park is on the right.

Fantasy Island

320 West 7th Street
Beach Haven, NJ (609) 492–4000
www.fantasyislandpark.com

Stopping at the top of the Ferris wheel here is quite a treat! Look one way and you'll see the Atlantic Ocean; look the other and you'll see the bay and the mainland. Look down and you'll see the entire Victorian-themed park and its 19 rides.

From the brick sidewalks and immaculate landscaping to the Tiffany-style lights in the arcade, the atmosphere here is totally Victorian. Occupying an entire block just 2 blocks from the beach, the park's casino is an adult playground with slot, poker, and blackjack machines. The winnings here don't come in the form of cash; you'll get tokens you can redeem for prizes.

 Season: Park is open Memorial Day through mid-September; the arcade, year-round on weekends and daily during summer.

Operating hours: The park opens at 5:00 P.M. daily, except for Fridays, when it opens at 2:00 P.M.; it closes at varying times, depending on crowds and weather. The arcade opens at noon.

 Admission policy: Free admission, with rides and attractions on a pay-as-you-play basis. Pay-one-price specials on Friday night, $20. Free parking.

 Top rides: Sea Dragon, a swinging pirate ship; tea cups; bumper cars; kiddie boats; a train ride; a carousel; Giant Wheel.

 Plan to stay: 4 hours.

 Best way to avoid crowds: Come on a sunny day; everyone else is at the beach.

 Directions: Take the Garden State Parkway to exit 63 (Route 72). Take Route 72 east until it dead-ends on Long Beach Island. Turn right and go 6.5 miles; the park is on the right. Follow the 65-foot-tall Giant Wheel to the park.

Fun Town Pier, see page 151.

Gillian's Island Waterpark, see page 152.

Jenkinson's Beach Boardwalk & Aquarium, see page 152.

Keansburg Amusement Park Runaway Rapids

275 Beachway, Keansburg, NJ
(732) 495–1400/(800) 805–4FUN
www.keansburgamusementpark.com

Conveniently located just south of the New York state line, this seaside family mecca overlooking Raritan Bay has

THE AMUSEMENT PARK GUIDE

plenty to offer, from a tower drop thrill ride to a Red Baron plane ride for the kids.

With 25 of its 43 rides especially for the kids, it's no wonder the park has been a favorite among local families since 1904. In all there are more than 150 rides, games, eateries, and attractions located along the quarter-mile walkway adjacent to the beach.

Runaway Rapids waterpark features 13 different slides, what they call the largest hot tub in the state, a lazy river, and a 10,000-square-foot children's interactive play area known as Splash, Rattle and Roll.

 Season: March through September.

 Operating hours: Opens daily at 10:00 A.M.; closes at 11:00 P.M. during the week and at midnight on weekends. Slides open at 10:00 A.M. and close at dusk.

 Admission policy: All rides and attractions on a pay-as-you-play basis. Pay-one-price available on weekdays, under $20. Each Friday is Family Day, with all rides discounted to $16. Admission to waterpark, pay-one-price, under $18. Combination ticket with ride park available, under $29. Parking charge in lot or park at meters on street.

 Top rides: Double Shot tower drop; Chaos; Frog Hopper; carousel; Spook House, a ride-through darkride; bumper cars; a Himalaya ride; Trabant; Skydiver; Pharaoh's Fury; Red Baron; kiddie flume.

 Roller coasters: Wild Cat, family (S); Sea Serpent, family (S).

 Plan to stay: 4 hours.

 Best way to avoid crowds: Mondays are the slowest; spring weekends are very seldom crowded.

 Directions: Take exit 117 off the Garden State Parkway. Follow Route 36 east for 4 miles. Turn right at the sign for Keansburg Beach (Laurel Avenue) and go 1½ miles; the park is on the left. Located just south of the New York State line.

Land of Make Believe

Route 611
Hope, NJ (908) 459-9000
www.Lomb.com

Land of Make Believe was founded in 1954 to provide a fun environment where children and parents could play together. While many changes have been made since then, the mission remains intact, and there are now enough activities to fill an entire day. Not only is there a full-scale amusement park with rides of all kinds, but there is also a waterpark with a wide array of family activities.

The amusement park section features 15 rides including a large merry-go-round; the Thriller, a scaled-down roller coaster; the Tornado; a Tilt-A-Whirl; Frog Hopper; and a train that circles the entire facility. Other activities include a genuine DC-3 cockpit, the Haunted Halloween House, a Petting Zoo, and the Candy Cane Forest. Also don't miss the Middle-Earth Theater, where the audience is encouraged to participate in the show, and Santa's Barn, the summer home of Santa Claus.

The waterpark includes 3 waterslides, an action river, a huge pool with a bunch of scaled-down slides and other water activities, and the U-shaped Sidewinder, the only attraction of its kind in the northeastern United States.

The park is open 10:00 A.M. to 6:00 P.M., daily from mid-June through Labor Day and weekends in early June and early September. One admission price, for under $20, gains admission to both the amusement park and the waterpark. Parking is free and picnic facilities are available.

Morey's Piers, see page 153.

Mountain Creek

Route 94
Vernon, NJ (973) 827-2000
www.mountaincreek.com

Not only is Mountain Creek the largest waterpark in New Jersey, it's also a year-round resort with snow skiing and snow tubing in the winter. The waterpark offers more than

2 million gallons of water in which to play. There are 12 large water slides, 2 kiddie slides, 2 tube slides, a raft ride, a 450,000-gallon wave pool, and several water play areas.

The 99-foot-tall H_2O OhNo speed slide offers quite a thrill, but officials say the most popular ride of them all is the low-tech Tarzan Swings, on which you swing out over the water on a rope and let go. Simple, but still thrilling.

For the skateboard activists in the family, there's a full-service, multi-element, 20,000-square-foot skateboard park.

The waterpark is open from mid-June through Labor Day, 11:00 A.M. to 7:00 P.M. during the week and 10:00 A.M. to 7:00 P.M. on weekends. Pay-one-price admission is available, under $30. The skate park is an extra charge.

 TiM'S TRiViA

Know any great trivia or some fun facts about your favorite park you'd like to share with the world? Did you notice a mistake in any of the listings? If so, e-mail author Tim O'Brien at tim@casaflamingo.com. He'd love to hear from you.

Playland Park, see page 155.

Six Flags Great Adventure
Route 537
Jackson, NJ (732) 928–1821
www.sixflags.com

You're about to enter the largest complex in the Six Flags family. With three distinct worlds of thrills, this is also the largest regional amusement facility in the United States. In addition to the 140-acre theme park, the world's largest drive-through safari and Six Flags Hurricane Harbor, a 45-acre waterpark (see following listing), are located next door.

The theme park has more rides than any theme park on the planet. More than 70 rides include 13 roller coasters and two children's areas, plus an array of family-style rides throughout nine themed lands. The 350-acre Six Flags Wild Safari features 1,200 animals from six continents roaming freely throughout the wildlife preserve. Giraffes, elephants, rhinos, bears, tigers, camels, ostriches, and more can be seen up close and personal as you drive your vehicle through the park.

Superman–Ultimate Flight flying coaster is a unique ride for this part of the country, and the distinctive English-made Savage carousel is a colorful and ornate family attraction. The old steam engine has been converted to compressed air and the entire ride runs clockwise.

 Special Events: A summer concert series features top-name rock, classic rock, country, Christian, and pop artists. Christian and gospel music festivals in the spring and fall, Coaster Celebration in September, Fright Fest in October.

 Season: Varies for each park. Theme park usually opens in April and runs through Halloween weekend. It then reopens for special Christmas lights festival.

 Operating hours: Safari opens 9:00 A.M., the ride park usually at 10:00 A.M. Spring and fall weekend hours vary, as do closing times throughout the year.

 Admission policy: Pay-one-price, which includes a free Safari ticket for both regular and junior admission, under $48. Discounted return ticket available with all tickets purchased through the end of September. Combination ticket available for all three parks. Parking charge.

 Top rides: Escape from Dino Island 3-D simulator; Houdini's Great Escape indoor illusion ride; 1890s Savage carousel; Congo Rapids, a whitewater rapids ride; 150-foot-tall Ferris wheel; Pendulum, a Frisbee; The Twister, a Top Spin; and Log Flume, a four-minute log ride.

 Roller coasters: Superman–Ultimate Flight, flying coaster (S); Nitro, hypercoaster (S); Medusa, floorless (S); Batman and Robin: The Chiller, twin-tracked LIM (S); Batman The Ride, inverted (S); Great American Scream Machine, 7-loop (S); Viper, heartline (S); Rolling Thunder, dual-track (W); Skull Mountain, indoor (S); Runaway Mine Train, family (S); Blackbeard's Lost Treasure Train, family (S); Road Runner Railway, kiddie (S).

 Plan to stay: Allow two full days for all three parks. Theme park requires 8 to 10 hours to ride everything, and the waterpark takes 6 to 8 hours. The safari takes 1½ to 2 hours.

Best way to avoid crowds: Avoid weekends from June through August if you want to stay clear of crowds. This is a big park, so planning is important!

 Directions: Take the NJ Turnpike to exit 7A, go east on I–195 to exit 16A, and head west on Route 537. Park entrance will be on your right. Or, take Garden State Parkway to exit 98, go west on I–195 to exit 16. Follow signs to the park. Located 50 miles from Philadelphia and 60 miles from New York City.

Six Flags Hurricane Harbor

Route 537
Jackson, NJ (732) 928–1821
www.sixflags.com

The tropics are alive and well and living adjacent to Six Flags Great Adventure in New Jersey! This beautiful and colorful 45-acre tropical-themed oasis is one of the country's most modern and largest waterpark attractions. There are nearly 20 high-speed thrill and family slides and a million-gallon wave pool that offers undulating waves from 2 to 5 feet in height.

Discovery Bay is a large family water playground with more than 75 interactive gadgets and two huge water buckets that drop thousands of gallons every few minutes on the crowds below. The TAAK It EEZ EE Creek is a half-mile-long lazy river, the Big Bamboo is a six-person raft ride from the top of a 6-story platform, and the Juhranimo is a 75-foot-tall speed slide.

Open Memorial Day through Labor Day, the park is located adjacent to Six Flags Great Adventure Theme Park. Admission is under $32 for adults, under $25 for children. Combo tickets with the theme park are available. Opens daily at 10:00 A.M., closes between 6:00 and 8:00 P.M., depending on day of week and weather conditions.

Steel Pier

Boardwalk at Virginia Avenue
Atlantic City, NJ (609) 345–4893
www.steelpier.com

The entrance to this seaside city's only pier park is like none other. Located across the boardwalk from Donald Trump's magnificent Taj Mahal hotel and casino, the entrance is through a covered area on the boardwalk. A slight incline up through a games arcade unveils the colorful pier a little bit at a time.

With 25 rides now in operation, Steel Pier is back and today serves as a great family-magnet to this casino town. Following its heyday during the early twentieth century, the pier fell into disrepair and was finally destroyed by a fire in 1982. Trump rebuilt the pier, and in 1993 the four Catanoso brothers started rebuilding an international legend.

Once again full of excitement, the pier offers up a blending of family, thrill, and kiddie rides; go-karts; a magnificent double-deck carousel; and the Rocket, a 220-foot-tall reverse-bungee ride. Helicopter tours off the end of the pier are also available.

No admission charge to the pier, with rides and activities on a pay-as-you-go basis. Pay-one-price is available on Wednesdays only, under $22. Open daily, June through mid-September, weekends in spring and fall.

 Roller coasters: Crazy Mouse, spinning wild mouse, family (S); Little Leaper, kiddie (S).

Storybook Land

6415 Black Horse Pike
Cardiff, NJ (609) 641–7847/646–0103
www.storybookland.com

You'll be greeted by a 25-foot-tall statue of Mother Goose as you approach this intriguing 20-acre park. The park is still operated by the Fricano family who began it in 1955 and today it's a tradition in the area. Folks who came here long ago are now bringing their own children to enjoy the fun.

This wonderful world of fantasy has 12 kiddie rides, including a train, a carousel, Fantasy Ferris Wheel, antique cars, and a flying elephant. A special month-long "Fantasy with Lights" Christmas celebration features more than 200,000 lights in the park and Mr. and Mrs. Santa in their home to welcome the kids.

A pay-one-price admission, under $15, gives access to all storybook attractions and unlimited rides on all the rides. Open mid-March through October; reopens for weekends in mid-November through December 30.

A visit to this great little park is a wonderful way to keep the spirit of childhood alive in each of us. It's a fun place! Hours vary; call first.

Wonderland Pier, see page 155.

NEW MEXICO

Cliff's Amusement Park

4800 Osuna NE
Albuquerque, NM (505) 881–9373
www.cliffsamusementpark.com

The addition of the New Mexico Rattler, the state's only wooden roller coaster, to the already worthy lineup of rides has put this laid-back family- and employee-owned park on the big-time map. It's now on the radar screen of every coaster fan in the world.

Located in the middle of the city, the 15-acre park has a strong Southwest and frontier motif to it. There are 25 rides, including a great little kiddieland of 10 adventures just for the wee ones. For those extra-hot days, there's the Water Monkey's Adventure, a fun, cool, and wet interactive family playground.

 Season: Open weekends only in April, May, and August through mid-October. Open Thursday through Sunday in June; Wednesday through Sunday in July.

Operating hours: Opens at 11:00 A.M. except for Sunday, when gates open at 1:00 P.M. Closing times vary.

Admission policy: General admission fee includes all entertainment, with rides and attractions on a pay-as-you-play basis. Pay-one-price available, under $19. Free parking.

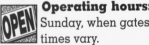 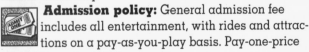 **Top rides:** Rocky Mountain Rapids, a log flume; Sky Glider, chairlift; Big Flush Water Coaster; Frog Hopper; Sea Dragon; Scrambler; bumper cars.

Roller coasters: New Mexico Rattler (W); Galaxi, family (S).

 Plan to stay: 4 hours.

 Best way to avoid crowds: Come on week-nights early in the week.

 Directions: Take the San Mateo exit off I–25, and go south on San Mateo for a short distance to Osuna. Turn left on Osuna; the park is a short distance on the left.

NEW YORK

Adventureland

2245 Broadhollow Road, Route 110
East Farmingdale, NY (631) 694–6868
www.adventurelandfamilyfun.com

As Long Island's only major amusement park, Adventureland offers a great lineup of fun activities and some great, high-tech rides. First opened in 1962, the park is located on 10 beautifully landscaped and well-kept acres. Decorative brick sidewalks lead you from one attraction to another and there's plenty of color and shade.

There are 28 rides, including several major spinning thrillers for the teens. A separate kiddieland offers up 12 rides, including a fun family coaster.

 Extras: The large 300-game arcade and restaurant are open year-round.

 Season: Palm Sunday through mid-September. Indoor kiddie rides open all year.

 Operating hours: 11:00 A.M. or noon to 11:00 P.M. or midnight.

THE AMUSEMENT PARK GUIDE

 Admission policy: Free admission, with rides and attractions on a pay-as-you-go basis. Pay-one-price also available, under $20. Parking is free.

 Top rides: Paul Bunyan Express; Adventure Falls, log flume; 1313 Cemetery Way, a ride-through haunted house; Capt. Willy's Wild Water Ride, bumper boats; antique cars; Top Scan; Venetian Carousel; Surf Dance; Ferris wheel.

 Roller coasters: Hurricane (S); Lady Bug Coaster; family (S).

 Plan to stay: 4 hours.

 Best way to avoid crowds: Come any week-night during the season, and you'll rarely have a long wait.

 Directions: Take exit 49 (Route 110) off the Long Island Expressway and head south for 2 miles. The park is on the left.

 # TiM'S TRiViA

Greetings from Coney Island. The roots of American amusement parks, rides, and attractions are planted deeply in this popular seaside area of Brooklyn, New York. For an in-depth look at the area, both past and present, go to Adam Sandy's Web site: http://history.amusement-parks.com.

Astroland Amusement Park

1000 Surf Avenue
Brooklyn/Coney Island, NY (718) 265–2100
www.astroland.com

The colorful roots of today's amusement and theme parks lie under the sandy beaches of Coney Island. This is where it all began in the United States. Once the haven of several parks and attractions, Coney Island today is home to two parks and a few additional clusters of rides, games, and attractions along the boardwalk and Surf Avenue.

The largest of the two seaside parks operating today is Astroland, with 24 rides, including the world-renowned

Cyclone wooden roller coaster. Built in 1927, the coaster is on city, state, and national historic structure registers and is still on the Top 10 list of many coaster enthusiasts from around the world.

TiM'S TRiViA

The Mermaid Parade is a wonderful event sponsored by a local historical group every June. For more information, see www.coneyisland.com/mermaid.shtml.

 Special events: Mermaid Parade, sponsored by a local historical group, June.

 Season: Palm Sunday through September.

 Operating hours: Noon to midnight, during summer.

 Admission policy: Free admission, with rides on a pay-as-you-go basis. Pay-one-price also offered for specific periods of time during the week and on weekends, under $15. Though parking is available at meters along the street, recommended parking is in the New York Aquarium parking lot adjacent to the park; the parking fee during the day includes admission to the aquarium.

 Top rides: A log flume; Dante's Inferno, a darkride; Breakdance; Enterprise; Power Surge; bumper cars; Pirate Ship; Astrotower, a 200-foot-tall observation tower providing a magnificent view of the entire Coney Island area.

 Roller coasters: Cyclone, circa 1927 (W); Big Apple Coaster, kiddie (S).

 Plan to stay: 3 hours.

 Best way to avoid crowds: The last 2 weeks in June are the least crowded during the season. Come early to avoid the big after-work crowd.

 Directions: Take exit 7 South (Ocean Parkway South) off the Belt Parkway. Ocean Parkway curves onto Surf Avenue. Follow Surf to West 10th

Street; the park is on the left. Via subway, take the W to the end of the line at Stillwell Avenue.

Deno's Wonder Wheel Park

**1025 Boardwalk
Brooklyn/Coney Island, NY
(718) 372-2592
www.wonderwheel.com**

The Wonder Wheel is the center of attention here at New York City's largest kiddie and family park. Overlooking the Atlantic Ocean and miles of Coney Island beaches, the 150-foot-tall wheel has been providing spectacular views since 1920 and is a genuine New York Historic Landmark.

In addition to the wheel, the park has 23 rides, most of which the entire family can ride and enjoy together. The Darkride and Funhouse Enthusiasts organization calls the park's classic Pretzel darkride, the Spook-A-Rama, "a masterpiece from the golden age of darkrides."

The wheel provides quite a ride! Sixteen of its 24 gondolas run down a short track and swing back and forth as it takes riders over the top. As a passenger, that movement can be quite disconcerting if you aren't expecting it!

 Roller coaster: Sea Serpent, family (S).

Located along the boardwalk and adjacent to Astroland, the park is close to all other Coney Island attractions, rides, and food outlets. Admission is free; rides are on a pay-as-you-play basis. The park is open from 11:00 A.M. daily and is in operation from mid-April through October. Sign on to Deno's Web site and you'll get an e-mail discount coupon back.

Enchanted Forest Water Safari

**Route 28
Old Forge, NY (315) 369-6145
www.watersafari.com**

With the beautiful Adirondack Mountains all around, this park is practically hidden from everything else in the area, including its own parking lot! All of the 33 attractions are tucked away in a canopy of trees and many of the rides use the area's topography to enhance the experience.

The 50-acre park is divided into four areas. Dawson City, a Western town, has most of the traditional park rides. Here you can enjoy a nice grouping of rides, such as a classic Herschell carousel, Round-Up, Rock-O-Planes, the Enchanted Forest Railroad, a Ferris wheel, old-time cars, a sky ride, bumper cars, and children's helicopters and boats.

The Water Safari is one of the largest waterparks in the state. One thoughtful touch is the fact that all the water is heated, which makes slides even more enjoyable. Favorite attractions include the Shadow, an enclosed slide just inside the entrance; Kiddie Car Wash, a play area that looks like the real thing; Killermanjaro, a terrain speed slide more than 280 feet long; and Amazon, a 1,100-foot-long family raft ride.

The other areas are Storybook Lane, a walk-through area reminiscent of many post-war kiddie parks for Baby Boomers, and Animal Lane, a petting zoo. The Calypso's Family Cove is located next door and offers go-karts, a climbing wall, batting cages, and miniature golf.

Located on the north side of Old Forge, the park opens daily from mid-June through Labor Day at 9:30 or 10:00 A.M. and closes at 6:00 or 7:00 P.M. A pay-one-price ticket for adults, under $23, provides unlimited access to the rides and slides. Guests who come in after 3:00 P.M. can enjoy the next day for free.

Fairyland Kiddie Park

**2361 Utica Avenue
Brooklyn, NY (718) 951-9302**

As we go to press, we are informed that Fairyland Kiddie Park, located along a commercial strip in Brooklyn, is closing down. Its rides will be sold at a Norton Auctioneers sale in May, 2003 and the land will be sold for commercial development.

The former owner of this Brooklyn gem was proud to admit that his park hadn't changed much during the past 50 years, and as a result Fairyland was one of the last true 1950s-style kiddielands still in operation. But, with the demise of this park, there are now less than a dozen 1950s-era kiddie parks in operation in the country, down from more than 150 during the 1960s. The one-acre park was founded by Irving Miller in 1952 and has remained in the family during its entire existence. This was a true piece of Americana.

Great Escape and Splashwater Kingdom Fun Park

Route 9
Lake George, NY (518) 792–3500
www.sixflags.com

Serving as the centerpiece of entertainment in this region renowned for its beauty and tranquility, Great Escape is nestled into the base of the Adirondack Mountains, a few miles from Lake George.

The 140-acre park was founded in 1954 by the legendary Charles Wood as a storybook land, and with time it grew into one of the state's unique parks. Today it boasts 44 rides and more than 80 other attractions and shows.

The park's star is the Comet roller coaster. It ran from 1948 until 1989 at the famous Crystal Beach Park in Ridgeway, Canada, across from Buffalo, New York. The coaster was placed in storage and reopened in 1994 at Great Escape. People from the world over travel to the park to ride what many consider to be one of designer Herbert Schmeck's greatest rides.

There are many rides here like the Blue Goose and Pony Carts that are geared to the kids in the family. In addition, there are several quaint attractions from another era like the Cinderella Carriage Coach, where families can ride around in a pumpkin, and Alice in Wonderland, where guests enter through the rabbit hole.

Splashwater Kingdom is the waterpark here and offers up a nice selection of water activities, including an adventure river, a wave pool, an interactive tree house, and several slides and play areas.

 Extras: Go-karts, rock wall, Turbo Bungee.

 Special events: Fright Fest, weekends in October.

Season: Daily Memorial Day through Labor Day, weekends in May, September, and October.

Operating hours: Opens at 10:00 A.M.; closing hours vary.

Admission policy: Pay-one-price, under $34. Free parking.

Top rides: Giant Wheel, a gondola-style Ferris wheel; Desperado Plunge, a log flume; Raging River, a raging-rapids ride.

Roller coasters: Canyon Blaster, mine train (S); Comet (W); Steamin' Demon, 2-corkscrew, loop (S); Coast-to-Coaster, boomerang (S); Alpine Bobsled (S); Nightmare, indoor (S).

Plan to stay: 7 to 8 hours.

Best way to avoid crowds: Come during the middle of the week.

Directions: Located a few miles outside Lake George on Route 9, between exits 19 and 20 of the Adirondack Northway (I–87).

Hoffman's Playland
Route 9
Latham, NY (518) 785–3842
www.hoffmansplayland.com

While other parks specialize in the tallest and fastest rides, this one makes sure there is a ride for each member of the family. Many of the park's attractions have run since opening in 1952. Many of the local patrons claim that their favorite thing to do is to bring their children back to enjoy the same rides they themselves loved as kids.

The 18 rides consist of 13 children's attractions and 5 major rides. The centerpiece is the 3-row 1952 Allan Herschell carousel. Other rides include a Ferris wheel, Balloon Flight, a kiddie boat ride, and bumper cars. Be sure to check out the large arcade and the miniature golf course and driving range, both of which are adjacent to the park.

Open from Easter Sunday through September. Park hours are noon to 10 P.M. daily; admission is free, with rides on a pay-as-you-go basis.

 Roller coaster: Lil Whipper Snapper, family (S).

Magic Forest

Route 9
Lake George, NY (518) 668-2448
www.magicforestpark.com

In a pine forest only minutes from Lake George, this 40-acre park has a winter holiday theme. It's divided into Christmas Village, the Storybook land, and the rides area. There are 25 rides to choose from, including a 3-row Allan Herschell carousel, a Ferris wheel, and a Tilt-A-Whirl.

 Roller coaster: Kiddie Coaster, kiddie (S).

The park also has some unique attractions like a Safari tram ride; the world's tallest Uncle Sam (at 36 feet); a circular slide; and Rex, the diving horse. Don't miss the Magic Forest magic show, which performs three times daily, and Santa Claus, who has made the park his summer home.

Open daily from Memorial Day through early September; call for hours. Admission is pay-one-price, under $15.

Martin's Fantasy Island

2400 Grand Island Boulevard
Grand Island, NY (716) 773-7591
www.martinsfantasyisland.com

Located only 10 minutes from Niagara Falls, this 80-acre facility has just what it takes for a family outing. Part ride park, part waterpark, and part Western town, this place has lots of things to keep you busy and happy all day long.

You can be shot up 100 feet on the Daredevil free-fall tower and get a great view of the area, be spun upside down 60 feet above the ground on the Patriot, or take a more relaxing trip on the Giant Gondola Wheel. The park has a kiddie area with lots to keep the little ones occupied, and the five themed areas offer 38 rides for the grown-ups.

 Extras: Cinema 180; miniature golf, paddle-boats, and a petting zoo are all included in the admission price. Haunted Fantasy Island is an all-age Halloween celebration, weekends in October.

 Season: Late May through mid-September.

 Operating hours: 11:30 A.M. to 8:30 P.M. Closed Mondays.

 Admission policy: Pay-one-price, under $18. Free parking.

 Top rides: Chaos; Old Mill Scream, a log flume; Dare-devil, shot and drop; Splash Creek, an active lazy-river raft ride; Giant Gondola Wheel; Super Sizzler.

 Roller coasters: The Silver Comet (W); Wildcat, family (S); Orient Express, kiddie (S).

 Plan to stay: 6 hours.

 Best way to avoid crowds: Come during the week and plan your visit around the show schedule.

 Directions: Take exit N19 off Highway 190, go west on Whitehaven Road to Baseline Road, turn left, and go to Grand Island Boulevard. The park can be seen from the highway.

Midway Park

Route 430
Maple Springs, NY (716) 386–3165
www.midway-park.com

You'll take a true step back in time when you pass through the front gate here. The hustle and bustle of today's world slows as you take a walk along the well-landscaped paths and take time to enjoy the peaceful atmosphere that others have enjoyed here, on the banks of Lake Chautauqua, since 1898.

TIM'S TRIVIA

There are several antique carousels operating in the New York City area; here are three of them:

- *A circa 1908 Stein & Goldstein has been operating in Manhattan's Central Park since 1950. It has 52 jumpers, 5 standers, and 2 chariots. A Ruth & Sohn band organ plays a Wurlitzer 150 music roll. Open year-round, daily during warmer months. 90 cents a ride. (212) 879–0244.*

- *The B&B Carousell (that's how it has been spelled for years) is located on Surf Avenue at 10th Street in Coney Island. It's a circa 1903 Mangels & Carmel machine, you can grab for the ring, and it costs $2.50 per ride. Open daily during warmer months.*

- *A circa 1912 Mangels & Carmel carousel has its own pavilion in Prospect Park in Brooklyn. The 3-row machine has 51 hand-carved horses, a lion, a giraffe, a dragon, and 3 chariots, with a Wurlitzer 153 band organ. Open April through October at the Willink entrance to the park. Rides are 50 cents. (718) 965–7777.*

There are 20 well-kept rides, including a 1946 3-row carousel from the Allan Herschell Company. The machine was meticulously restored for the park's one hundredth season and the rounding boards display paintings of the surrounding region.

Other unique attractions include a roller rink on the second story of the circa 1915 ballroom and a big, patriotic July 4 picnic and fireworks show. It's the sixteenth-oldest park in the United States and one of only 12 remaining trolley parks from the end of the nineteenth century.

 Extras: Museum highlighting the park and the trolley and railroad companies that started it, free. Roller skating, miniature golf, go-karts, bumper boats, and family paddleboat excursions on the lake, all for extra charges.

 Season: Memorial Day weekend through Labor Day weekend. Closed non-holiday Mondays.

 Operating hours: 1:00 P.M. until dusk.

 Admission policy: Free admission to the park, with rides on a pay-as-you-go basis. Pay-one-price available on weekends.

Top rides: Tidal Wave, pirate ship; Tubs of Fun, a spinning ride; Tilt-A-Whirl; a giant slide; 7 Allan Herschell kiddie rides.

 Roller coasters: Dragon Coaster, family (S); Little Dipper, kiddie (S).

 Plan to stay: 3 hours.

 Best way to avoid crowds: Come during the week and be there when the rides open.

 Directions: Located on Route 430 on Lake Chautauqua in Maple Springs.

Nellie Bly Park

1824 Shore Parkway
Brooklyn, NY (718) 996–4002
www.nellieblypark.com

A few blocks away from the famous Coney Island district of Brooklyn, this family and kiddie park may very well be the best bargain around. It's a compact, friendly little facility with 18 rides, including 8 just for the little ones.

Also available are go-karts, miniature golf, batting cages, and a petting farm. A fun walk through Haunted House is among the offerings. It's a great place for birthday parties, and don't be surprised if the employees know the names of the guests. It's a neighborhood park and the locals love the fact that it's "their" facility. The park was named after the country's first female newspaper reporter.

 Season: Easter through October, or as long as the weather holds out.

 Operating hours: 11:00 A.M. or noon to 10:00 P.M.

Admission policy: Admission is free, with rides and attractions on a pay-as-you-play basis. Pay-one-price available on Tuesday and Thursday from 11:00 A.M. to 2:00 P.M. and on Wednesday evenings, 7:30 to 10:30 P.M., under $10. Free parking.

Top rides: Tilt-A-Whirl; bumper cars; Crazy Bus; Scrambler; Frog Hopper, a kids'-size tower drop; giant slide; Convoy, a kiddie truck ride; Red Baron, a kiddie plane ride; and a carousel.

 Plan to stay: 2 hours.

 Best way to avoid crowds: Wednesdays are the slowest days.

 Directions: Take exit 5 off the Belt Parkway and travel ½ mile to 25th Street; the park is on the right.

Playland Park

Playland Parkway and the Beach
Rye, NY (914) 813–7010
www.ryeplayland.org

Nostalgia galore on the New York shore! Overlooking the Long Island Sound, this traditional park was built in 1928 and still holds much of its original charm and appeal. It's truly a slice of Americana, with a cool mix of original Art Deco elements and rides of the late 1920s with modern rides and attractions.

 TiM'S TRiViA

America's first master-planned amusement park was Playland in Rye, New York. It opened in 1928. The park still entertains guests today and features Art Deco buildings and beautiful landscaping, all on the shores of Long Island Sound.

The county-owned complex features a beach and board-walk, an 80-acre lake, and more than 50 rides and attractions, including a separate kiddieland with 20 rides. If you're into darkrides, you'll party here! The Zombie Castle and Ye Old Mill were completely restored and expanded and reopened in 2002 with the latest in animatronics and scare tactics, and the traditional Flying Witch is a funky trip in the dark.

A circa 1915 Mangels & Carmel carousel with 66 horses has a great-sounding Gavioli band organ. The 1927 Prior &

Church Racing Derby still spins in the same building where it was placed in 1928 and is one of only two such machines still operating in the United States, with the other being at Cedar Point in Ohio.

 Extras: Olympic-size swimming pool, miniature golf, pedal boats, beach swimming, all extra. Don't miss the House of Mirrors, complete with a maze and strobe lights.

 Season: Mid-May through mid-September.

 Operating hours: Opens at noon and closes at various hours during the evening, depending on crowds and weather. Closed Mondays.

 Admission policy: Free admission, with all rides and attractions on a pay-as-you-go basis. Parking charge.

 Top rides: Double-Shot, free fall; Inverter; Power Surge; Playland Plunge, shoot-the-chute; Skyflyer, pendulum; The Log Flume, with 2 drops; Giant Gondola Wheel; Chaos; and Auto Scooter, bumper cars.

 Roller coasters: Zig Zag Coaster, family (S); Hurricane (S); Dragon Coaster (W); Kiddy Coaster, junior (W); Family Flyer, family (S).

 Plan to stay: 4 hours.

 Best way to avoid crowds: Tuesdays are the slowest, but Thursdays are the most fun. Come early, have dinner, hear a free concert, and see the fireworks.

 Directions: Take exit 19 (Playland Parkway) off I-95. Follow the parkway 1½ miles to the beach where the road dead-ends at the park.

Santa's Workshop

Whiteface Memorial Highway
North Pole, NY (800) 806-0215
www.northpolenewyork.com

This fun little family park fits quite well up here in the green hills of northern New York. The park dates from 1949 and still has the charm of a local post-war kiddie park, the kind that dotted the American landscape through the 1950s.

The story goes that Mr. Claus needed a place to relax during the summer, so he created this place and didn't try to keep it a secret. That's why it's so easy for children to find him here, along with his reindeer and a replica of the actual frozen North Pole. You're allowed to touch it but sticking your tongue on it is discouraged.

Santa's Workshop has 4 rides: the Kiddie Bobsleds; a Christmas Tree Ride in which children pilot giant tree ornaments; the Candy Cane Express, a train ride for the entire family; and a carousel. One of the park's unique features is a post office with a special North Pole postmark.

The park is open mid-June through mid-October and Saturdays and Sundays in December through the last weekend before Christmas. Pay-one-price admission is under $17. To get to the park take Highway 86 west from Wilmington for 11 miles. It's located in the Adirondack Forest Preserve.

Seabreeze Amusement Park Raging Rivers Waterpark

4600 Culver Road
Rochester, NY (585) 323–1900
www.seabreeze.com

Few park owners have the same commitment to tradition as the owners of Seabreeze. Its original antique carousel burned in a 1994 fire, and instead of finding a high-tech thrill ride to replace it, the Norris family decided to buy an antique Philadelphia Toboggan Company (#31) frame and refurbish it. The owners then commissioned 38 new horses to be hand-carved to accompany the 4 horses spared from the fire. The grove where the carousel now turns in a new pavilion is one of the more beautiful places in any American amusement park.

Founded in 1879, Seabreeze is the fourth-oldest continuously operated amusement park in North America. Located on a high bluff overlooking Lake Ontario, the park combines the charm of a city garden with the excitement of a family-oriented traditional amusement park.

Other attractions include 23 rides and a waterpark with a wave pool, a lazy river, speed and tube slides, and the Soak

Zone interactive play area, complete with a huge dump bucket that provides a very thorough soaking every few minutes.

 Season: Early May through Labor Day.

 Operating hours: Open weekends in May; daily operation mid-June through Labor Day, noon to 10:00 P.M.

 Admission policy: General admission, includes entrance and 2 rides, under $6. Pay-one-price available; includes all rides and waterpark, under $19. Free parking.

 Top rides: Screamin' Eagle, a Hawk ride; a carousel; Sea Dragon; Gyro-Sphere, a dome with a Scrambler, complete with sound and light show; a log flume; bumper cars; Tilt-A-Whirl.

 Roller coasters: Jack Rabbit (W); Quantum Loop, 2-loop (S); Bobsleds (S); Bear Trax, junior (S).

 Plan to stay: 6 hours.

 Best way to avoid crowds: Come Monday, Tuesday, or Wednesday.

 Directions: Take I–490 off the New York State Thruway (I–90) to I–590. Go north toward Lake Ontario. Take a left at the Seabreeze traffic circle; then take the next right onto Culver Road. The park is a few blocks down on the right.

Six Flags Darien Lake
Route 77
Darien Center, NY (585) 599–4641
www.sixflags.com

Pack your bags if you're headed to Six Flags Darien Lake. Recognized as New York State's largest theme park and entertainment complex, there's plenty to do during your stay at this fun amusement resort and there are several lodging options to choose from if you want to stay overnight. You can stay in the 163-room Lodge on the Lake hotel or, for campers, there are nearly 400 RV spots and more than 680 campsites. And if a park with more than 100 rides, shows, and attractions isn't enough, there is also a full-scale waterpark and a 20,000-seat performing arts center that showcases several national acts each summer.

TiM'S TRiViA

A great way to keep up with the latest information about roller coasters is to become a member of the American Coaster Enthusiasts (ACE). The organization publishes a glossy quarterly magazine with some great photos and a bimonthly newsletter all about roller coasters. Visit them at www.aceonline.org.

Included among the rides are 5 roller coasters, one of which is the 208-foot-tall Superman Ride of Steel. Looney Tunes Seaport for kids offers 10 different rides and activities for younger guests. A don't-miss show is Laserblast, a state-of-the-art visual display that combines the latest in aerial fireworks, pyrotechnics, laser animation, lights, sounds, and musical choreography and is performed nightly Memorial Day through Labor Day at the Lakeside Amphitheater.

The waterpark is included with admission and features Crocodile Isle, a million-gallon wave pool and Hook's Lagoon, an interactive family play area complete with a giant treehouse and Barracuda Bay water slides.

And if you do decide to stay on property, all accommodations include theme park admission. What a deal!

 Extras: Paddleboats, miniature golf, go-Karts, batting cages, Skycoaster, Turbobungy, and Slingshot, a new reverse-bungee thrill ride are all available for an additional cost.

 Special events: Fright Fest, weekends in October.

 Season: May through October.

 Operating hours: 10:30 A.M. to 10:00 P.M. daily, except in May, June, September, and October, when the park is open only on weekends.

Admission policy: Pay-one-price, under $33. Discount tickets available at Tops Markets throughout the area. Parking charge.

 Top rides: Grizzly Run, a raging-rapids ride; Giant Wheel, a 165-foot-tall Ferris wheel; Shipwreck Falls, shoot-the-chute; Skycoaster; Ranger, a looping ship ride; Slingshot.

 Roller coasters: Superman Ride of Steel, hypercoaster (S); Boomerang (S); Brain Teaser, family (S); Mind Eraser, inverted (S); Predator (W); Viper, multi-element (S).

 Plan to stay: 8 to 10 hours or overnight.

 Best way to avoid crowds: Come early in the day on all days. Mondays and Tuesdays, except for holidays, are the slowest.

 Directions: Located midway between Rochester and Buffalo. Take exit 48A off the New York State Thruway and head south 5 miles on Route 77. Pay attention to and use the recommended alternate traffic route posted on the Web site and along the route on high-volume days.

 # TiM'S TRiViA

The beautifully restored Philadelphia Toboggan Company #18 carousel spins proudly each day at the Carousel Center Mall, 9090 Carousel Center in Syracuse, N.Y. The 1909 machine has 42-hand carved horses, of which 38 are jumpers. Music is supplied by an Artizan band organ that plays Wurlitzer 150 rolls. Open during mall hours, it costs $1 to ride. (315) 466–6000. For a history and photos, go to www.carouselcenter.com.

Splish Splash

Exit 72W off the Long Island Expressway
Riverhead, NY (631) 727–3600
www.splishsplashlongisland.com

Nestled deep in a pine forest, 60 miles east of New York City, Splish Splash has a unique rural setting, where once you enter, you'll be shut off from the rest of the real world. But don't let its location fool you. This park is one of the best waterparks in the country, and it's run by one of the best management teams in the business.

Few waterparks have entered the themed-ride business, in which individual rides have a strong story line that interacts with riders and creates a more immersive experience. In 2002, Splish Splash delved into storytelling when it debuted the Hollywood Stunt Rider, which combines an enclosed family raft ride with heavy theming, a fun story line, and a very New Yorkish animatronic Hollywood director. Plus, it's a great ride to start with!

The park offers 16 adult slides of all sizes, speeds, and shapes; Monsoon Lagoon, an interactive family area with all sorts of watery elements to play with; and the Mammoth River Rapids, a five-person tube ride. Additionally, there's a 1,300-foot-long lazy river with waves; a wave pool; Kiddie Cove, a children's activity area featuring 4 different pools and a kiddie car wash; and 2 daily shows, a high-dive show, and a tropical bird presentation.

There are 2 restaurants, a food court, 2 gift shops, and plenty of parking. Open 9:30 A.M. to 7:00 P.M., daily, Memorial Day through Labor Day, under $28. After 4:00 P.M., $20. Parking charge.

Sylvan Beach Amusement Park

Park Avenue, Route 13
Sylvan Beach, NY (315) 762–5212
www.sylvanbeach.org/amusementpark/
index.html

Truly, a park of summers gone by. The sounds and lights of this nostalgic playland, located on the shores of Oneida Lake, transport visitors back 50 years as they take an evening stroll down the midway. The park has survived pretty much intact and is a good example of a traditional Northeast resort park.

The park's centerpiece is a darkride called Laff-Land from the defunct Pretzel Company of New Jersey. It was added in 1954 and is one of the best-kept Pretzel rides remaining in the country. Many of the stunts, such as the famed Al E. Gator and Jersey Devil, are original to the ride and quite rare in their own right.

There are some other attractions unique to amusement parks today like a Crazy Dazy tea cup ride, a carousel, and a Bubble Bounce called the Tip Top. With more than 21 rides, 10 designed for children, and fun activities such as Skee-Ball and Fascination, families find plenty to keep them busy.

 Special events: Old-Fashioned Weekend, observed opening weekend in April, with all rides 25 cents each; Thank-You Weekend, last weekend of the season, with all rides 25 cents each.

 Season: Late April through September.

 Operating hours: Noon to 11:00 P.M.

 Admission policy: Free gate, with rides and attractions on a pay-as-you-go basis. A pay-one-price special, under $9, is available every Friday night after 6:00 P.M.

 Top rides: Bumper cars; bumper boats; Superslide; Scrambler; Tilt-A-Whirl; and a carousel.

 Roller coaster: Galaxi, family (S).

 Plan to stay: 2 hours.

 Best way to avoid crowds: Since rides are on a pay-as-you-go basis, there usually isn't a crowd rushing from one ride to another. The pace is slower here; the park is very seldom crowded, especially during the week.

 Directions: Located in the Village of Sylvan Beach on Route 13, 4 miles north of Route 31 and 8 miles north of exit 34 (Route 13) off I–90, the New York Thruway. About halfway between Utica and Syracuse.

NORTH CAROLINA

Ghost Town in the Sky

U.S. Route 19
Maggie Valley, NC
(828) 926–1140/(800) GHOSTOWN
www.ghosttowninthesky.com

There are few, if any, other amusement parks in the country that have this rugged of a setting. The park is spread out on five different levels of the mountain and the only way you can get up to the lowest level is via a 3,370-foot-long ride on a chairlift. From there you can walk to the other levels, or a shuttle bus will help save you a few vertical steps.

Several of the rides at the very top are positioned to swing out over the edge of the mountain, giving the rider quite a view and quite an adrenaline rush at the same time. (The park has fallen into some disrepair as of late and several of the attractions are not as good as they could be, but the uniqueness of the park makes the trip well worthwhile.)

Begun in 1961 as a ghost-town attraction, the facility has added rides and other elements through the years. There are 20 rides, including 8 for children. But the best attraction of all is the splendid view of the expansive Maggie Valley, a mile below.

Divided into four towns, the park offers the original Ghost Town, Fort Cherokee, Mining Town, and the Mile-High Ride area.

 Extras: Sunday church services are held in the Chapel on Main Street in Ghost Town. The Mystery Shack is a unique gravity tilt house, free with admission. Five different shows, including cancan dancers, gunfights, and Cherokee Indian dancers.

 Season: May through October.

 Operating hours: 9:00 A.M. to 6:00 P.M. The chairlifts and incline quit taking guests up to the park 2 hours before the official closing time.

"Yo-Yo," Ghost Town in the Sky, Maggie Valley, North Carolina
Photo by Tim O'Brien

 Admission policy: Pay-one-price, under $21. Free parking.

 Top rides: Global Swings, unique flying swings in a metal globe; Black Widow, an indoor Scrambler; Ghost Mine; walk-through fun house; Sea Dragon; Tilt-A-Whirl; bumper cars; carousel.

 Roller coaster: Red Devil, looping, with drop off side of mountain (S). (This unique coaster has been under renovation and has not been open for several seasons. The owner told me he has set forth a plan that will get it open for the 2003 season. If your trip is based on this, or any other ride in the park, please call first.)

 Plan to stay: 4 hours.

 Best way to avoid crowds: The smallest crowds come in late May and late August. Monday is the slowest day of the week.

 Directions: Located on Highway 19, west of Maggie Valley. The park is 35 miles from Asheville via I–40 and 90 miles east of Knoxville, Tennessee, via I–40.

Goldston's Beach and Pavilion

White Lake Road at the Beach
White Lake, NC (910) 862–4064

Situated on 1,275-acre White Lake, this small park offers 9 rides, including a Flying Bob's and an old carousel, a large video and games-of-skill arcade, miniature golf, piers and swimming areas, cottages, a motel, and a Dairy Queen restaurant. In mid-May, there's an annual festival featuring water shows, a parade, and firemen's Olympics.

The entire facility is open from 9:00 A.M. to 11:00 P.M., with the rides in operation only during the evening. Admission is free during the week, with a pay-as-you-play policy for the rides, attractions, and beach facilities. There is a small general admission fee on weekends.

Jubilee Park

Highway 421
Carolina Beach, NC (910) 458–9017
www.jubileepark.com

Located 3 blocks from the oceanside boardwalk, this 7½-acre park has 18 rides, including 7 for kids. Flat, paved walkways between the rides make this an easy park to get around in.

 Extras: Go-karts; water slides, speed slides, and a kiddie play pool; large arcade with pool tables; gift shop.

 Season: Easter through mid-September.

 Operating hours: July is considered peak season, with hours 10:00 A.M. to 11:00 P.M. Slides open first and close first; rides open later and close last.

 Admission policy: Free admission, with rides on a pay-as-you-go basis. Pay-one-price also available, under $18.

 Top rides: Carousel, Tilt-A-Whirl; Ferris wheel; Rock-O-Plane; Scrambler; swings; Octopus; Viking Ship.

Roller coaster: Little Dipper, kiddie (S).

 Plan to stay: 3 hours.

 Best way to avoid crowds: Tuesdays are the slowest days. July is the busiest month.

 Directions: Located on Highway 421, about ¾ mile past the Pleasure Island Bridge, 8 miles south of Wilmington.

Paramount's Carowinds WaterWorks

Carowinds Boulevard
Charlotte, NC (704) 588–2600
www.carowinds.com

This park can claim something no other park can: It has the North Carolina–South Carolina state line running right down the middle of its main street. There's a line marking the border painted on the street, so you can catch some fun photos of you and yours standing in both states simultaneously.

The main entrance to the 100-acre park is through Plantation Plaza, an area reminiscent of the Old South. The architecture, mature trees, and landscaping provide a calming contrast to the 12 roller coasters and the other 26 high-tech rides. In 2003, a new kids' area called Nickelodeon Central opened, featuring the Rugrats Runaway Reptar, a new suspended coaster for the entire family. The new SpongeBob SquarePants ride is also a fun family adventure.

The 13-acre WaterWorks waterpark includes a new 80-foot-tall multi-slide tower called Pipeline Peak, many speed slides, activity pools, family slides, and a wave pool. There's no additional fee to enter the waterpark.

 Special events: Scarowinds, October.

 Season: Mid-March through late October.

THE AMUSEMENT PARK GUIDE

Operating hours: 10:00 A.M. to 8:00 P.M. Stays open until 10:00 P.M. on Friday and Saturday during peak season.

Admission policy: Pay-one-price, under $40. An after 5:00 P.M. ticket is available, under $29. Parking charge.

Top rides: Scooby-Doo's Haunted Mansion, interactive darkride; Meteor Attack, motion simulator; Stan Lee's 7th Portal, 3-D simulator; Drop Zone, free fall; Rip Roarin' Rapids, rapids ride; White Water Falls, shoot-the-chute.

Roller coasters: Richochet, wild mouse (S); Nickelodeon Flying Super Saturator, suspended with water elements, family (S); Top Gun, inverted (S); Taxi Jam, junior (S); Rugrats Runaway Reptar, family (S); Carolina Goldrusher mine train (S); Scooby Doo's Ghoster Coaster, junior (W); Carolina Cyclone, 2-loop/corkscrew (S); Hurler (W); Thunder Road, racer (W); Vortex, stand-up (S).

Plan to stay: 10 hours.

Best way to avoid crowds: Come on weekends during the morning hours and ride the popular rides before the midday crunch arrives.

Directions: Take exit 90 (Carowinds Boulevard) off I–77, 10 miles south of Charlotte.

Santa's Land
Theme Park & Zoo

Route 1
Cherokee, NC (828) 497–9191
www.santaslandnc.com

Mr. and Mrs. Claus never had it so good! What a place to call your summer home. This cool, 16-acre park, located in the Great Smoky Mountains, is a beautiful, lush respite from the busy tourist areas in the Cherokee region. It's a true gem hidden away under a canopy of tall pine, with its 9 rides, great shopping, and various tableaus including a

"Rudicoaster," Santa's Land, Cherokee, North Carolina
Photo by Tim O'Brien

Nativity scene, Santa's School, the Three Wise Men, and a super-tall snowman and his house.

Divided into three areas, Santa's Land, Zoo Land, and Fun Land, the park has working vegetable gardens, a redemption arcade, live magic and bear-feeding shows, and a lot of comfortable resting areas. Mr. and Mrs. Claus are always on duty and if you can't find them in their own house, located just inside the front gate, they're probably out walking and greeting the guests. You might even find them on their favorite ride, the Rudicoaster!

There is no pavement in the park, only gravel sidewalks, so come prepared with good walking shoes.

 Extras: A chance to sit on Santa's lap; free paddleboats on a lake surrounding two islands full of monkeys; a chance to pet a reindeer; see a turn-of-the-twentieth-century mill. Employees wear what may be the neatest costumes of any park in the country . . . some, including management, are dressed as elves.

Special events: Harvest Festival, weekends in October, a celebration of mountain heritage with crafts, food, apple cider pressing, mountain music, and clogging.

THE AMUSEMENT PARK GUIDE

 Season: April through November.

 Operating hours: 9:00 A.M. to 5:00 P.M.

 Admission policy: Pay-one-price, under $15. Free parking.

 Top rides: A train ride, a mile-long jaunt; paddleboats; a Ferris wheel; a carousel.

 Roller coaster: Rudicoaster, Rudolph-themed family ride (S).

 Plan to stay: 3 hours.

 Best way to avoid crowds: Weekdays are least crowded. Park officials say the best time to visit is during the Harvest Festival.

 Directions: 3 miles north of Cherokee, on U.S. Highway 19.

Tweetsie Railroad

Highway 221/321
Blowing Rock, NC
(828) 264-9061/(800) 526-5740
www.tweetsie.com

Amusement rides, live shows, a deer petting zoo, and a unique mountain Old West environment combine to create a fun, family entertainment park here on Roundhouse Mountain. The facility opened in 1956 as a train excursion and in the years since, a neat little theme park has been created with the 3-mile steam train ride as its centerpiece.

The overall atmosphere is one of an Old West railroad town. You enter the park through an old depot building and proceed down a Western-style street. Specific areas include Tweetsie Square, Miner's Mountain, and Country Fair, where the 9 family rides are located.

Apart from the rides and the train, a chairlift takes you up to Miner's Mountain, where you can pan for gold, visit a shaded deer park, or take a miniature train ride through Mouse Mine and see small, animated mice busy at work.

TiM'S TRiViA

North Carolina's Tweetsie Railroad is much more than a classic ride up and around the mountain on an authentic and historic train. The family-owned facility is a unique theme park with rides, shows, and attractions.

 Extras: Wild West, a coin-operated shooting gallery, and the Railroad Museum. During the 3-mile train ride, guests get robbed by bandits and attacked by Indians. Entertainment includes a clogging show, saloon cancan, and a bluegrass music band.

 Special events: July 4 Week celebration; Halloween Festival and the Ghost Train, October.

 Season: May through October.

 Operating hours: 9:00 A.M. to 6:00 P.M. daily.

 Admission policy: Pay-one-price, under $25. In after 3:00 P.M., the next day is free. Free parking.

 Top rides: A chairlift to Miner's Mountain; bumper cars; a Ferris wheel; bumper boats; a train ride; a carousel.

 Plan to stay: 5 hours.

 Best way to avoid crowds: Come at opening time on Monday or Friday, avoiding weekends and holidays if possible. Once you take the train ride located just inside the front gate, take the chairlift to the top and work your way back down.

 Directions: Located 3 miles from Blowing Rock and 3 miles from Boone, on Highway 321/221.

Wet 'n Wild Emerald Pointe Water Park

3800 South Holden Road
Greensboro, NC
(336) 852-9721/(800) 555-5900
www.emeraldpointe.com

The new, high-tech Hydra Fighter II interactive roller coaster takes you through walls of cascading water while you are drenched by geysers and water cannons. It's the only steel roller coaster in a waterpark in the world!

Surf's up! The Thunder Bay wave pool produces some of the largest man-made waves in the world, at 6 feet tall and 84 feet wide, and that means big-time fun for adventure seekers at this thrill-packed park. Although you might be tempted to surf these big waves, no boards are allowed in the pool; body surfing is permitted, however, as is tube riding.

The Dare Devil Drop provides the tallest and fastest speed drop of any waterslide on the East Coast. The Twin Twisters are identical enclosed black water chutes. In addition, there are 13 slides, 4 kiddie activity pools, 3 family activity pools, the Lazee River, and Cyclone Zone, a fast-moving circular river.

There are a sand volleyball court, 5 snack stands, a beach and gift shop, and a 3-point basketball court. Open mid-May through mid-September, 10:00 A.M. to 8:00 P.M. An "All-Day Splash" ticket is under $25; an after 4:00 P.M. ticket, good until closing, is available, under $16. The Skycoaster charges $12.50 for individual riders.

 Roller coaster: Hydra Fighter II, family (S).

NORTH DAKOTA

Lucy's Amusement Park

Highway 83 South
Minot, ND (701) 839-2320

Nicely laid out on a well-kept 2-acre treed and grassy lot, just outside of the city limits, the park's challenging miniature golf course is as popular as its 6 mechanical rides.

Among the rides are both adult and kiddie bumper cars, airplanes, an orbiter, and a giant slide. Everything here is on a pay-as-you-go basis. Open daily from mid-morning to 10:00 or 11:00 P.M., with the miniature golf course staying open later than the rides.

OHIO

The Beach
Kings Mill Road (Exit 25) at I–71
Mason, OH (513) 398–SWIM
www.thebeachwaterpark.com

Die-hard waterpark fans from across the country list The Beach as one of their favorites and as a must-do each summer. It features 35 acres of watery fun combined with 35 slides, so everyone is sure to find something that makes them wet and wild.

The detailed theming on attractions like the Aztec Adventure will amaze first-time visitors. Guests dart through ancient ruins and speed down hills on the Midwest's first water coaster. Thrill-seekers also enjoy the Cliff, a 5-story slide that dives underground before emptying into a pool.

For those looking for relaxation, be sure to check out the Lazy Miami River, a 1,200-foot river; Thunder Beach, a wave pool that holds more than 750,000 gallons and has waves as big as the ocean's; and the Pearl, a pool where the temperature is kept at 85 degrees. For fish out of water, the park offers 3 sand volleyball courts, 2 basketball courts, and the Pirates Den Arcade.

The park is located across the interstate from Kings Island. Open mid-May through early September, the tickets are under $26.

Cedar Point Amusement Park & Resort

**On a Lake Erie Peninsula
Sandusky, OH (419) 627–2350
www.cedarpoint.com**

As the grand dame of Midwest parks, this 364-acre facility, founded in 1870, is the second-oldest continuously operated amusement park in North America and the largest and most complete regional amusement resort in the country.

A trip to Cedar Point can be either a fun-packed day trip or a more leisurely multi-day experience. In addition to the well-known amusement park, there is Soak City, an 18-acre waterpark; Challenge Park action area; and a supervised beach on Lake Erie for swimming and other water sports.

 TiM'S TRiViA

College football legend and Notre Dame great Knute Rockne worked as a lifeguard at Cedar Point with teammate Gus Dorian. During their free time during the summer of 1913, they perfected the forward pass on the Cedar Point beach. No word on where the Hail Mary pass was created.

Additional resort amenities include a 665-slip marina only a few steps from the park's entrance, 4 hotels with nearly 1,500 rooms, 283 RV campsites, 50 lakeside cottages, 10 rustic cabins, and 59 luxury RV campsites. Numerous pools, spas, and restaurants dot the peninsula and a lakeside boardwalk connects everything together.

Cedar Point Amusement Park

Cedar Point was the first park ever to introduce a roller coaster over 200 feet tall in 1989 with the debut of the Magnum XL-200 at 205 feet. In 2000, it was the first park to go beyond the 300-foot threshold with the 310-foot-tall Millennium Force.

In May 2003, the $25 million Top Thrill Dragster will debut. Riders are "launched" out of the station and go from 0 to 120 mph in 4 seconds, up the 420-foot hill at a 90 degree angle, go over the top, and drop 400 feet straight down, again

Snoopy on the Midway, Cedar Point, Sandusky, Ohio
Photo by Tim O'Brien

reaching speeds of 120 mph. It's the tallest and fastest roller coaster with the longest drop in the world.

While some of the areas are themed, Cedar Point has no aspirations to be a theme park. On the other hand, one could argue that the traditional park atmosphere combined with 68 rides, including 16 roller coasters, in itself represents the theme of the popular park.

One themed area is Camp Snoopy. That's where Snoopy and all his pals hang out each season. In addition to the character meet-and-greets, this family area has 8 rides, including a 31-foot-tall family roller coaster and a huge Snoopy bounce for the kids.

It's a heavily wooded, well-landscaped, big park. A walk from the front of the park to the back, along the Frontier Trail, is a 1-mile jaunt. The many tall rides provide a great bird's-eye view of Lake Erie and the rest of the park spread out over the peninsula.

To save a few steps, utilize the park's transportation system. The Sky Ride provides a one-way trip between the front and the back, and the Cedar Point and Lake Erie Railroad has a stop in the back of the park in Frontiertown.

The park's history is chronicled in the Town Hall Museum in Frontiertown, and the region's crafts history is revealed along the Frontier Trail, where you'll find several crafts-people creating and then selling their wares from rustic log cabins. A fun petting zoo area can be found along the same trail. There are several live entertainment shows in the park, including a high-dive show and the popular ice skating show *Snoopy Rocks! On Ice.*

Several turn-of-the-twentieth-century buildings, including the recently restored ballroom, are still in operation and some of the popular food items from that era, the Cedar Point French Fry and Cedar Point Custard, are still available.

 # TiM'S TRiViA

The Merry-Go-Round Museum, located in the old post office building in downtown Sandusky, Ohio, just a few miles from the Cedar Point Causeway, provides a glimpse into the world of carousel carving and preservation. On exhibit is a collection of tools, benches, and animals from the Dentzel carving shop of 1867. A circa 1930 Allan Herschell carousel is in operation, with a collection of different antique as well as modern carved wooden horses. Open year-round. (419) 626-6111.

Soak City and Challenge Park

The waterpark and action park are located between the amusement park and the resort hotels and campground at the outer end of the peninsula. Soak City is probably the only waterpark in the world with a world-class roller coaster dividing it in half. The Magnum steel coaster cuts through the park, with passageways leading from one side to another. Among the elements are a wave pool, 14 slides, and the popular Bubbles Swim-up Bar for those over 21.

Challenge Park is located adjacent to Soak City and has two 18-hole miniature golf courses, go-karts, and a Skycoaster, with all attractions on a pay-as-you-go basis.

 Special events: CoasterMania, a day for enthusiasts, early June; in-water boat show, September; HalloWeekends, late September through October.

 Season: May through October for amusement park and Challenge Park; Memorial Day to Labor Day for Soak City.

 Operating hours: Open daily, 10:00 A.M. to 10:00 P.M. or midnight; weekends only after Labor Day.

Admission policy: Pay-one-price, under $45. Combination tickets are available. Parking charge.

 Top rides: Power Tower complex of 4,240-foot-tall free falls; 3 antique carousels; Thunder Canyon, a raging-rapids ride; Giant Wheel, a 15-story-tall Ferris wheel with gondola-style seating; Snake River Falls, a shoot-the-chute.

 Roller coasters: Top Thrill Dragster, hyper-coaster (S); Wicked Twister, LIM Impulse (S); Millennium Force, hypercoaster (S); Mantis, stand-up (S); Raptor, inverted (S); Blue Streak (W); Mean Streak (W); Corkscrew (S); Disaster Transport, indoor bob-sleds (S); Cedar Creek Mine Ride (S); Iron Dragon (S); Gemini, twin racing (S); Magnum XL200 (S); Jr. Gemini, junior (S); Wildcat (S); Woodstock Express, family (S).

 Plan to stay: A 2-day visit is a must, in order to enjoy the park to its fullest.

 Best way to avoid crowds: Come before mid-June or during the last week in August. Sundays in September are wonderful times to visit the Point. Be there early; the causeway leading out to the park becomes a bottleneck once the masses start arriving.

Directions: Located midway between Toledo and Cleveland. Take exit 7 off the Ohio Turnpike (I–80), go north on Route 250 into Sandusky, and then follow the signs to the causeway.

Coney Island

6201 Kellogg Avenue
Cincinnati, OH (513) 232–8230
www.coneyislandpark.com

Sunlite Pool, one of the largest swimming pools in the world, is the glue that has held this little park together through the years and is still the major draw today.

First opened in 1886, the park was often referred to as Coney Island West, but in reality it had very little except for its name in common with the famous Coney Island in Brooklyn, New York. People came up the river by steamboat from Cincinnati by the thousands to picnic and play. In

1972, the owners closed down the ride side of the park and moved many of the rides to Kings Island, a new park they built 20 miles north of Cincinnati.

The pool continued to operate, however, and the little park refused to roll over. New owners came along and the park began to grow again. Today, there are 21 family and kiddie rides, an 18-hole miniature golf course, and pedal boats and bumper boats on Lake Como. Additional rides include Flying Bobs, Super Roundup, bumper cars, Tempest, and a Giant Slide.

In the pool area there are 2 major water-slide complexes and 6 diving boards to add to the watery thrills.

 Roller coaster: Python, Zyklon family (S).

The historic Moonlite Gardens ballroom, now restored, features live concerts, including big band dances several times a year. Open May through September. Free admission, with all rides on a pay-as-you-go basis. A value pass, good for the pool and the rides, is available.

 # TiM'S TRiViA

The ability to run first-class amusement parks must be in the water in Ohio. As of 2003, the top officials of 3 amusement park chains are from the Buckeye state. Richard Kinzel of Cedar Fair; Al Weber of Paramount Parks; and Gary Story of Six Flags are all Ohio natives. In addition, more than 20 parks in North America have Ohio natives as members of the top management staff.

Erieview Park

5483 Lake Road
Geneva-on-the-Lake, OH (440) 466–8650
www.erieviewpark.com

In the heart of a popular summer resort community in northeast Ohio, this family-owned park offers 19 rides, a waterslide complex, and a winery. Nearly hidden behind the stores and restaurants that line the busy and colorful strip, the 3-acre park is located on a bluff overlooking Lake Erie.

Among the unique and classic rides are a 24-gauge train built by the National Amusement Company and a rare Bill

Tracey darkride that is being restored with the help of several members of the Darkride and Funhouse Enthusiasts organization.

 Extras: A large shooting gallery and Woody's World Arcade are adjacent to the park entrance. The Firehouse Winery makes its own wine.

 Season: Mother's Day through Labor Day, daily from early June through late August.

 Operating hours: Open daily 2:00 to 10:00 P.M. Wild Water Works is open daily, noon to 9:00 P.M.

 Admission policy: Free gate, with rides on a pay-as-you-go basis. An all-day "ride and slide," pay-one-price ticket is available, under $16. Parking free if you buy ride tickets.

 Top rides: Ferris wheel; Roll-O-Plane; a darkride; bumper cars; a carousel; Flying Skooters.

 Roller coaster: The Brat, kiddie (S).

 Plan to stay: If you intend to use both rides and water slides, plan to stay 4 to 5 hours.

 Best way to avoid crowds: Come early in the week or at midday on weekends. The park is busiest in the evening, when the town itself is hopping.

 Directions: Take the Geneva-on-the-Lake exit (Route 534 North) off I–90 and drive north about 7 miles into the village. The park is on your left, with parking next to the water slide and Woody's World Arcade.

 TiM'S TRiViA

The National Carousel Association has a great Web site. In addition to the normal membership and convention information, there is an easy-to-use inventory of the country's operating antique carousels, an on-line shop, a history of the popular ride, and links to other carousel-related sites. See www.nca-usa.com.

LeSourdsville Lake Amusement Park

**5757 Middletown–Hamilton Road
State Route 4
Middletown, OH (513) 539–2193
www.lesourdsvillelake.com**

Following several years of financial instability and two seasons of being closed to the public after a new owner purchased it, Americana Amusement Park reopened in 2002 under the name it had when it originally opened in 1921.

Positioning itself as a local picnic facility, the park now has 40 rides surrounding the tranquil lake, a lake cruise on a paddlewheel boat, pedal boats, a swimming pool, plenty of picnic pavilions, and a fun kiddieland removed from the rest of the park.

 Roller coasters: Screechin' Eagle (W); The Serpent (S); Little Dipper, kiddie (S).

Among the popular rides are the Raging Thunder log flume, a train ride that takes guests to the back of the park, and the traditional Flying Scooters.

It's good to see this traditional park come back to life with a management that cares and is willing to invest while at the same time keeping the park a working-class, neighborhood park that is priced right for the young family.

LeSourdsville Lake, Americana Amusement Park, Middletown, Ohio   Photo by Tim O'Brien

Open May through October. General admission is $3 per person. Rides can be purchased individually or an unlimited ride ticket can be purchased once inside the park, under $17.

Memphis Kiddie Park

10340 Memphis Avenue
Brooklyn, OH (216) 941-5995
www.memphiskiddiepark.com

Talk about taking care of your equipment! Nine of the 11 rides still in operation here today were here when the park opened in 1952. One was added in 1969, and the cool little crank cars were added in 1999, replacing the original ones that had worn out. Most of the rides were built by Allan Herschell and were purchased new for this park.

The neat part is that they all look like new. They are renovated and painted practically every year and the effort to keep them in top shape is paying off. Many who bring their children to the park today rode the same rides at the same park. A few third-generation Kiddie Park fans are starting to show up now.

In a state filled with megaparks, this quaint little kiddie park is truly a breath of fresh air. In addition to the rides, there are birthday party quarters, a championship miniature golf course, and several games.

 Roller coaster: Little Dipper, kiddie (S).

Open daily 10:00 A.M. to 9:00 P.M., April through September. It's pay-as-you-go, with each ride taking one ticket; tickets cost from 65 cents to 95 cents depending on how many you buy.

Paramount's Kings Island WaterWorks Waterpark

Kings Island Drive
Kings Island, OH
(513) 754-5700/ (800) 288-0808
www.pki.com

Here, it's not a question of what to do, but rather, where to start! There's so much here that it can be a bit overwhelming for many first-timers. Sure, you've heard of this 30-year-old-park, but if you've never been here, you will certainly be surprised at its size, its ride and attraction lineups, its mature landscaping, and its clean midways.

TiM'S TRiViA

In 1972, less than two years after construction began, Kings Island opened about 20 miles north of Cincinnati. Built by Taft Broadcasting, the park welcomed 7,000 people on opening day, April 29. Slightly more than 2 million attended the park that season. In 1984, the park was purchased through a leveraged buyout by a team of top park officials who called themselves Kings Entertainment Company. In 1987, that team sold Kings Island to American Financial Corporation, while continuing to manage it under contract. Paramount Communications purchased the park in 1992 and it became known as Paramount's Kings Island.

Where should you start? A good way to orient yourself is to grab a park map and take an elevator ride to the top of the 332-foot-tall Eiffel Tower. You can't miss this massive landmark at the end of the fountains on International Street at the entrance.

As you look below, check out the massive wood structure lurking in the corner of the park. That's The Beast, arguably one of the best and most famous wooden coasters in the world. More than two decades have passed since it first opened and this ride is still the longest wooden roller coaster in the world at 7,400 feet. Steel coaster fans can have fun as well on Flight of Fear. Linear induction magnets launch the trains to 54 mph in seconds before they are catapulted through 4 inversions in the dark. Now that's a coaster ride.

Delirium is an amazing thrill ride. Just its size is enough to intimidate the casual thrill-seeker. Check it out in the Thrill Zone area. There's nothing like it anywhere else in the world!

If you want to take things at a slower pace, be sure to enjoy the interactive darkride, Scooby Doo and the Haunted Castle. Guests join Scooby and "those meddling kids" as they journey along in the Mystery Machine searching for ghosts. Points can be scored by "scaring" away the ghosts by aiming the Fright Light ghost blasters at them. SpongeBob SquarePants is a fun motion-based simulator ride for the entire family.

"Face Off," Paramount's Kings Island, Kings Island, Ohio Photo by Adam Sandy

The park's carousel, Philadelphia Toboggan Company #79, was built for Cincinnati's Coney Island in 1926. After that park closed in September 1971, the ride was moved to Kings Island for its opening the following spring. There are several individually themed children's areas, including the 6-acre Nickelodeon Central. Four different family coasters can be found in the kids' areas. Check out the junior woodie, Beastie.

With 46 rides to choose from, you'll find that your day here will be packed full of activity. If you need to cool off, be sure to check out WaterWorks, an adjacent 30-acre waterpark with 19 additional rides and activities for no additional charge. Season-pass holders have their own entrance to the waterpark as well as preferred parking closer to that entrance.

 TIM'S TRIVIA

Built nearly 25 years ago, The Beast wooden roller coaster at Paramount's Kings Island near Cincinnati is still in the Top Ten of most coaster aficionados. Designed and built by Kings Island personnel, the ride was designed to fit into the rugged terrain of 35 densely wooded acres. It is so wooded back there that riders can't see the tunnels, hills, and drops coming, which adds a great element of surprise. The ride is still studied by coaster designers from all over the world and continues to be the benchmark by which other wooden coasters are measured.

 Season: Mid-April through Halloween.

 Operating hours: 9:00 A.M. to 11:00 P.M.

 Admission policy: Pay-one-price, under $40. A specially priced second-day ticket is available. Parking charge. Season passes good at all 5 Paramount parks.

 Top rides: Tomb Raider: The Ride, a themed special effects–filled indoor thrill ride featuring a Giant Top Spin; Wild Thornberry's River Adventure, a family log flume; Delirium, a swinging pendulum taking riders 137 feet high; Drop Zone, a 315-foot-tall gyro-drop tower; The Flying Eagles, a Flying Skooter ride; Wipe Out Beach, a wave surfer, and Rushing River tube ride, both in WaterWorks.

 Roller coasters: Son of Beast, looping (W); Runaway Reptar, Rugrats-themed inverted coaster (S); Face/Off, inverted boomerang (S); Racer, twin racing (W); The Beast (W); The Beastie, junior (W); Vortex, 6-loop (S); Adventure Express mine train (S); Scooby's Ghoster Coaster, suspended kiddie (S); Top Gun, suspended (S); Flight of Fear, indoor (S); TopCat's Taxi Jam, junior (S).

 Plan to stay: 10 hours.

Best way to avoid crowds: Work your way around the circular layout and finish each area as you go; doubling back is time-consuming. Use a map to plan your voyage.

 Directions: Located 24 miles north of Cincinnati, 80 miles south of Columbus, off I–71. Take the Kings Island Drive exit and go east to the park entrance.

 # TiM'S TRiViA

The coaster wars continue! Cedar Point in Sandusky, Ohio, which had the most coasters of any park on the planet for many years, has been challenged lately by Six Flags Magic Mountain in Valencia, California, for that bragging right. In 2001 Magic Mountain caught up with Cedar Point at 14. They both added one in 2002, keeping them tied at 15, and they were both set to open one more in 2003, keeping them even at 16.

Six Flags Worlds of Adventure

1060 North Aurora Road
Aurora, OH (330) 562–7131
www.sixflags.com

What do you get when you combine a world-class marine park, a major waterpark, a high-thrill theme park, and a motel and campground? Six Flags calls this example of park convergence a 750-acre super park. All the facilities are adjacent to one another and surround the 55-acre Geauga Lake.

In addition to the 100 rides and attractions on the "ride side" of the park, the waterpark, complete with 28 slides, features a 25,000-square-foot wave pool, a lazy river, and two areas just for the smaller kids and their families.

On the "wildlife side," on the grounds of the former SeaWorld of Ohio, there are numerous marine mammal and animal shows, including a killer whale show and a Bengal tiger exhibit and presentation on Tiger Island. The park has an extensive wildlife collection, including penguins, seals and sea lions, a walrus, bottlenose dolphins, and a diverse aquarium collection.

THE AMUSEMENT PARK GUIDE

The ride park has 10 roller coasters, including the X-Flight, a coaster ride that gives you the sensation of flying. At times, you are lying down, horizontal to the ground. What a trip! There are three woodies here, including The Villain. The high-tech Batman Knight Flight floorless coaster is a unique ride to the Midwest, and Superman–Ultimate Escape is a vertical spiraling LIM coaster.

Looney Tunes Boomtown is a larger-than-life interactive family playground with 7 rides and a foam factory playland. Batman appears daily in the Batman Thrill Spectacular stunt show and Bugs Bunny and his friends star in the Looney Tunes Road Show.

 Extras: Red Canyon Rock Climbing Wall, Geronimo Sky Swing Skycoaster, and go-karts, all for an extra fee.

 Special events: Fright Fest, weekends in October.

 Season: Daily Memorial Day through August. Weekends in May, September, and October.

 Operating hours: Opens at 11:00 A.M. during the week; 10:00 A.M. on weekends. Closes daily at 10:00 P.M. Hours vary during spring and fall.

 Admission policy: Pay-one-price, under $40. Parking charge.

 Top rides: Texas Twister, Top Spin; Mr. Hyde's Nasty Fall, free fall; Shipwreck Falls, shoot-the-chute; 1926 Marcus Illions Carousel.

 Roller coasters: X-Flight, flying (S); Big Dipper (W); Raging Wolf Bobs (W); The Villain (W); Serial Thriller, inverted (S); Double Loop, looping (S); Mind Eraser, boomerang (S); Road Runner Express, family (S); Batman Knight Flight, floorless (S); Superman–Ultimate Escape, LIM vertical spiral (S).

 Plan to stay: 8 to 10 hours if you play in the waterpark.

 Best way to avoid crowds: There are 2 gates to the park, one on the marine park side, the other on the ride side. Go into the park through the gate that corresponds with the activity you want to experience first. On the ride side, go to the back and work your way, against the crowds, to the front. Lines for the big rides tend to shorten by mid-afternoon.

 Directions: Take exit 13 off Ohio Turnpike (I–80) and go north 9 miles on State Route 43 (North Aurora Road). Located 30 miles southeast of Cleveland and 26 miles north of Akron.

Swings 'N' Things

8501 Stearns Road
Olmsted Township, OH
(440) 235-4420
www.swings-n-things.com

You won't have a problem finding something to do here. Outside at this 13-acre family fun park, you can ride the adult and rookie go-kart tracks, bumper boats, and a few children's rides; play on the 2 miniature golf courses; or practice in the batting cages.

There's a lot more to do inside. Here you'll challenge the Ground Zero laser tag game; little ones can play in the Kids Korner soft-play area and win prizes in the arcade. Don't miss the homemade ice cream in Just Scoops . . . I love it!!

The indoor activities operate year-round, with most outdoor attractions open daily during the summer and weekends the rest of the year, weather permitting.

Tuscora Park

Off Tuscora Avenue
New Philadelphia, OH (330) 343-4644
www.tuscora.park.net

This fun and laid-back 37-acre community recreation area, located a few blocks from downtown, has several family attractions, including a small rides area. The fun Mini Coaster junior coaster and a Ferris wheel are among the 8 family and kiddie rides.

The most popular attraction is the 1929 Herschell/ Spillman carousel. Bought by the city in 1940, this 3-row machine features 36 hand-carved figures and 2 chariots. The beautiful music that sounds throughout the area comes from a Wurlitzer 153 organ.

The city-owned park also offers an 18-hole miniature golf course, batting cages, picnic facilities, and a swimming pool.

Open Monday through Thursday at 5:00 P.M. and Friday through Sunday at noon, Memorial Day through Labor Day. Closes daily at 9:30 P.M. The rides are on a pay-as-you-go basis for only 50 cents each. What a deal!

Wyandot Lake

10101 Riverside Drive
Powell, OH (614) 889–9283
www.sixflags.com

If you can't decide whether you want to go to a waterpark or an amusement park, you might want to come to this true hybrid that offers an eclectic lineup of rides, slides, and activities. This is one of the few parks where you can ride and scream on a wooden roller coaster and then walk a few yards, jump in the water, and body surf in the Wild Tide wave pool, all for one admission price. The waterpark and the amusement park are intertwined.

There are 16 mechanical rides, with half of them located in a great, shaded kiddie area. Right off kiddieland is the kiddie waterpark, featuring a 5-story interactive play element, Christopher's Island. Other mechanical rides include the circa 1956 John Allen–designed Sea Serpent junior wooden coaster, a carousel, a scrambler, and a classic Eli Ferris wheel.

In addition to the wave pool, there are 10 water elements, including a great action river, tube slides, and body slides.

Owned by Six Flags Inc., the park features the branded Fright Fest Halloween events on weekends in October. It is open mid-May through mid-September, then reopens for Fright Fest the first weekend in October.

Roller coaster: Sea Dragon (W).

All rides and slides are included in the pay-one-price admission, under $27. A combination ticket with the adjacent Columbus Zoo is available. The world-famous zoo features a C.P. Huntington train and a 1914 Mangels-Illions carousel. The two facilities share the same parking area.

Bell's Amusement Park

3900 East 21st Street
Tulsa State Fairgrounds
Tulsa, OK (918) 744–1991
www.bellsamusement.com

Doing business in the southwest corner of the Tulsa State Fairgrounds since 1951, this park has become a local tradition and generations have enjoyed the hospitality of the Bell family.

The 10-acre facility houses 27 rides, including the Zingo wooden roller coaster, which goes under one side of a concession stand and out the other. The grounds are clean, compact, and well-groomed and become part of the midway of the Tulsa State Fair each fall.

The Phantasmagoria is a classic Bill Tracey darkride and the White Lightning log flume guarantees a fun splashdown, especially on a hot Oklahoma afternoon! Additional rides include a Tilt-A-Whirl and a Himalaya.

 Roller coaster: Zingo (W).

The Bells love to hand out great deals. Twenty-five-cent ride nights during the week, a $5 unlimited ride pass during the week, and a low $3 general admission pass are deals you can find all summer long. Regular prices are a $3 general admission fee, with a $16 all-you-can-ride pass or rides on an individual basis.

Open mid-April through the closing of the fair, in early October, the park operates from 6:00 to 10:00 P.M. during the week and 1:00 to 11:00 P.M. on weekends. Take the Harvard

Street exit off I–244, go south 1¾ miles, turn east on 17th Street, and go a short distance to the fairgrounds.

Frontier City

11501 Northeast Expressway
Oklahoma City, OK (405) 478–2412
www.sixflags.com

The theme park version of the Wild West is alive and a lot of fun at this 40-acre park owned by Six Flags. You'll enter through a replica of an 1880s Western town with all architecture, landscaping, and activities themed to that period. There are several shows, including a traditional gunfighters presentation.

In keeping with the theming, the kiddie rides can be found in the O.K. Kid's Korral, and Paul Bunyan's Buzzsaw Company is an interactive wet/dry play area. Of the 32 rides, 11 are for the young ones. Geronimo, a 113-foot-tall Skycoaster, and NASCAR-style go-karts are also available for an extra fee.

 Special events: Fright Fest, weekends in October.

 Season: Mid-April through October.

 Operating hours: Opens 10:30 A.M. daily; closes most nights at 10:00 P.M.

 Admission policy: Pay-one-price, under $28. Parking charge.

 Top rides: ErUPtion!, a sky sling; Mindbender, Inverter; Grand Centennial Ferris wheel, located on the highest point in the park; Tomahawk, a 360-degree swinging pendulum; Mystery River, a log flume; Prairie Schooner, a swinging pirate ship; Renegade, a raging-rapids ride.

 Roller coasters: Silver Bullet, looping (S); Diamond Back, shuttle loop (S); Wildcat (W); Nightmare, indoor family (S); Wild Kitty, kiddie (S).

Plan to stay: 6 hours.

 Best way to avoid crowds: Come on week-days or Sundays.

 Directions: Take the 122nd Street exit off I–35, about 20 minutes north of downtown Oklahoma City. The park is just south of 122nd Street on the west side of the interstate.

Kiddie Park
In Johnstone Park

200 North Cherokee
Bartlesville, OK (918) 336–5337
www.tulsawalk.com/parks-places/
johnstone-index.html

A true relic from the past, this little park has been provid-ing fun for area toddlers and grade school kids since 1947. Promoting itself as a park that has "15 brightly colored rides that don't go very fast, far, or high," it is owned by the local playground association.

Among the rides are a Ferris wheel, airplanes, bumper cars, a train, and a carousel. Open Monday through Saturday only, from 7:00 to 9:30 p.m. Each ride takes 1 ticket and each ticket costs 30 cents. Now that's a deal!

White Water Bay

3908 West Reno
Oklahoma City, OK (405) 943–9687
www.sixflags.com

A tropical watery oasis in the middle of Oklahoma is a wonderful site during the midsummer heat! There are 25 acres full of exciting and cooling water rides and attrac-tions here, plus a lot of shade and peaceful areas to sit back, have a cool drink, and watch the world go by.

For the adventurous, there's Cannonball Falls, 2 high-speed slides; Acapulco Cliff dive, a 65-foot free-fall slide; and the Bermuda Triangle, a 7-story tower with 3 different slides. For those searching for calmer waters, there is a Castaway Creek leisure river, and for the little family members, Kids' Kove offers plenty of water play activities. Keelhaul Falls is a fast, active shallow tube ride and Big Kahuna is a 6-passenger family tube ride.

Open May through Labor Day daily at 10:30 A.M., with closing at either 8:00, 9:00, or 11:00 P.M. Admission charge is under $26. Come late afternoons during the week to avoid the crowds.

OREGON

Enchanted Forest

8462 Enchanted Way SE
Turner, OR (503) 363–3060
www.enchantedforest.com

The greatest fairy tales of all time come alive at Enchanted Forest, a heavily forested park with storybook characters' homes as the main attraction. There's a slide in the Old Lady in the Shoe's house, a maze at the bottom of the Rabbit Hole in the Alice in Wonderland area, and at the Crooked Man's House visitors meet gravity head-on.

There are also 3 additional attractions for the kids, bumper boats, a Frog Hopper free fall, and a pint-size Ferris wheel.

There's a shooting gallery and Indian Caves to explore in the Western area; in the Old World Village area, don't miss Fantasy Fountains, a dazzling water and light show. In addition, there are the Big Timber Log Ride, the Ice Mountain Bobsleds roller coaster, and the park's famous Haunted House.

 Season: Mid-March through September. May through Labor Day, daily. Spring and fall, weekends only.

Operating hours: 9:30 A.M. to 6:00 P.M.

Admission policy: General admission, under $8. Haunted House and mechanical rides cost extra.

Roller coaster: Ice Mountain Bobsled, family (S).

Plan to stay: 2 hours.

Directions: Located 7 miles south of Salem, just off exit 248 of I–5.

Oaks Park

Southeast Oaks Parkway
Portland, OR (503) 236–5722
www.oakspark.com

Situated along the banks of the Willamette River and surrounded by the stately trees for which it was named, Oaks Park is approaching its one hundredth anniversary, a feat that only 24 other U.S. parks have ever reached.

The 44-acre park opened on May 30, 1905, as a trolley park for the Oregon Water Power & Navigation Company, to coincide with the Lewis and Clark World Expo. Today, with 20 rides, the park blends nostalgia and high technology to create a fun family experience. But even with the fancy new rides, the park is still a prime example of a well-kept and well-loved traditional park.

Extras: Go-karts and miniature golf, extra charge. The Oaks Museum presents a nostalgic look at the park with photos and memorabilia.

Season: Mid-March through October. Roller skating rink is open year-round.

Operating hours: Open daily at noon; closes at 9:00 or 10:00 P.M. Closed non-holiday Mondays.

Admission policy: Free admission, with rides and attractions on a pay-as-you-go basis. Pay-one-price available for 5-hour period, $13. Free parking.

 Top rides: Scream-n-Eagle, swinging pendulum; Sea Dragon; Tilt-A-Whirl; bumper cars; Scrambler; a Ferris wheel; a circa 1911 Herschell/Spillman 3-row carousel; Haunted Mine, a darkride; Rock & Roll, 1950s-themed Matterhorn; a train ride around the park and along the river.

 Roller coasters: Looping Thunder, 1-loop (S); Zoooom Coaster, family (S).

 Plan to stay: 5 hours.

 Best way to avoid crowds: Visit Tuesday or Friday during the day or on weekends before Memorial Day or after Labor Day.

 Directions: Take exit 299A, Lake Oswego, off I–5 and follow the signs to Lake Oswego, which will take you to Macadam Avenue. Proceed south on Macadam until you get to the Sellwood Bridge. Cross the bridge and make a left onto 6th Avenue, then make a left onto Southeast Spokane Street. The park is on your left. Located 8 miles from downtown.

Thrill-Ville USA

8372 Enchanted Way
Turner, OR (503) 363–7616
www.thrillvilleusa.homestead.com

There are thrill parks, there are family parks, and there are extreme parks. Here, you'll find a bit of all three. Serving the Portland area since 1984, the park features 16 thrill and kiddie rides including several classic oldies, go-karts, bumper boats, miniature golf, and water slides.

The lineup of extreme rides is superb. Featured are The Big Sling, a slingshot-style ride that catapults riders 275 feet into the air; the Turbo Force, where riders spin at the end of a 140-foot-long propeller; the Skycoaster; a Scad Dive that provides a pure free fall with no ropes or cables attached; a Euro-Bungy trampoline; and a rock wall. The extreme rides are often taken out of the park and booked on as attractions at major fairs across the country, so if you're going for a specific ride, call first to make sure it's there.

 Roller coaster: Ripper, family (S).

It's free to enter the park, with rides on a pay-as-you-go basis. An unlimited pass, which is good for all the rides and slides except for the extreme rides, go-karts, and miniature golf, is available for $15. Open daily, Memorial Day through Labor Day starting at 11:00 A.M., open weekends in spring and fall.

PENNSYLVANIA

Bucktail Family Fun Park & Camping Resort

1029 Mann Creek Road
Mansfield, PA (570) 662–2923
www.bucktailcamping.com

If you come to camp AND to play, you'll be sleeping right in the middle of things. In addition to the swimming pool, hiking trails, miniature golf, and a great playground, the place has 8 attractions, including a ¾-mile train ride, tower slide (using burlap bags), moon bounce, Venetian Swings, and merry-go-round.

 # TIM'S TRIVIA

Pennsylvania has long been a true amusement park mecca. Through the years, nearly 400 amusement parks have operated in the state. From the early 1900s to the mid-1960s, there were more parks operating in Pennsylvania than in any other state.

The fee for lodging, which ranges from a primitive camping site to the "Dream Lodge," includes all activities except for bingo and the arcade games. The summer is full of events, ranging from rock-and-roll concerts and a chocolate festival to free pancake breakfasts.

It's rustic, it's quiet, and it's a great place to spend quality time with the family!

Bushkill Park

2100 Bushkill Park Drive
Easton, PA (610) 258-6941
www.bushkillpark.com

Only 24 parks in the United States have been around long enough to celebrate their 100th anniversary. In 2002, Bushkill became the 8th Pennsylvania park to do just that. This 17-acre traditional park offers a lot of shade, nostalgic buildings, classic amusement rides, and antique charm.

There are 17 rides, with half of them just for the kids. Included in the mix are a Merry Mixer, a Tilt-A-Whirl, a train, and a circa 1924 Allan Herschell carousel with 42 jumpers, 2 chariots, and a Wurlitzer band organ. You can grab for the brass ring on this machine, one of less than a dozen carousels in the United States where you can still partake in this fun.

 Roller coaster: Kiddie Coaster, family (S).

The walk-through fun house, dating back to the park's early days, is known as The Barl of Fun. Its name has been misspelled for as long as anyone can remember, and when the owners restored it, they repainted the sign as it was. The haunted Pretzel darkride is a classic amusement park ride and the oldest of its type still in operation.

The roller skating rink is open to the public only on Saturday nights, 8:00 to 11:00 P.M. There's an 18-hole miniature golf course and an arcade with video and midway games.

Open Wednesday through Sunday, Memorial Day weekend through Labor Day weekend. The park opens at noon and closes at 6:00 P.M. during the week, 9:00 P.M. on Fridays and Saturdays. Free admission during the week, with rides on a pay-as-you-go basis or $15 for an all-day unlimited ride pass. There's a $3 general admission charge on Saturday and Sunday if a $15 unlimited ride pass is not purchased. Every Wednesday is Wacky Wednesday, featuring a $10 all-day unlimited ride pass. Free parking.

Camelbeach Waterpark

Exit 299 off I-80
Tannersville, PA (570) 629-1661
www.camelbeach.com

What do you do with a popular snow ski area in the summer? The owners of the Camelback Ski Area came up with the answer several years ago when they created Camelbeach, a full-scale, fun-filled waterpark.

Highlighting the action are 2 bowl slides. On Vortex you ride on a tube, and on the Spin Cycle you body slide. On both, you head down a chute to build up speed, then slide into a bowl and go around and around. As you slow, you move closer to the bottom and eventually drop through the hole at the bottom into a pool below, kind of like a funnel. Triple Venom, new for 2003, is a 6-story-tall complex of three body slides.

The Kahuna Lagoon Wave Pool delivers waves 4 to 6 feet tall, Camel Cove is a fun family interactive water play area, the Titan is an 8-story-tall 5-passenger tube ride, and the Blue Nile Adventure River is a 1,000-foot-long action river. In addition, there are a swimming pool, bumper boats, miniature golf, an Alpine slide, and a free chairlift ride to the top of the mountain, where you can enjoy lunch and a great view.

Open weekends May through mid-June, daily until Labor Day. Opens at 10:00 A.M., closes at 7:00 P.M. during the summer. Admission, under $25. Come in after 4:00 P.M. and get the next day free.

Carousel Village at Indian Walk

591 Durham Road/State Route 413
Wrightstown, PA (215) 598-0707
www.shearerpenn.com/village

One would expect to see some great color and awesome landscaping in an amusement park located inside a garden center, and that's exactly what you'll find here. The owner of the Christmas tree farm and garden center found a historic carousel in the late 1980s, had it restored, and since then has added a family fun side to his horticultural endeavors.

The carousel is a Herschell/Spillman, originally built sometime around the turn of the century, and is mounted on a circus wagon. It is thought to be the last of its kind in operation. It has 36 jumpers and 2 chariots and is located under a colorful canvas top.

The train ride takes passengers past animals, including buffalo, deer, and goats. Other rides include antique cars, a moon bounce, classic pony cart and fire engine kiddie rides, a swing ride, Red Baron airplanes, and a classic Allan Herschell kiddie roller coaster.

 Roller coaster: Roller Coaster, kiddie (S).

The rides are open weekends, weather permitting, from April through December. They are open daily during the summer months. Everything is priced on a pay-as-you-go basis.

Conneaut Lake Park

Highway 618
Conneaut Lake Park, PA
(814) 382-5115/(877) 782-5115
www.conneautlakepark.com

Rides, attractions, and summer cottages are all mixed together at this unique summer resort. For more than a century the park dominated the entertainment world in this part of the state. Financial problems threatened to close it down, but through creative measures, the community has been able to hold it together.

Today the park has made a great comeback and has 31 rides, including the famous Blue Streak wooden roller coaster. Among the rides are the Flying Skooters, a train ride, Paratrooper, and a 1905 D.C. Muller/T. M. Harton carousel. All the Muller horses are now gone, but have been replaced by Carousel Works carved animals. The Harton frame is original. The Devil's Den is one of the few Pretzel Company gravity darkrides still in operation.

TIM'S TRIVIA

Pennsylvania has several unique carousels that are not in amusement parks. Here are a couple you might want to visit.

- *Albion Boro Park, 15 Smock Avenue, Albion. Home of the third oldest operating carousel in the United States. Manufactured during the 1890s by the U. S. Merry-Go-Round Company, the ride has 2 rows with 14 jumpers and 4 chariots. It's been here since 1947 and is open on weekends only, June through Labor Day. (814) 756-3660.*

- *Peddler's Village, Route 202/Route 263, Lahaska. Built on a restored frame of a circa 1922 Philadelphia Toboggan Company carousel (#59), this ride is populated with mostly new carvings, including 36 jumpers, 10 standers, and 2 chariots. Open daily, year-round. (214) 794-8960. www.peddlersvillage.com.*

There's a waterpark with several slides and a lazy river, a sandy beach on the lake, Camperland campground, boat rentals, and the Hotel Conneaut, a classic summer resort hotel where crooner Perry Como was discovered while working as the hotel's barber.

 Roller coasters: Blue Streak (W); Toboggan (S); Little Dipper (S).

Open Wednesday through Sunday at noon. Rides close at varying times, between 8:00 and 10:00 P.M. Free admission, with rides on a pay-as-you-go basis. Pay-one-price, under $15, includes waterpark. On Wednesday, Thursday, and Friday, the all-day pay-one-price is under $10, which includes all rides and water activities.

DelGrosso's Amusement Park

Route 220
Tipton, PA (814) 684-3538
www.delgrossos.com

This cool little park gets its name from the family that purchased the facility in 1946 as a place to manufacture their famous spaghetti sauce. While the sauce is now produced in its own factory, food still defines the park—from the

THE AMUSEMENT PARK GUIDE

Italian specialties made fresh at the park's sprawling kitchen to their famous potato salad.

The park dates back to 1907, when a carnival set up residence on what was then the Bland family farm. Today you'll find great food, fun rides, and immaculate midways.

The park's carousel is a beautiful 3-row machine dating from 1924, was built by the Herschell/Spillman Company, and comes complete with a beautiful-sounding Wurlitzer band organ. The Zyklon roller coaster is a perfect fit for the park and everyone, from thrill-seekers to first-time riders, will enjoy its collection of drops and turns. Be sure to take a ride on the Tipton Creek Railroad for a fun trip through the woods.

If the 30 kiddie and adult rides aren't enough for you, take a walk across the street for the water rides. WaterWorks has several slides and the Tipton Rapids is a fun interactive water play area.

 Season: Weekends in May and September; daily June through August. Rides closed Mondays; waterpark, golf, and speedway open every day.

 Operating hours: Noon to 9:00 P.M. Closed Mondays.

 Admission policy: Free admission with 2 different pricing packages to choose from, an all-day ride package or an all-day package that includes rides, water slides, and water playground; prices range from $9 to $13. Individual ride tickets are also available. Free parking.

 Top rides: Space Odyssey, an indoor caterpillar with a sound and light show; Scrambler; Sea Dragon; bumper cars; Paratrooper.

 Roller coaster: Zyklon, family (S).

 Plan to stay: 4 hours.

 Best way to avoid crowds: Tuesdays are the least crowded. Small crowds and beautiful weather prevail on weekends in spring and fall.

 Directions: Take exit 23 (Highway 220) off I–80. Follow Highway 220 south for 35 miles; the park is on the right, 3 miles south of Tyrone.

"Meteor," Dorney Park & Wild Water Kingdom, Allentown, Pennsylvania
Photo by Adam Sandy

Dorney Park & Wild Water Kingdom

3830 Dorney Park Road
Allentown, PA (610) 395-3724
www.dorneypark.com

Part tradition, part thrills, and part water, this park is all fun and is not your basic chain-owned park. This one has traditional park roots and many of them have been preserved.

Founded in 1884, the park is the fifth-oldest, continuously operated park in North America, and there are several rides here that you won't find in most corporate-owned parks. The Whip ride is one of the best in the country and a treat for those wanting to enjoy the rides of yesteryear. Another great old attraction is the Zephyr train ride, which is patterned after the Burlington train of the 1930s.

Just inside the entrance is the park's 1921 Dentzel carousel. The 4-row machine was moved from Dorney's sister park, Cedar Point, in 1995. There are lots of beautiful carvings on this menagerie machine including a deer, lion, and chariot that features an angel sounding a trumpet.

THE AMUSEMENT PARK GUIDE

There are twenty-first-century thrills here as well. Next to the carousel is the imposing Talon inverted steel roller coaster. The ride stands 135 feet tall and takes riders through 4 inversions over 3,110 feet of track before hitting the brakes. Another exciting attraction is the Meteor. Here riders are strapped in three abreast and as their feet dangle they are tossed head over heels 65 feet in the air. On hot days be sure to check out the Thunder Creek Mountain log flume. It uses the natural terrain to give riders a tour under the Hercules roller coaster before soaking them.

Wild Water Kingdom is included in the admission price and features more than 40 slides and activities. Rides like the new Patriot's Plunge, Jumpin' Jack Splash, the Aqua Blast raft ride, Torpedo Tubes speed slides, 2 action rivers, and a wave pool are sure to keep you wet and happy.

 Season: May through October.

 Operating hours: Opens at 10:00 A.M.; closing times vary.

 Admission policy: Pay-one-price, under $35, includes both the ride and waterpark. Special after-5:00 P.M. rates available; special junior rate, under $7.

 Top rides: Dominator, space shot/free-fall towers; Ferris wheel, set on a hillside providing a great view of the park; Wave Swinger, fast swing ride above the midway; White Water Landing, a wet splashdown ride; and the nostalgic Swan Boats.

 Roller coasters: Talon, inverted (S); Steel Force (S); Hercules (W); Thunderhawk (W); Lazer, 2-loop (S); Little Lazer, junior (S); Dragon, family (S); Wild Mouse, family (S); Woodstock Express, family (S).

 Plan to stay: 10 hours if you visit both parks.

 Best way to avoid crowds: Most people visit the ride park until noon, next go to the waterpark until around 5:00 P.M., and then go back to ride park until closing. To avoid the crowds, do the opposite.

 Directions: Take I–78 to exit 16 (Route 222/Hamilton Boulevard). Follow signs to park.

Dutch Wonderland

2249 Route 30 East
Lancaster, PA
(717) 291-1888/(866) 386-2839
www.dutchwonderland.com

There aren't too many parks in this country that are loved more by their local community than Dutch Wonderland. While the park's primary target is families with young children, parents and older kids alike find plenty of things to do and to ride in this eclectic and beautiful 44-acre park.

After passing through the Castle entrance you'll notice unique attributes like the Old Woman's Shoe, the Wishing Well, and the Gingerbread House. Be sure to partake of the gondola boat ride that takes you past the Eiffel Tower, a Japanese pagoda, and other famous international landmarks.

When your kids are old enough to have their first wooden coaster ride, the Sky Princess is the attraction to take them on. It has a fun layout that will bring them back with a smile on their face. The kiddie Ferris wheel is built to resemble a Dutch windmill.

Now owned by Hershey Entertainment Company, the same people who own nearby Hershey Park, the wonderland has 27 rides.

 Extras: The Wonder House is a fascinating attraction: You sit still while the whole room spins, making you feel like you're tumbling. Other extras, also included in admission, are a giant slide inside a barnyard silo and an opportunity to milk a make-believe cow. Don't miss the pretzels!

 Special events: Happy Hauntings, family Halloween activities, last three weekends in September.

 Season: Mid-April through October.

 Operating hours: Opens at 10:00 A.M., closing times vary from 6:00 to 8:00 P.M.

 Admission policy: Pay-one-price, under $24. Free parking. Buy a full-price ticket within 3 hours of closing and receive a free pass for the following day.

THE AMUSEMENT PARK GUIDE

 Top rides: VR Voyager, motion-based simulator; Flying Trapeze, flying swings; skyride, going from the front to the back of the park; Turnpike Ride, antique cars; Monorail, a trip around the park; Tug Boat Ride; River Boat Ride; the Ripcord, family parachute drop; Double Splash Flume, a log flume with 2 drops.

 Roller coasters: Sky Princess, junior (W); The Joust, family (S).

 Plan to stay: 3½ hours.

 Best way to avoid crowds: Come early in the week; take the sky ride to the back of the park and work your way forward.

 Directions: Located on Route 30, 4 miles east of Lancaster.

Hersheypark

100 West Hersheypark Drive
Hershey, PA
(717) 534–3900/(800) HERSHEY
www.hersheypark.com

It surprises many people that the park that chocolate money built doesn't have an actual chocolate theme to it, but in reality, the presence of the chocolate company pervades and gives such a theme to the entire city of Hershey.

The ambience created by wonderful old trees, a rolling terrain, mature landscaping, and plenty of shaded areas is the true theme here. There's also a lot of man-made fun. With more than 60 rides and attractions including 9 roller coasters, 7 water rides, and 22 rides just for the kids, this park has the largest collection of activities in the state.

Unique areas within the park include ZooAmerica, an 11-acre zoo, and Midway America, a re-creation of an old-time amusement park and country fair, complete with classic rides and 2 of the park's 3 wooden roller coasters.

Many consider the park's carousel, Philadelphia Toboggan Company #47, the most beautiful machine ever carved. Master carver John Zalar created the 4-row ride in 1919, and the horses are full of his personal touches, such as swords carved on the horses and sensitive looks on the animals' faces.

For a great view of all that the park has to offer, check out the 250-foot Kissing Tower. The unique double-armed Giant Wheel and the Ferris wheel also let visitors look out over the park. The Roller Soaker roller coaster is one of the few attractions in the country that combines water guns and a wet coaster experience.

TiM'S TRiViA

Hersheypark opened on April 24, 1907, as a recreational playground for Hershey chocolate factory workers and their families. In addition to building his factory in the area, Milton S. Hershey created an entire community that would be pleasant and fun not only for himself, but for his entire group of dedicated employees. The first ride in the park was a carousel added in time for a July 4 celebration in 1908.

 Extras: Chocolate World, located next to the park, presents a ride-through tour of how chocolate is made (free).

 Special events: Creatures of the Night at ZooAmerica, October; Hersheypark in the Dark, October; the Hersheypark Christmas Candylane, mid-November through December. Free admission for October through December events.

 Season: May through September; see also Special events.

 Operating hours: 10:00 A.M. to 10:00 P.M.

 Admission policy: Pay-one-price, under $36, includes admission to ZooAmerica. A 2-day and a 3-day ticket are also available. Special evening rates and a next-day-free plan are great ways to save money.

 Top rides: Claw Revolution; Frontier Flyers, flying scooters; Coal Cracker, a log flume; Flying Falcon, a spinning ride that takes guests above the trees; Canyon River Rapids, a raging-rapids ride; Starship America, a jet ride from the 1950s; Dry Gulch Railroad, a steam-powered train; Tidal Force, a shoot-the-chute ride; and the Giant Wheel, a 100-foot-tall Ferris wheel with gondola seating.

THE AMUSEMENT PARK GUIDE

 Roller coasters: Lightning Racer, twin racing (W); Great Bear, inverted (S); Roller Soaker, suspended with water features (S); Wild Mouse, family (S); Wildcat (W); Comet (W); Sidewinder, boomerang (S); Sooperdooperlooper, looping (S); Trailblazer, mine train (S).

 Plan to stay: 8 hours.

 Best way to avoid crowds: Mondays and Tuesdays are the slowest days during the season. Avoid weekends. The park opens a half-hour before the rides do; come early, stake your claim on your favorite ride, and go from there.

 Directions: Take exit 20 off the Pennsylvania Turnpike to Route 322. Follow Route 322 to Hershey and take Route 39 West to Hersheypark Drive; the park is on the right.

Idlewild Park & Soak Zone

Route 30
Ligonier, PA (724) 238–3666
www.idlewild.com

Few will disagree that this is one of the most beautiful traditional parks in America. Started more than 120 years ago as a stop on the Ligonier Valley Railroad, the 90-acre park is situated deep in the mountain woodlands of central Pennsylvania.

The 35 rides, including 12 just for the kids, are top-notch and represent a good mix of the old and the new. The park is divided into seven themed areas, including Soak Zone, a waterpark with 12 waterslides, a swimming pool, several water activities, and a play area for the kids. Kids can walk through their favorite storybook character's home in the Story Book section, and Jumpin Jungle is a participatory play area. All the kiddie rides are located in Raccoon Lagoon, and the traditional rides, foods, and games are located in Old Idlewild.

Extras: Miniature golf, paddleboats, pony rides, and electric boats, extra fee. Confusion Hill is a walk-through house of illusions.

Special events: Old Fashion Days, mid-July; Ligonier Highland Games, September (the Scottish games are sponsored by an outside group, not the park, but they are held here annually).

Season: Late May through Labor Day.

Operating hours: Gates open at 10:00 A.M. with closing time posted each day; closed non-holiday Mondays.

Admission policy: Pay-one-price, under $20, includes waterpark attractions. Free parking.

Top rides: Dizzy Lizzy's Four Quarters Saloon, an illusion ride; Tri-Star, cars spin while entire ride spins; Mister Rogers' Neighborhood, a one-of-a-kind trolley ride through the neighborhood of make-believe popularized by TV's late Fred Rogers; Rafters Run, a twin-tube water slide; a circa 1931 Philadelphia Toboggan Company carousel; Skooters, bumper cars; Caterpillar, with canvas top.

Roller coasters: Wild Mouse, family (S); Rollo Coaster (W).

Plan to stay: 8 hours.

Best way to avoid crowds: Come early afternoon on any weekday.

Directions: Take exit 7 (Irwin) off Pennsylvania Turnpike, go east on Route 30. The park is 50 miles from Pittsburgh, 60 from Altoona.

Kennywood

Route 837
West Mifflin, PA (412) 461–0500
www.kennywood.com

High on a bluff overlooking the Monongahela River, the 40-acre park is one of the best and most-loved traditional amusement parks in the country. You'd expect a great deal from a park that is listed as a National Historic Landmark, and Kennywood definitely fulfills any promise a designation of that sort implies.

There are 45 rides, including 6 roller coasters, 3 water rides, and 14 kiddie rides. Phantom's Revenge is a great hyper-coaster that utilizes the terrain along the river, and the Auto Race, a zippy little car ride, is the last of its kind in the world.

Noah's Ark is a classic dark walk-through, the Turtle is one of only three Tumble Bug rides still in existence in the world, and The Old Mill, the second-oldest ride in the park, is an old-fashioned tunnel of love dating back to 1901.

 Special events: Grand Victorian Festival, July 4 weekend; plus a dozen different ethnic and community days throughout the summer. The different nationalities come out, cook and sell food, have their own entertainment, and draw visitors from a three-state area.

 Season: Late April through September.

 Operating hours: 11:00 A.M. to 10:00 P.M.

 Admission policy: General admission fee, with rides on a pay-as-you-go basis. Pay-one-price also available, under $26. Free and paid parking.

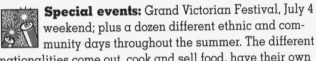 **Top rides:** Auto Race, circa 1930 car ride; Gold Rusher, a darkride; Pittsburg Plunge, shoot-the-chute; Skycoaster (extra fee); Pitt Fall, a 255-foot-tall free-fall ride, which from the top allows you to see downtown Pittsburgh; Log Jammer, a log flume; Raging Rapids, a raging-rapids ride; Turtle, the classic Tumble Bug ride; Old Mill, a circa 1901 ride-through tunnel of love in wooden boats; a circa 1926 Dentzel carousel with band organ.

 Roller coasters: The Exterminator, indoor wild mouse (S); Phantom's Revenge, hyper-coaster (S); Thunderbolt (W); Jack Rabbit (W); Racer (W); Lil' Phantom, junior (S).

 Plan to stay: 7 hours.

 Best way to avoid crowds: Come on weekdays in July and August. This is not a tourist park, so crowd patterns do not reflect tourist patterns.

It's wise to call ahead to learn when the major groups are booked, so that you can avoid those days.

 Directions: Take exit 9 (Swissvale) off I–376 (Penn–Lincoln Parkway). Go south, across the river, until the road dead-ends. Turn left onto Highway 837 and go about 1½ miles. The park is on your left; free parking is on your right. Located 8 miles from downtown Pittsburgh. Note: The park is famous for its big yellow arrows pointing the way.

Knoebels Amusement Resort

Route 487
Elysburg, PA
(570) 672–2572/(800) ITS4–FUN
www.knoebels.com

If you're looking for a true piece of Americana, you've found it here in the hills of east-central Pennsylvania. There is nothing like it anywhere. Knoebels is a traditional amusement park with all the nostalgia and comfort you'd expect at a 75-year-old rural park, but it also has some of the newest amusement rides and attractions in the market.

Although situated out in the middle of nowhere, the park offers 50 rides, including 2 world-class wooden roller coasters, the best traditional Haunted House in the country, a great picnic grounds, and the largest swimming pool in the state. A campground and rental cottages make this a true family resort.

 ## TiM'S TRiViA

In addition to having 2 antique carousels in operation in the park, Knoebels Amusement Resort has the Brass Ring Carousel Museum, featuring more than 20 antique horses, memorabilia, and a huge selection of carousel-related gift items. Open during park hours. (570) 672–2572.

Roaring Creek meanders through a pine forest that serves as a canopy over most of the park's rides. Just walking along the shaded walkways past the old, beautifully maintained buildings is a treat in itself.

The Amusement Park Guide

The new scenic Sky Ride takes you on a vertical climb of 354 feet up the side of the mountain. There are two antique carousels in operation, along with 5 working band organs. The Grand Carousel is a 4-row 1913 Kremers Karousel Works/Carmel machine, complete with a ring mechanism allowing guest to grab for that elusive brass ring. It has been in the park since 1941. The Kiddieland Carousel is a 1910 Stein & Goldstein 2-row portable carousel. It was operated by the family both in the park and on the fair circuit until it was sold in the early 1950s. In the mid-1970s, it was found, repurchased, restored, and put back into operation in time for the park's fiftieth anniversary season in 1976.

Various fan organizations have annually voted the food at Knoebels as the best amusement park food in North America. It's particularly known for the pizza and the french fries, but it also serves up a tempting dish of chicken and waffles, a regional favorite. The same groups of fans say "bring your pocketbook," because Knoebels has the best souvenirs of any park in North America.

 Extras: Anthracite Coal Museum; Brass Ring Carousel Museum, featuring more than 40 hand-carved figures; The Knoebels Museum, chronicling 75 years of park history, all free. Miniature golf, 4 water slides, a 900,000-gallon swimming pool with several slides, and a new kiddie participatory play area, all available for a fee.

 Special events: Covered Bridge Arts Festival and the Phoenix Phall Phunfest, both on the first weekend in October.

 Season: Late April through late September.

 Operating hours: 11:00 A.M. to 10:00 P.M. during peak season.

 Admission policy: Free gate, with rides and attractions on a pay-as-you-go basis. Pay-one-price available only during the week, under $28 (does not include the Haunted Mansion). After 5:00 P.M. ticket saves you $10. Free parking.

 Top rides: Power Surge, rotating ride with a 360-degree spin around 2 axes; Super Round-Up; Italian Trapeze, swing ride; Skloosh, a 50-foot-tall shoot-the-chute; 110-foot giant Ferris wheel, the tallest in the state; Haunted Mansion; 1001 Nacht; Scooter, bumper cars that still use original Lusse cars; a log flume; and Cosomotron, an indoor, all-dark ride on a Himalaya.

 Roller coasters: Twister (W); Phoenix (W); High Speed Thrill Coaster, junior (S); Whirlwind, split corkscrew (S).

 Plan to stay: 6 hours is the average, but if you plan to swim and eat here, add a couple of hours—you'll probably want to make it an all-day affair.

 Best way to avoid crowds: Tuesdays are the slowest, followed by other midweek days. Weekends are busiest, but because of the number of high-capacity rides, most lines move swiftly.

 Directions: Located on Highway 487 between Elysburg and Catawissa, in the east-central part of the state. Take exit 224 (Danville) off I–80 and head to Danville on Highway 54. Follow Highway 54 east through Danville to Elysburg, then 487 North to park.

Lakemont Park
Island Waterpark

Routes I–99 & 36
Altoona, PA
(814) 949-PARK/(800) 434-8006
www.lakemontparkfun.com

The circa 1902 Leap the Dips, the oldest operating roller coaster in the world, is this park's claim to fame. The ride was on the chopping block for several years but was restored and reopened for the 1999 season. The park, only a few years older than the coaster, opened in 1894. It now has more than 30 rides and attractions, including 5 roller coasters.

You'll find many classic American rides here like the Monster, the Twister, and Antique Cars. The Island Waterpark and Pirate's Cove kiddie play area are included in the admission price and offer ways to cool off during the hot summer afternoons. There are also 2 go-kart tracks, Traintown Miniature Golf, and Galactic Ice, the area's only indoor ice-skating rink.

 Roller coasters: Leap the Dips (W); Mad Mouse, family (S); Skyliner (W); Little Leaper, family (S); Toboggan, family (S).

Open May through mid-September, and then reopens from Thanksgiving weekend through the first week of January for Holiday Lights on the Lake promotion. Open daily 11:00 A.M. to 9:00 P.M., during peak season. Free admission and free parking, with rides on a pay-as-you-go basis. A pay-one-price ride and slide pass, good for everything but go-karts and miniature golf, under $10; after 5:00 P.M., under $8. The area's Double A Baseball team, Altoona Curve, plays in the stadium adjacent to the park.

Pocono Play Park

Route 6111
Bartonsville, PA (570) 620-0820
www.poconogokarts.com

Truly a family park with an eclectic offering! The site includes 8 amusement rides, 4 go-kart tracks, a climbing wall, a trampoline, miniature golf, a skate park, and several paintball galleries.

Among the kiddie rides are a pony cart and a Whip. A Scrambler offers some teen fun, and the Mangels kiddie coaster is a small family coaster that delivers more thrills than it appears it could!

Open weekends April through November, daily Memorial Day through Labor Day. Some sports activities are open year-round.

Sandcastle

1000 Sandcastle Drive
West Homestead, PA (412) 462-6666
www.sandcastlewaterpark.com

Sandcastle waterpark is two parks in one. Located along the banks of the Monongahela River in this Pittsburgh suburb, it's a fun family waterpark by day and the city's coolest hot spot on Friday and Saturday nights when it turns into a popular hangout for the over-21 crowd.

Among its offerings are 15 slides and flumes; a lazy river; Wet Willie's children's area, with slides and interactive activities; an adult activity pool; a wave pool; a large hot tub; a marina on the Monongahela River; food service; beach shop; sand volleyball courts; shuffleboard courts; and a 1,400-foot boardwalk overlooking the river. Miniature golf and a Formula 1 Speedway are available for an extra fee.

An all-day slide and pool pass sells for under $22. A 5-visit pass is $46. Open Memorial Day through Labor Day weekend, 11:00 A.M. to 7:00 P.M.

At 5:00 P.M. on Fridays and Saturdays, the park turns into an adult entertainment center for ages 21 and over. Several bars and clubs are open for dining, drinking, and dancing. The swimming pool, hot tubs, fire pits, and sand volleyball are open throughout the evening. There is a $4 charge. At 6:30 P.M. on Sunday nights, the park becomes an oldies dance club, with dancing and a pool party. That event runs to 10:30 P.M., and when live music is featured, admission is $10. When DJ's are in action, it's $6.

Sesame Place

New Oxford Road
Langhorne, PA (215) 752-7070
www.4adventure.com

Kids, and those of us who grew up with the Sesame Street gang, never seem to get enough of this place. That's because being here is almost like being on the "real" Sesame Street. The Sesame Neighborhood is great. It's a full-size replica of the TV show set and all our favorite costumed characters from the show hang out on the street most of the day. There's even a parade!

In addition, there are 40 outdoor play activities; 15 water activities, including Big Bird's Rambling River lazy river; and the Vapor Trail family roller coaster. Most of the activities are kid-powered, so count on a quiet ride home!

You'll definitely want to book a time for Breakfast and/or Dinner with Big Bird and Friends. Held throughout the season, these activities promise you a good meal and some one-on-one face time with the characters. There are many seasonal events here as well, including Elmo's Lowdown Hoedown and the Count's Halloween Spooktacular.

 Roller coaster: Vapor Trail, family (S).

The park is open May through October; hours are from 9:00 A.M. to 8:00 P.M. during the summer season (hours vary during the rest of the season). Tickets are under $37, and if it rains be sure to ask for the Sunny Day guarantee. Located on New Oxford Valley Road off U.S. Route 1 near Oxford Valley Mall, 7 miles southwest of Trenton and 20 miles northeast of downtown Philadelphia.

Twin Grove Park and Campground

Route 443
Pine Grove, PA (717) 865–4602
www.twingroveparkcampground.com

When Twin Grove Amusement Park closed in the 1980s, most people thought they had seen the last of this nostalgic roadside amusement stop. Fortunately, we all have been proven wrong.

A new ownership group purchased Twin Grove Park and launched a major renovation and expansion and expects to open in 2003. The revitalized amusement park will feature nearly a dozen rides, including a restored Airplane Swing; a Flying Scooter; a miniature train; and a merry-go-round. Other rides will be announced as the renovation reaches completion. The complex offers much more than a few rides. You'll also find a large KOA Campground, a brand-new swimming pool, an ice-cream parlor, and a restaurant.

The owners are also planning several other activities to turn Twin Grove Park into a year-round entertainment facility. Located 7 miles west of the town of Twin Grove, on Highway 443.

Waldameer Water World

Route 832/Peninsula Drive
Erie, PA (814) 838–3591
www.waldameer.com

Great shows, new rides, old rides, wet rides, water rides, and plenty of shade from great big mature trees. In a nutshell that pretty well sums up wonderful Waldameer.

Founded in 1896 as a trolley park, the park today has an amazing diversity of offerings for its size. There are 24 rides in the amusement park, including 8 just for the little ones, and 18 different slides, a giant hot tub, a kids' activity pool, and a lazy river in the waterpark.

 Extras: Pirates Cove is a walk-through fun house, one of two known walk-through attractions created by darkride genius Bill Tracey. The park's Tracey-created Whacky Shack is perennially named as darkride fans' favorite classic darkride.

 Season: Mother's Day through Labor Day.

 Operating hours: During peak season, the ride park is open from 1:00 to 10:00 P.M.; the waterpark, from 11:00 A.M. to 7:30 P.M. Both facilities closed Mondays.

 Admission policy: Free gate, with rides and attractions on a pay-as-you-go basis. Pay-one-price also available, good for all rides and attractions in both parks, under $20. Free parking and free use of the tubes in the waterpark.

 Top rides: Ali Baba, flying carpet; Frog Hopper, kiddie free fall; Thunder River, log flume; a 100-foot-tall gondola Ferris wheel; Sea Dragon; Wipeout; train ride, a scenic 15-minute ride; Whacky Shack, a 2-decker darkride; a carousel.

 Roller coasters: Comet, junior (W); Ravine Flyer 3, kiddie (S).

 Plan to stay: 4 hours if you only go on the rides; 7 hours if you also visit the waterpark.

 Directions: Take exit 5N off I–90 and go north on Route 832 for about 8 miles. The park is on the left, just before you enter the parkway to Presque Isle State Park.

Weona Park

Route 512
Pen Argyl, PA (610) 863–9249
www.pahs.org/OurTown/carousel.html

The circa 1900 Dentzel carousel is the centerpiece attraction in the 17-acre town park, which was created in 1920 by a local group that felt that Pen Argyl should have a park. Once a swimming pool, ball fields, bathhouse, and picnic grounds were built, a name for the park was needed. Hundreds of names were submitted, but it was Corienne Board who submitted the winning name, Weona Park, as in "we-own-a-park."

In 1923, enough money was raised to buy the used Dentzel carousel. It has 44 animals, all stationary, including 34 horses and 10 menagerie animals including goats, deer, and a zebra. It still runs every weekend, from Memorial Day through Labor Day. There is also a jeep ride for the kids and a Ferris wheel. Rides are open on weekends, on a pay-as-you-go-basis, with the rest of the park's amenities open daily.

Williams Grove Amusement Park & Speedway

Off Route 74 on Williams Grove Road
Mechanicsburg, PA (717) 697–8266
www.williamsgrovepark.com

Bright lights and screams of delight from teens riding thrill rides are but two of the many sensory stimulants you'll experience as you walk down the historic midway of this heavily wooded, traditional amusement park that has entertained hundreds of thousands since opening more than 135 years ago.

During late August each year, the park is home to the Grange Fair. Between 400 and 500 steam aficionados display their working steam engines of all sizes during the 9-day event. There is a daily steam parade, a 60-acre flea market, and live country music bands every night.

Among the nostalgia and the well-kept old buildings are 22 rides and attractions, including a Disco Star music ride, Twister, Musik Express, and a Monster. There are 9 kids' rides, most of which are located along the lake in the middle of the park. The 4-story-tall kiddie maze will keep the smaller ones busy for hours. In addition, there's a laser tag arena and a go-kart track and several live shows are performed daily.

You can bring in your own food and beverages and enjoy a nice, shaded picnic, or you can eat in the park's cafeteria or one of its fast-food and snack locations.

 Roller coasters: The Cyclone (W); Wildcat, family (S).

The Speedway is the nation's top-rated dirt track and is the host of several national races each season. The park is open from Memorial Day through Labor Day. Call for hours and days of operation and admission prices.

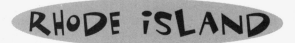

Enchanted Forest

Route 3
Hope Valley, RI (401) 539–7711
www.enchantedforest-ri.com

This neat little family park is as colorful as a children's storybook! In fact, it started out in 1970 with a storybook theme, and through the years it has been able to maintain the fantasy as well as the wonderful canopy of shade provided by the mature trees.

It's a great place to let your kids' imagination run wild as they explore various storybook exhibits such as the Three Little Pigs' house, the Little Red Schoolhouse, the home of the Old Woman Who Lived in a Shoe, and Quack-Quack's Pirate Ship.

In addition to the storybook features, the park has 11 kiddie and family rides, including airplanes, a merry-go-round, a Ferris wheel, bumper cars, a Tilt-A-Whirl, and a Scrambler. There's a kiddie roller coaster, batting cages, a miniature golf course, a go-kart track, and a petting zoo.

 Roller coaster: Roller coaster, kiddie (S).

Open May through September, 11:00 A.M. to 5:00 P.M. daily, with a pay-one-price admission, under $15. Located 30 miles south of Providence. Take exit 2 off I–95 to Route 3; follow signs to the park in Hope Valley.

TiM'S TRiViA

There are many antique carousels operating in Rhode Island. In addition to the ones already listed, here are three more:

- Crescent Park Carousel, East Providence: This circa 1895 Looff, originally built as a showcase for prospective buyers, is the largest and most elaborate of all Charles Looff's works. It has 62 hand-carved figures and 4 chariots. It's open Easter through mid-October, mostly on weekends. (401) 435–7518.

- Flying Horse Carousel, Watch Hill: In this circa 1884 model by Charles Dare, hand-carved wooden horses swing on chains freely. The 22 horses have leather saddles and horsehair manes and tails. One of the oldest operating carousels in the United States, it's open during summer months in a tourist area next to the bay. (401) 596–7761.

- Looff Carousel at Slater Memorial Park, Pawtucket: This circa 1895, restored machine has 48 horses and 2 chariots. Located in its own pavilion within the city park, it operates Easter through mid-October, mostly on weekends. (401) 728–0500.

Roger Williams Park
Elmwood Avenue at I–95
Providence, RI (401) 785–9450
www.rogerwilliamsparkzoo.com

Truly a Rhode Island landmark, this 435-acre city park near downtown Providence has been the center of family outings and family fun since the 1880s. There's a neat little zoo here, the Museum of Natural History, nicely kept gardens, and several historic structures, and with 105 acres of waterways with rowboats and paddleboats, there's plenty of physical activity if that's what you're looking for.

However, for the purpose of this book, the centerpiece of the park is Carousel Village, a laid-back little family amusement ride area. The 60-animal carousel in its own pavilion is a popular family ride, while outside under a canopy of trees are several kiddie rides, including a train and a dinosaur roundabout. There are also pony rides and the Boundless Playground, with Mr. Potato Head at the gate to greet you.

The park's trolley stops here and can be an easy link to the zoo, the museum, and the historic Victorian boathouse, where boats can be rented. Open spring through fall, daily at 11:00 A.M., with closing times varying with the season. The zoo opens at 9:00 A.M. daily year-round.

SOUTH CAROLINA

Broadway at the Beach

Between 21st & 29th Streets
Highway 17 Bypass
Myrtle Beach, SC (843) 444–3200
www.broadwayatthebeach.com

The contemporary Ripley's Aquarium, an IMAX theater, the NASCAR Speedpark, the NASCAR Cafe, Planet Hollywood, and more than 100 more retail stores, nightclubs, and restaurants can be found on this 350-acre complex, just 10 blocks from the beach.

This is where you'll find the entertainment after spending the day at the beach or on the golf course. The action is all built around a 23-acre lake.

There are 4 kiddie rides, paddleboats, a games arcade, and the Dragon's Lair miniature golf course, featuring a 28-foot-tall animatronic, fire-breathing dragon. All rides and attractions are on a pay-as-you-go basis. Open during store hours, year-round.

Family Kingdom Amusement Park & Water Park

3rd Avenue South
Myrtle Beach, SC (843) 626–3447
www.family-kingdom.com

Snuggled up against the Atlantic Ocean, along the popular Grand Strand, this park is home to both the state's tallest

Ferris wheel and the renowned Swamp Fox wooden roller coaster.

You'll find 30 rides here, including 16 for the little ones. The Great Pistolero Round-Up is a great interactive darkride for the entire family. An arcade provides some great video-game fun and a games-of-skill area is located along the midway.

 Roller coaster: Swamp Fox (W).

Admission is free, with rides on a pay-as-you-go basis. Pay-one-price available, under $20. Open daily, mid-April through September. Hours vary with season.

The Ocean Front Waterpark, located across the street from Family Kingdom, offers several fun water activities for the entire family. A joint admission pass can be purchased for both parks.

Grand Prix Family Thrill Park

**3900 Highway 17 South
North Myrtle Beach, SC (843) 272–7770
www.mbgrandprix.com**

People usually come to Myrtle Beach looking for some excitement and this park is ready to deliver. The Thrill Zone has 7 rides, the most popular of which is the spinning Crazy Mouse roller coaster. Be sure not to miss the Top Star Tour, a unique ride that turns riders head over heels in more ways than you can count. Other rides include a Tilt-A-Whirl, bumper cars, and a rock and roll–themed Music Express. There are 11 rides in the kids' zone, including a family steel coaster called the Wacky Worm, a small double-decker carousel, and the Jumping Jack children's free fall.

The Race Zone has 6 go-kart tracks, bumper boats, and a simulator. The go-kart tracks offer lots of different skill levels, from Junior Racers to the Formula Grand Prix EXP 1, which goes in excess of 50 mph.

The park is open March through September. It opens at 1:00 P.M., with closing times varying to as late as midnight. Free parking and admission and rides can be purchased on a pay-as-you-go or a pay-one-price (under $35) basis.

"Crazy Mouse, "Grand Prix Family Thrill Park, North Myrtle Beach, South Carolina   Photo by Adam Sandy

 Roller coasters: Crazy Mouse, spinning wild mouse, family (S); Wacky Worm, kiddie (S).

Myrtle Beach Pavilion and Amusement Park

Ocean & 9th Avenues
Myrtle Beach, SC (843) 448–6456
www.mbpavilion.com

Smack dab in the middle of the city's downtown area, this 11½-acre complex serves as the hub of a 5-block area of beachside entertainment attractions, shops, and restaurants. With more than 40 rides and a great wooden coaster, this is the largest seaside ride park south of New Jersey.

The park, in business since 1949, is intersected by Ocean Avenue. The pavilion, teenage club, arcade, go-kart tracks, boardwalk games, shops, and restaurants are located on the beach side of the avenue, while the amusement park, including its 40 rides, is located on the other.

 Extras: Two go-kart tracks, extra charge. The large arcade is open from 8:00 A.M. to 2:00 A.M. daily. The Pavilion has the Attic, an 1,800-seat auditorium that is regularly used as an alcohol-free teenage club. On occasion, name entertainment is booked in.

Season: March through October.

Operating hours: Rides are open from 1:00 P.M. to midnight. Boardwalk shops and attractions are open from 8:00 A.M. to 2:00 A.M.

Admission policy: Gate admission, with rides on a pay-as-you-go basis. Pay-one-price available, under $25. In exchange for $5 general admission, you get $5 worth of ride tickets. Parking charge.

Top rides: Chaos; Top Spin; Hydro Surge, rapids ride; Log Flume, 2 drops and a tunnel; a circa 1912 Herschell/Spillman carousel with 50 horses and animals; Haunted Inn, a darkride; Super Skooter, bumper cars; Siberian Sleigh Ride, a Himalaya; Scrambler; Caterpillar, with canvas top.

Roller coasters: Hurricane Category 5 (W); Mad Mouse, family (S); Little Eagle, junior (S).

Plan to stay: 3½ hours.

Best way to avoid crowds: Most people come here for the beaches and play at the park when they can't be at the shore. Therefore, daytime hours are the least crowded. Business picks up when the sun goes down or when the sky is overcast.

Directions: Take Route 17 to Myrtle Beach. Turn east on 8th Avenue and go 4 blocks to Ocean Avenue. The park is located between 8th and 9th Avenues, on Ocean Avenue.

Myrtle Waves Water Park

Highway 17 Bypass at 10th Avenue North
Myrtle Beach, SC (843) 448–1026
www.myrtlewaves.com

The speed slides coming off the Turbo Twisters tower here are considered the three largest tubular slides in the world. They are 10 stories tall!

Although those slides stand out from the rest because of their height (and the screams coming from them), the park has several other unique rides and slides, including the

Racing River. Located inside the Splash Zone area of the park, the river has a current of 10 mph, and riders hang on to floats as they speed around a figure-8 course.

The Night Flight is a black, fog-filled enclosed tube slide, and the Ocean in Motion is the wave pool. Tadpole is the children's activity area, and the Bubble Bay is a leisure pool, with bubbles and rain trees. In all, there are more than 30 rides and activities.

Open 10:00 A.M. to 6:00 P.M. during the peak summer season, the park is open from mid-May through mid-September. Located adjacent to Broadway at the Beach.

South of the Border Pedroland Park

I–95 at U.S. 301/501
Hamer, SC (843) 774-2411
www.pedroland.com

Serving as a pit stop for the weary traveler and an oasis for those in search of pure funk, this curious mix of Old Dixie and Old Mexico is roadside America at its finest! It's located about a mile south of the North Carolina/South Carolina border, and you'll see its numerous billboards long before you arrive. As you near, the giant Sombrero Tower will help guide the way. As you pull into the parking lot, a 97-foot-tall statue of Pedro, the first Mexican to work here, greets you.

Known for stocking one of the largest inventories of fireworks in the country, this spot also offers gas, clean restrooms, restaurants, a motel, campgrounds, Mexican souvenir shops, and Pedro's Pleasure Dome's indoor pool, bar, and Jacuzzi.

Pedroland Park has 11 rides operating year-round, weather permitting, including a wild mouse roller coaster, a Himalaya, bumper cars, a carousel, antique cars, a Ferris wheel, airplanes, and a train. Three arcades round out your playtime options.

Make sure you take a ride to the top of the 20-story-tall tower, where you can walk around the rim of the sombrero and take in the vast pine forests that surround this oasis. The complex is open 365 days a year. The locals call this place SOB, and everyone who works here, regardless of gender, race, creed, or color, is called Pedro.

Wild Water—Water & Race Theme Park

910 Highway 17 South
Surfside Beach, SC (843) 238-9453
www.wild-water.com

On the Grand Strand, just south of Myrtle Beach, this park features a wide array of water and play activities for the entire family, ranging from water speed slides to fast-paced go-karts.

Among the waterpark offerings are an adult lounge pool with bubble jets; an interactive children's play area with slides, crawls, and pools; the Wipeout wave pool; 3 tube slides; 4 mat slides; and 4 speed slides. The Head Rush is an amazing head-first toboggan mat slide. It's quite an experience going down a slide headfirst!

The lazy river meanders through a shipwreck and offers riders an opportunity to divert off into a unique wave channel. Live concerts take place on the stage adjacent to the wave pool.

In addition, there are 5 go-kart tracks, bumper boats, pirate-themed miniature golf, an arcade, and a food court. Open daily from Memorial Day to Labor Day, 10:00 A.M. to 7:00 P.M. Waterpark admission, under $25, with all other activities on a pay-as-you-go basis. A Slide and Ride pass is available and includes the waterpark and three additional rides or activities, under $30.

SOUTH DAKOTA

Flintstones Bedrock City

West Highway 16 & Highway 385
Custer, SD (605) 673-4079
www.flintstonesbedrockcity.com

"Hey Wilma, look here—I've found a nifty amusement park named after me!" Yes, that's Fred Flintstone, who you'll meet if you stop by this colorful little park. You'll also get a chance to meet Fred's neighbor, Barney Rubble.

Founded in 1966, the park replicates Bedrock, the Flintstones' hometown. Visitors can peek into the 20 Flintstone-style buildings or romp in the prehistoric playground.

A train ride takes guests around the park. Two old Volkswagens converted into Flintstone-style cars also give visitors a ride around the town. In the movie theater, you'll find a continuous showing of Flintstone cartoons; on the stage, an animated trio singing a happy song.

The food available at the Bedrock Drive-in—where Wilma and Betty work—includes Bronto Burgers, Dino Dogs, and Chick-a-Saurus sandwiches.

There's a 125-site campground and a Mountain Music live show each night. Open mid-May through Labor Day. Admission is pay-one-price, under $6. Hours vary; call first.

TENNESSEE

Dolly's Splash Country

1020 Dollywood Lane
Pigeon Forge, TN (865) 428-9488
www.dollysplashcountry.com

When this park opened in 2001, it broke many of the traditional rules of waterpark design. Instead of being set out in the open on a slab of concrete with few trees around, Dolly's Splash Country was tucked back into the woods. Instead of the typical waterpark tropical theme, designers utilized the area's rustic Smoky Mountain ambience. The park is located just a stone's throw from Dollywood and is set down in a holler (as they call valleys around here) and out of sight. First-time visitors are surprised when the woodsy oasis suddenly appears as they cross the entrance bridge.

You'll find the Mountain Twist in the new Raintree Hollow section of the park. It's a popular ride that utilizes the hilly terrain. Guests on the Mountain Scream choose from 4-drop or corkscrewing tunnel slides. Kids and families alike will enjoy themselves in the interactive Little Creek Falls water play area.

In total, there are 15 slides, 2 play areas, a lazy river, and a wave pool. Most of the attractions use the land's natural topography to provide the thrills.

Open mid-May through early September. Admission, under $28, is separate from Dollywood; however, Splash-n-Play tickets, which are good for 3 days and accepted at both parks, sell for under $60.

TiM'S TRiViA

So many people were traveling through the Smoky Mountains with their pets and stopping by Dollywood that park officials decided to build a new kennel to cater to the canine travelers. Doggywood, a $200,000, 1,600-square-foot kennel, opened in late 2002. The climate-controlled indoor dog care facility provides each dog a private kennel with its own water supply for $7 a day. More elaborate dog cottages are also available for $30 per day.

Dollywood

1020 Dollywood Lane
Pigeon Forge, TN (865) 428-9488
www.dollywood.com

Set back into the foothills of the Great Smoky Mountains, this park has a lot of unique attractions packed into its 100 acres. Country music superstar Dolly Parton grew up in this part of the state and many of her kin work in the park. She'll usually show up a couple or three times a summer.

Upon entering, you'll see one of the park's newest attractions, The Smoky Mountain Wilderness Adventure, a simulator ride that takes you on a whimsical aerial tour of the region.

While this is considered a large theme park, it's free from the hustle and bustle found at so many other larger parks. Instead you'll have the opportunity to meander through at a leisurely pace and take time out to enjoy the crafts, shows, and unique displays. There are lots of authentic mountain touches, such as a blacksmith creating his own wares, an old time schoolhouse, and a 2-room replica of Dolly's home. Unique attractions such as these set this park apart from the rest.

With more than 20 rides, Dollywood hasn't forgotten the thrill-seekers. The Tennessee Tornado steel roller coaster

"Daredevil Falls," Dollywood, Pigeon Forge, Tennessee
Photo by Adam Sandy

marks the back of the park. Like many of the attractions here, it utilizes the mountainside and dives down a 128-foot drop and through 3 inversions before returning riders to the station. The indoor Blazing Fury is part darkride and part roller coaster. You'll slowly roll through a burning town before splashing down into the grand finale. Children love the Dreamland Forest. From jumping fountains to large water guns to a room filled with 50,000 balls, the little ones can play all day here.

Don't forget to stop and eat between shows and rides. Dollywood has some of the best food you'll ever find in a park. The Hickory House BBQ is superb and Grannie Ogle's Ham 'n Beans is Southern cooking at its best.

 Extras: In the Eagle Mountain Sanctuary, you'll find the largest presentation of non-releasable bald eagles in the country.

 Special events: Festival of Nations, international festival, April; Harvest Celebration, October; Smoky Mountain Christmas, featuring 300,000 lights, Thanksgiving through New Year's Day.

Season: Early April through October. Reopens mid-November through December for its Christmas celebration.

The Amusement Park Guide

Operating hours: 9:00 A.M. to 6:00 or 9:00 P.M.

Admission policy: Pay-one-price, under $36. All rides and shows, except in Celebrity Theatre, are included. Parking charge.

Top rides: Daredevil Falls, shoot-the-chute; Smoky Mountain Rampage, a raging-rapids ride; Mountain Slidewinder, a fast, downhill toboggan run in a rubber boat; Dollywood Express, a 5-mile excursion up the mountain on a 110-ton, coal-fired steam train; Blazing Fury, a combination roller coaster, darkride, and water ride that takes riders through a burning town.

Roller coaster: Tennessee Tornado, multi-element (S).

Plan to stay: 5 hours.

Best way to avoid crowds: Come on Mondays, Thursdays, or Fridays.

Directions: Located 1 mile east of Highway 441 in Pigeon Forge, about 5 miles north of Gatlinburg. Turn at the Dollywood Information Center, located below the area's largest billboard and beside a 110-ton Dollywood Express locomotive.

Libertyland

Mid-South Fairgrounds
940 Early Maxwell Boulevard
Memphis, TN (901) 274–1776
www.libertyland.com

It's hard to find anything in Memphis that isn't connected in some way to Elvis Presley, and this 26-acre park has a strong claim to the King of Rock & Roll. Elvis would rent out the park for his entourage, and his daughter and her friends would come along to ride his favorite wooden roller coaster, the park's Zippin Pippin.

Opened on July 4, 1976, the nation's bicentennial, the park has a colonial feel to it. As you enter, one of the first things you'll see is a replication of the Liberty Bell and Independence Hall. You'll also discover a few pioneer cabins and an antique 1909 Dentzel carousel with 48 carved wooden horses, a rare ride because of its all-horse platform. It has been on the fairgrounds since 1923 and in the park since its opening in 1976.

In addition to 23 rides, the park has a great reputation for its live shows.

 Special events: July 4 Birthday Party; Libertyland Remembers Elvis, mid-August.

 Season: Mid-April through Labor Day.

 Operating hours: Opens at 10:00 A.M. or noon and closes at 8:00 P.M. Open daily from mid-June to mid-August. Closed Mondays and Tuesdays.

 Admission policy: An $8 general admission ticket includes all shows, kiddie rides, antique cars, the Grand Carousel, and the train. For an additional $10, you get all the thrill rides as well. There's a big discount after 5:00 P.M. Free rides and admission for anyone 55 years or older.

 Top rides: Rebellion, a free-fall tower; Casey's Cannonball, a 15-minute train ride around the park; Turnpike, antique cars; Wipe Out; Kamikaze; Sea Dragon; the Old Hickory Log Flume; and Surf City Slide, a double water slide on fiberglass sleds.

 Roller coasters: Zippin Pippin (W); Revolution, corkscrew/loop (S).

 Plan to stay: 4 hours.

 Best way to avoid crowds: Come Wednesday and plan your rides around the show schedule.

 Directions: Located 7 miles from downtown Memphis, on the fairgrounds. Take the Airways exit off I–240 to East Parkway. The park entrance is 2 miles north, between Central and Southern.

Nashville Shores Waterpark

4001 Bell Road
Hermitage, TN (615) 889-7050
www.nashvilleshores.com

With 385 acres of rolling, wooded land and more than 3 miles of shoreline on Percy Priest Lake, this place would be a fun day out even if it didn't have all those waterslides, a wave pool, an action/lazy river, and several great, fun play areas for the entire family.

White sandy beaches on this beautiful Army Corps of Engineers lake, only 10 miles east of downtown Nashville, help provide a fun lake experience, while all the slides and pools provide the waterpark action experience. Combined, it's a full day of eclectic watery fun.

In addition to the get-wet water activities, there is a miniature golf course and plenty of volleyball courts, horseshoe pits, and open areas to play and picnic. You can rent jet skis or a pontoon boat, or you can board the *Nashville Shoreliner* paddlewheel boat for a 45-minute excursion on the lake, free with a paid admission to the park.

Art students from local schools have added plenty of whimsy and color to the park. They came out and painted murals on just about anything that wasn't moving, including the fences and several patio floors.

There is a Halloween festival and a Christmas drive-through light show. The waterpark is open on weekends in May and September and daily during the summer. Gates open at 10:00 A.M., with closing times varying during the summer. Take the Old Hickory Boulevard exit (221 B) off I-40 and go south to Bell Road, then take a right and follow the signs.

Ober Gatlinburg
All Seasons Resort

1001 Parkway
Gatlinburg, TN (865) 436-5423
www.obergatlinburg.com

No matter when you're in Gatlinburg, there's always something going on at this wonderful, four seasons resort. Indoors, there are ice skating, a video arcade, a miniature golf course, a great fudge shop, a souvenir shop, several eateries, and more. Snow skiing dominates the outdoor activities during the winter.

In summer there's plenty to do as well, including go-karts, an Alpine slide, water slides, and a kiddieland with 4 rides and a play area. You'll also find a black bear habitat, an arts and crafts area, and various eateries.

A fun way to reach the top is via a tramway. It's located near Traffic Light No. 9. The tram carries 120 passengers more than 2 miles up the side of the mountain during the 10-minute journey. However, it's quite pricey at $8 a person for a round trip. You can drive up Ski Mountain Road to the top, and it's $2 per car for parking. Be careful, the road is a typical, curvy mountain road.

All attractions, including the tram and bungee jump, are on a pay-as-you-go basis. Hours vary according to the time of year and the weather. It's best to call ahead.

 # TiM'S TRiViA

Memphis has the largest Putt Putt in the world, but Gatlinburg, about two-thirds of the way across Tennessee, has the most interactive miniature golf course. Davy Crockett Mini-Golf opened in 2002 by Ripley's Entertainment. The woodland setting provides a "fort" atmosphere, while animatronic animals will talk to you and chide you if you miss a putt. Great fun at Traffic Light #1. (865) 430–8851.

Putt Putt Family Park

5484 Summer Avenue
Memphis, TN (901) 386–2992
www.puttputtmemphis.com

More than 40 acres of go-karts, miniature golf, driving ranges, and kiddie rides combine to make this the largest Putt Putt Family Park in the world. In operation since 1966, the park, with 3 courses containing 54 holes of miniature golf, has gained quite a reputation and is the site of several sanctioned tournaments each year.

In addition to the mini golf, there is a popular driving range, 3 kiddie rides, bumper boats, go-karts, batting cages, a large video and redemption arcade, a MaxFlight roller coaster simulator, and a 7,000-square-foot LaserTron arena.

Open daily year-round. Opens at 8:00 A.M.; closing times vary, between 11:00 P.M. and 1:00 A.M.

TEXAS

Downtown Aquarium

410 Bagby/ I-45 & Memorial Parkway
Houston, TX (713) 223–FISH
www.downtownaquarium.com

There is much more than fish here in the old Fire Station No. 1 building. What you'll find is an amazingly new and fresh approach to aquatic-oriented family entertainment and dining. Located in a 6-acre complex in downtown Houston, the $40 million facility is owned and operated by Landry's Restaurants.

The centerpiece of the property is a public aquarium with more than 200 species of fish in a variety of themed tanks. In addition, you'll be able to dine in boats as you watch vintage sea-based movie clips and TV programs at the cool Marina Matinee Cafe; enjoy a seafood meal in the highly themed Aquarium Restaurant; and enjoy a drink in the Dive Lounge.

The custom-created rides, all supplied by Chance Rides, include The Diving Bell Ferris Wheel, with diving bell–themed gondolas; a carousel with sea creatures on which to ride; The Periscope, a revolving observation tower that provides views of the downtown skyline; and perhaps one of the most interesting C.P. Huntington train rides of all time. The 10-minute train trek travels throughout the complex and into an acrylic tunnel through a 200,000-gallon shark tank. An audio presentation takes place as the train stops among the sharks.

In addition, there are 6 midway games and The Dancing Fountains area, where you can frolic in the cool water. Everything is priced individually, with rides costing approximately $2 each and entry into the aquarium in the $6 range. Open daily; call for hours.

Joyland Amusement Park

Mackenzie State Park
Lubbock, TX (806) 763–2719
www.joylandpark.com

Occupying its own 14-acre site within the Mackenzie State Park, Joyland has 30 rides and 60 years of tradition. This family-owned traditional park began its life in the late

1940s as the Mackenzie Park Playground. In 1973, the Dean family purchased it, changed its name, and began to expand it by adding more adult-oriented rides. Today the second generation of the Dean family and their families run the well-maintained, colorful local park.

 Season: Mid-March through mid-September.

 Operating hours: Opens at 7:00 P.M. during the week and 2:00 P.M. on weekends; closes nightly at 10:00 P.M.

 Admission policy: General admission, plus rides on a pay-as-you-go basis; pay-one-price also available, under $14. Free parking.

 Top rides: Wild River, log flume; Vortex, a water coaster; bumper cars; Rock-O-Plane; Roll-O-Plane; Musik Express, a sky ride; carousel; Paratrooper.

 Roller coasters: Mad Mouse, family (S); Galaxi, family (S); Little Coaster, kiddie (S).

 Plan to stay: 3 hours.

 Best way to avoid crowds: Tuesday nights are the least crowded.

 Directions: Take 4th Street exit off I–27 and enter the state park. Follow the signs to Joyland.

Kemah Boardwalk

Bradford & 2nd Street
Kemah, TX (281) 535–0201
www.kemahboardwalk.com

In the little seaside community of Kemah, Texas, about halfway between Houston and Galveston, the Landry Seafood Restaurants company has created a fun, and I might add delicious, complex overlooking Galveston Bay.

A boardwalk along the bay leads from the boutique hotel, past 7 Landry-owned restaurants, midway games, retail shops, and 4 amusement rides. The C. P. Huntington train winds itself through the complex, and a Pharaoh's Fury, a carousel, and a gondola Ferris wheel are located at one end. There's a 30-minute boat tour of the bay available as well.

Joe's Crab Shack, Landry's Seafood House, and the Aquarium restaurant are among the dining opportunities. Festivals and concerts are presented weekly, a dancing water fountain the kids can play in, and great food all add to the fun. Restaurants and shops are open daily, the rides on a weather-permitting basis.

Kiddie Park

3015 Broadway
San Antonio, TX (210) 824-4351
www.kiddiepark.com

A true piece of amusement park history rests at the edge of the sprawling Brackenridge City Park, 2 miles north of downtown. Established in 1925, this is America's oldest operating kiddieland, now serving its fourth generation of kids.

There are 9 rides, including the beautiful, hand-carved horses on the 1918 Herschell/Spillman carousel. The 1-acre park is situated under a shade canopy created by beautiful, mature elm trees.

The park operates daily, year-round, opening at 10:00 A.M. during the week and 11:00 A.M. on Sundays, with closing times during the summer at 10:00 P.M., earlier during the rest of the year. Admission is free, with rides on a pay-as-you-play basis. An all-you-can-ride wristband is available for $7.25. Adults can ride free with their children on the carousel.

The adjacent city park is a great deal of fun in itself. The San Antonio Zoo is there, as is the Brackenridge Eagle, a 2.5-mile train ride around the park. You'll find acres of walking trails and plenty of picnic areas, all at the head of the San Antonio River. For more information on the park, call (210) 734-7183.

 # TiM'S TRiViA

The Rainforest Café in Galveston is the first in the chain to build a ride within its wildlife-themed restaurant. The Lost River Ride is an 8-minute ride in a 5-person raft through the rain forests of the world, complete with animatronic animals, sounds, and waterfalls. Located at 5310 Seawall Boulevard. (409) 744-6000.

TiM'S TRiViA

EVERYONE IS GOING TO THE PARKS!
In 2002, nearly 320 million visits were registered at U.S. amusement parks and theme parks. Add another 62 million who went to waterparks. That's more visitation than to all the major league sports combined! Here, courtesy of *Amusement Business* magazine, which has been tracking the business to business side of the industry since 1894, is estimated attendance at the most-attended parks in 2002:

TOP TEN NORTH AMERICAN PARKS

- *The Magic Kingdom at Walt Disney World Resort, Lake Buena Vista, FL, 14,044,800*
- *Disneyland, Anaheim, CA, 12,720,500*
- *Epcot at Walt Disney World Resort, 8,289,200*
- *Disney-MGM Studios at Walt Disney World Resort, 8,031,360*
- *Disney's Animal Kingdom at Walt Disney World, 7,305,586*
- *Universal Studios at Universal Orlando, FL, 6,852,600*
- *Islands of Adventure at Universal Orlando, FL, 6,072,000*
- *Universal Studios Hollywood, Universal City, CA, 5,200,000*
- *SeaWorld Florida, Orlando, 5,000,000*
- *Disney's California Adventure, Anaheim, 4,700,000*

TOP FIVE U.S. WATERPARKS

- *Blizzard Beach at Walt Disney World Resort, Lake Buena Vista, FL, 1,723,000*
- *Typhoon Lagoon at Walt Disney World Resort, 1,556,640*
- *Wet 'n Wild, Orlando, FL, 1,246,440*
- *Schlitterbahn, New Braunfels, TX, 810,000*
- *Water Country USA, Williamsburg, VA, 700,000*

Sandy Lake Amusement Park

1800 Sandy Lake Road
Dallas, TX (972) 242-7449
www.sandylake.com

Talk about a neighborhood park! You'll find everyone here from the local church women's club to the local day care crowd. It's the local swimming hole as well as the local picnic grounds as well as the local amusement park. It's also the only outdoor amusement facility in Dallas County.

THE AMUSEMENT PARK GUIDE

With 96 acres, 20 rides, and a real "Texas-size" swimming pool, there is a great deal of room here to wander around, to picnic, and to rest under a big shade tree. There are a miniature golf course and paddleboats on the 2-acre lake. Each April and May, more than 1,200 school bands, choirs, and choral groups come to compete in FunFest. It's down-home Americana entertainment at its best!

 Season: Easter through mid-September, daily June through mid-August. Pool open Memorial Day through Labor Day.

 Operating hours: Daily, 10:00 A.M. to 5:00 or 6:00 P.M. (The park has never been open after dark.)

 Admission policy: General admission, plus rides. Free parking.

 Top rides: Fun House, a classic Pretzel dark-ride; a train ride around the park; Tilt-A-Whirl; Scrambler; Rock-O-Plane; bumper cars; and a Paratrooper.

 Roller coaster: Little Dipper, kiddie (S).

 Plan to stay: 3 hours.

 Best way to avoid crowds: Come on Sunday afternoons, when crowds tend to be moderate—just enough people to make things interesting, but not so many as to slow you down.

 Directions: 15 miles north of Dallas at exit 444 (Sandy Lake) off I–35.

 # TiM'S TRiViA

Sandy Lake Amusement Park hosts more than 50,000 Texas music students each spring during FunFest. From late March through late May, more than 1,500 bands, choirs, and orchestras travel to the park to take part in the competition. The concerts are free to park-goers.

Schlitterbahn Waterpark & Resort

**305 West Austin
New Braunfels, TX (830) 625-2351
www.schlitterbahn.com**

Not only is this North America's most attended seasonal waterpark, with more than 40 rides, the 65-acre park is the largest waterpark in the state and one of the most diverse in the world. It not only has rides, slides, and pools, it also has plenty of fun activities, restaurants, cottages, motel rooms, and condominiums. It's a true riverside family resort with a German feel.

Located along the banks of the spring-fed Comal River, known for its tubing activities, the park features more than 3 miles of inner-tubing adventures. There are 16 different tubing experiences, from single tubes to four-person tubes. Guests can experience natural rivers, lazy rivers, fast rivers, and torrential rivers, and one downhill tubing river is more than a quarter-mile long!

TiM'S TRiViA

What the owners are calling the first ever "line-less" waterpark opened in 2001 on South Padre Island, Texas. Schlitterbahn Beach Waterpark is owned by the same family that owns the original Schlitterbahn in New Braunfels, Texas. Much of the new park is interconnected by rivers, pools, and channels that transport guests to 12 different ride and slide elements. Riders partake of all this without ever getting out of the water or their tube. You go down one slide into a river, which transports you to another element, and they all link together. (956) 772-SURF, www.schlitterbahn.com.

In addition, there are body slides, a family wave pool, 3 uphill water coasters, 5 swimming pools, 5 hot tubs, and 7 children's water playgrounds. There are plenty of places to grab a bite, and plenty of places to sneak a rest under some big old trees.

The Blastenhoff area is where you'll find the extreme rides, there are plenty of small-fry activities in Kinderlund, the world's first surf machine is in Surfenburg, and the Das Lagune features plenty of family activities. The park is owned by the same family that owns NBGS, a top water ride manufacturer, and that means the park gets the "world's first" models of most of the company's newest slides and rides.

You can buy an all-day ticket (under $30), a half-day pass, or a 2-day pass, which is the best deal if you have the time. Stay around for 2 days—you'll be glad you did!

Open May through mid-September, from 10:00 A.M. to 8:00 P.M. You get a lot of free stuff with your admission ticket, including free parking, free inner tubes, free life vests, and free body boards. You are permitted to bring food and beverages into the park.

SeaWorld Adventure Park Lost Lagoon

10500 SeaWorld Drive
San Antonio, TX (210) 523–3611
www.seaworld.com

Shamu is a name we all know and love. But there are other names here at SeaWorld that we should be familiar with as well. How about Seamore and Clyde, the Steel Eel, the Rio Loco, The Great White, or R.L. Stine? Well, they are all part of the entertainment lineup here at the most diverse SeaWorld of them all.

SeaWorld San Antonio is four parks in one. It's a show park, a rides and slides park, a waterpark, and, at 250 acres, it's the world's largest marine life park.

This was the first SeaWorld park to add a roller coaster and it now has two of the thrill machines, including the tall, fast, and wonderful Steel Eel. *R.L. Stine's Haunted Lighthouse* is a multisensory family adventure. Starring Christopher Lloyd, among others, it's quite a unique horror presentation that the entire family can enjoy together.

The 5-acre Lost Lagoon waterpark is a perfect, cool, and wet supplement to the other attractions. Included in park admission, it's a great way to cool off after visiting the animals and watching shows for several hours. Among the waterpark attractions is the 3-story-tall Splash Attack interactive family fun house, complete with slides, climbs, and thousands of ways to get wet. Sky Tubin' is a 5-story-tall, 500-foot-long tube slide. In addition, there's a wave pool and Li'l Gators Lagoon activity pool for the kids.

Shamu's Happy Harbor is a 3-acre themed play area for the kids, with all sorts of wet and dry interactive elements.

Season: March through October.

Operating hours: 10:00 A.M. to 6:00, 8:00, or 10:00 P.M.

Admission policy: Pay-one-price, under $40. Parking charge.

Top rides: Texas Splashdown, a flume; the Rio Loco, a raging-rapids ride. There are several kiddie rides, including mini tea cups, a Ferris wheel, and a kiddie free fall.

Roller coasters: Steel Eel (S); The Great White, inverted (S). (This was the first SeaWorld park to add a roller coaster.)

Plan to stay: 7 hours.

Best way to avoid crowds: Come during the week, just before dinnertime.

Directions: Located 16 miles northwest of downtown San Antonio, off State Highway 151 between Loop 410 and Loop 1604, on SeaWorld Drive.

Six Flags AstroWorld
Six Flags WaterWorld

9001 Kirby Drive
Houston, TX (713) 799-1234
www.sixflags.com

Houston's premier entertainment complex, Six Flags Astro-World features 100 acres of fun activities. Among its offerings is an eclectic mix of 32 rides, including 10 coasters with more than 4 miles of twists and turns. You'll find several world-class concerts each season in the Southern Star Amphitheater; entertaining festivals; Broadway-style musical shows, and the action-packed WaterWorld, a waterpark that is now included with the price of admission.

The Amusement Park Guide

Little ones will love Looney Tunes Town, a cartoon city designed just for guests 48 inches tall and under.

Located across from the Reliant Park Stadium and the AstroDome, AstroWorld incorporated the waterpark into its one-price system in 2002 and is now a much better deal than ever. Not only do you get the rides and coasters, but also 15 acres of water rides, slides, and attractions, a lazy river, a 30,000-square-foot wave pool, and Hook's Lagoon, a multilevel treehouse interactive play area, all for one admission price.

 Special events: Christian Youth Days, April; Gospel Celebration, June; Un Dia Padre, June; Fourth of July Celebration, July; and Fright Fest, weekends in October.

 Season: March through October; WaterWorld open late April through early September.

 Operating hours: Opens daily at 10:00 A.M. Closings vary.

 Admission policy: Pay-one-price, under $40. Parking charge.

 Top rides: Diablo Falls, a spinning rapids ride; SWAT, sky swatter, a fast and tall swing thrill ride; Dungeon Drop, a themed free fall; Thunder River, the world's first white-water raging-rapids ride; Antique Taxis, antique cars; a circa 1895 Dentzel carousel; Tidal Wave, shoot-the-chute; Astroway, a cable-car ride 100 feet above the park.

 Roller coasters: Serial Thriller, inverted (S); Batman The Escape, stand-up (S); Mayan Mindbender, indoor (S); Greezed Lightnin', shuttle loop (S); Serpent, mini-mine train (S); Texas Cyclone (W); Viper, looping (S); XLR-8, suspended (S); Ultra Twister (S).

 Plan to stay: 8 hours.

 Best way to avoid crowds: Come during the week. The park is easy to get around in: Though spread out, it has a circular pattern. Take your time, see things as you go, and you won't have to double back.

 Directions: From the 610 South Loop take the Fannin exit. Guest parking is located across 610 from AstroWorld at Reliant Park. Head west on the

610 feeder road and the entrance will be on the right, just east of Kirby Drive.

Six Flags Fiesta Texas Armadillo Beach

I–10 and Loop 1604
San Antonio, TX (210) 697–5050
www.sixflags.com

Of all the parks in the country, this one was created in one of the most striking locations. The 200-acre park is situated in a once rattlesnake-infested abandoned stone quarry with dramatic 100-foot-tall limestone cliffs surrounding nearly three sides.

Developed in 1992 as a show park highlighting the music, culture, and history of this area of Texas, the park has grown into a great family thrill park that also has some great shows and entertainment. Since becoming a Six Flags park in 1996, Fiesta Texas has added more than 17 new rides and attractions, including Superman Krypton Coaster, the Southwest's only floorless coaster, and the wonderfully fun Scooby-Doo Ghostblasters—The Mystery of the Haunted Mansion, an interactive family darkride.

Armadillo Beach is free with park admission and is a most welcome oasis during hot afternoons, offering 20 water-based activities for the entire family. Included among its watery fun are a 1- million-gallon Texas-shaped wave pool, a 5-acre activity pool, and the Texas Treehouse, a 5-story interactive structure featuring more than 75 wet and wild water gadgets, slides, and climbs. The water dump bucket at the top of the structure is a 400-gallon cowboy hat.

 Extras: Each night during peak season, The Lone Star Spectacular laser and fireworks show is projected onto the quarry walls in the back of the park. Great sound, great visuals. You've never seen anything like this. Skycoaster and Climbing Wall, extra fee.

 Season: March through October.

 Operating hours: Opens at 10:00 A.M.; closes at varying times through the season.

THE AMUSEMENT PARK GUIDE

 Admission policy: Pay-one-price, under $40. Parking charge.

 Top rides: Scooby-Doo Ghostblasters—The Mystery of the Haunted Mansion, an interactive darkride; Frisbee; Scream, a 164-foot free fall; Bugs' White Water Rapids; The Gully Washer, raging rapids; Stop 39 Train, takes riders around park and through a tunnel in the cliffs; The Power Surge, shoot-the-chute; Motorama, a ride in 1950s-era gas-powered cars; Crow's Nest Ferris Wheel; The Wipeout.

 Roller coasters: Superman Krypton Coaster, floorless (S); Poltergeist, LIM-powered (S); Boomerang (S); Roadrunner Express, mine train (S); The Rattler (W); Der Rollschuhcoaster, family (S).

 Plan to stay: 8 to 10 hours.

 Best way to avoid crowds: Crowds generally tend to head to roller coasters first and to the waterpark during the hot afternoon. To avoid the long lines, do the opposite.

 Directions: Located 15 miles northwest of downtown San Antonio, off Anderson Loop 1604. Take the La Cantera exit (555) off I–10, then follow signs to the park.

Six Flags Hurricane Harbor

1800 East Lamar Boulevard
Arlington, TX (817) 265–3356
www.sixflags.com

Hurricane Harbor, which originally opened as Wet 'n Wild more than 20 years ago, is one of the world's first full-scale waterparks. Today, there are 32 major water rides, slides, and attractions in five different areas of this 52-acre oasis. There are more than 3 million cool, fresh gallons of water flowing down the slides and through three major pool areas and around the Lazy River.

Lagoona Beach, a 7-acre themed area, features Hook's Lagoon for the smaller set. This 3-story interactive water treehouse has slides, a rope crossing, and a giant bucket that drops thousands of gallons of water every 3 minutes.

This area also offers 4 sand volleyball courts and plenty of space to lay out and catch a few rays.

Picnics are allowed in the park, and there are a swim shop and a gift shop, just in case you forgot something. Open daily mid-May through mid-August. Hours vary with the season. Admission is under $30, and there is a parking fee.

Six Flags Over Texas

2201 Road to Six Flags
Arlington, TX (817) 640–8900
www.sixflags.com

This Texas legend has set the standards for all other regional parks throughout the world. As the mother ship of the fleet of Six Flags theme parks, it opened in 1961 as the first Six Flags facility and the first regional theme park in the world. It's a beautiful park, both by day and by night. The lush, natural landscaping offers a wonderful contrast to all the high-tech rides and attractions during the day, and at night, the color-ful lighting creates an energy-filled haven of fun.

The 212-acre park has 37 rides, including the new Superman Tower of Power free-fall ride, which the park claims to be the tallest free fall in the world. The themed areas here reflect the architecture, fun, and atmosphere of Texas culture. USA, Boomtown, Spain, Mexico, Gotham City, Tower, France, Texas, Old South, and Looney Tunes USA, a sprawling and colorful area for the kids, are some of the fun areas you can visit.

 Extras: Two of the original attractions are still in operation: the Casa Magnetica (a tilt house) fea-turing gravity illusions, and the Six Flags Railroad, taking visitors on a trip around the park. Climbing wall, go-karts, and Skycoaster, all for an addi-tional fee.

 Special events: Fright Fest, weekends in October; Holiday in the Park, Thanksgiving through New Year's Day.

 Season: March through October. Reopens for Holiday in the Park.

 Operating hours: Opens daily at 10:00 A.M.; closes at varying times all season long.

THE AMUSEMENT PARK GUIDE

"Titan," Six Flags Over Texas, Arlington, Texas
Photo by Tim O'Brien

 Admission policy: Pay-one-price, under $44. Kids, half price. Parking charge.

 Top rides: Superman Tower of Power, a free fall; Yosemite Sam and the Gold River Adventure, a boat ride through a cartoon; Log Flume, the very first of its kind in the world; La Salle's River Rapids, raging rapids; Splash Water, shoot-the-chute; Escape from Dino Island, a 3-D motion-based adventure; Texas Chute Out, 200-foot-tall parachute ride; Oil Derrick, an observation tower; Silver Star Carousel, a circa 1926 Dentzel carousel.

 Roller coasters: Titan, hypercoaster (S); Wile E. Coyote's Grand Canyon Blaster, family (S); Batman The Ride, inverted (S); Mr. Freeze, LIM shuttle (S); Runaway Mountain, indoor (S); Texas Giant (W); Flashback, boomerang (S); Shock Wave, 2-loop (S); Judge Roy Scream (W); Mine Train (S); Mini Mine Train (S); La Vibora, bobsleds (S).

 Plan to stay: 8 hours.

 Best way to avoid crowds: Come on Sundays in fall or spring, or come early in the day during midweek in peak season. Avoid Saturdays any time of the year if you want to stay out of crowds.

Directions: In Arlington, halfway between Dallas and Fort Worth, off I–30. Signs will give you fair warning that the exits to the park are approaching, and a huge electronic sign and the observation tower will mark the spot quite nicely.

Splashtown Waterpark

21300 I–45 North
Houston, TX (281) 355–3300
www.sixflags.com

There's plenty of action packed into this modern, well-kept waterpark, just minutes from downtown Houston in the community of Spring. A member of the Six Flags theme parks family, the park has more than 40 rides, slides, and attractions.

Water daredevils will love the 8-story-tall Texas Freefall speed slides, and Thunder Run inline tube slide could scare the toughest of us. The totally enclosed Space Rapids family raft ride is great fun, as is the amazing Big Spin, where you come shooting down and go into a funnel-shaped bowl; as you slow down and go lower in the bowl, you fall through the hole in the middle, just like a marble in a funnel! Tree House Island is a cool interactive playground, Crocodile Isle is a fun kids' area, and, with 500,000 gallons of water, the Wild Wave Pool is one of the state's largest.

Open weekends in April, May, late August, and September, and daily from late May through mid-August. Opens daily at 10:00 A.M., closing times vary from 6:00 to 11:00 P.M. Pay-one-price, under $28.

Western Playland

6900 Delta
El Paso, TX (915) 772–3953
www.westernplayland.com

As you ride slowly across the tops of the trees on the Sky Ride, look out over the river and you'll see Mexico. That's how close this park is to the border. Located in Ascarate

THE AMUSEMENT PARK GUIDE

County Park, the facility has 25 rides, including 10 just for the wee ones, on 16 acres.

With its Spanish motif, the park features an abundance of colorful gardens, shade trees, benches, and adobe buildings.

 Season: March through mid-October, Wednesdays through Sundays, June through mid-August, only.

 Operating hours: Opens at 6:30 P.M. during the week and at 2:00 or 3:00 P.M. weekends, depending on season. Closes nightly during peak season at 10:00 P.M.

 Admission policy: Pay-one-price, under $16. Also general admission, plus rides on a pay-as-you-go basis. Free parking.

 Top rides: Tsunami, shoot-the-chute; Frog Hopper, kiddie free fall; Pharaoh's Fury; Snake Mountain, a dry ride down a steep water slide; Splashdown, a log flume; a train ride, a 2½-mile trek around the park.

 Roller coaster: El Bandito, Zyklon, family (S).

 Plan to stay: 4 hours.

 Best way to avoid crowds: Come on weekday nights or Sunday afternoons.

 Directions: Take the Trobridge exit off I–10. Go left and proceed through three traffic lights, turning right onto Delta. The park is located about 1 mile after you cross over an overpass.

Wet 'n Wild Waterworld
Service Road, I–10 at Exit 0
Anthony (El Paso), TX (915) 886–2222
www.wetwild.com

It gets hot in El Paso, and the folks down here love their local waterpark. With more than 24 wet and wild rides and attractions spread out over 37 acres, there is virtually something for everyone. Hundreds of shade trees and some funky thatched huts offer plenty of shade. Centerpiece attractions include the Wild Island Waves, a wave pool; Volcano River, an inner-tube rapids ride; The Screamer, a 6-story-tall body slide; the Shotgun, a short slide with a long drop; Volcano Lake, an interactive play area for the kids; and The Amazon, a fast, dark, and sometimes scary slide.

There's a wide selection of games in the Volcano Arcade. (This park is not affiliated with the Wet'n Wild waterpark chain.)

Open daily, late May through Labor Day, at 10:00 a.m. or noon and closes at either 6:00 or 7:00 P.M. Admission price is under $18.

Wonderland Park

Highway 287 North
Amarillo, TX (806) 383-3344
www.wonderlandpark.com

The family that created all this in 1951 still owns and operates it! Right from the beginning, this park has been about one family providing fun and entertainment for all the families of Amarillo. Calling itself "Texas' Greatest Amusement Park," it must be doing a grand job.

Today, the third generation of the founders is welcoming the third generation of customers. Warm, family hospitality hasn't changed since 1951, but what has changed through the years has been the ride lineup. Big coaster and thrill rides today rule the midway.

There are 25 rides, including 6 just for the wee ones. There's a 19-hole miniature golf course and a nice-sized arcade with both traditional and high-tech games. Located in the city's largest greenbelt, Thompson Park, Wonderland has a flat, paved midway, with plenty of shade and benches.

 Season: Mid-March through Labor Day. Daily June through mid-August.

 Operating hours: Open weekdays 7:00 to 10:30 P.M., weekends 1:00 to 10:00 P.M.

THE AMUSEMENT PARK GUIDE

 Admission policy: General admission, plus rides, or a pay-one-price ticket is available for weeknights, under $12, and on weekends, under $18 (the looping coaster and the darkride are not included in the pay-one-price). Free parking.

 Top rides: Pipeline Plunge, a dry ride down a water chute; Pirate Ship; Rattlesnake River, a raging-rapids ride; Shoot-the-Chute; Fantastic Journey, darkride; Big Splash, a log flume.

 Roller coasters: Texas Tornado, 2-loop (S); Big Coaster, family (S); Cyclone, family (S).

 Plan to stay: 3 hours.

 Best way to avoid crowds: Come during June. Thursday evenings are the slowest times.

 Directions: Located in the Texas Panhandle. Take the 24th Street or River Road exit off Highway 287; the park is located inside Thompson Park and is easily visible from the road.

Zero Gravity Thrill Amusement Park

11131 Malibu Drive
Dallas, TX (972) I–DO–JUMP
www.gojump.com

Anyone with vertigo should stay away from this thrill zone! There are only 4 attractions here, but they are the best of their kind. Nothin' But Net is the latest in extreme rides. You are dropped 100 feet into a net, with nothing attached to you. It's a straight free fall and it's quite a rush! The Texas Blast-Off is a reverse bungee ride where riders are catapulted 150 feet into the air, from a standstill to 70 mph in 1.2 seconds.

In addition, there is a 110-foot-tall Skycoaster, and bungee jumping is from 7 stories up. The rides are all priced separately, but you can get a ticket for all 4 for about $100. Open Wednesday through Sunday, year-round.

UTAH

Lagoon Park
Lagoon A Beach

I-15 & Lagoon Drive
Farmington, UT
(801) 451-8000/(800) 748-5246
www.lagoonpark.com

When you visit any state's largest amusement facility, there is a level of expectation of excitement and thrills that you take along with you. Well, this place is going to not only meet those expectations, but will far exceed them. With 38 rides, there's plenty to keep everyone, from your 2-year-old to the teen thrill-seeker, happy.

In addition to the amusement park, there is Lagoon A Beach, a 6-acre waterpark with a full lineup of slides, rides, and pools, and the 15-acre Pioneer Village, which features crafts, foods, and architecture from the pre-1900 Utah frontier. Everything is included in the price of admission.

A historic carousel, built by the Herschell/Spillman Company near the turn of the twentieth century, has been in the park since 1906. It has 21 jumping and 2 standing, horses and a group of 22 menagerie animals. There are also 2 fun, family darkrides.

The X-Venture Zone has been created to feature the park's extreme rides, including go-karts; Skycoaster; Top Eliminator Dragster; and the Catapult, in which riders sit in an open capsule and are launched 200 feet into the air. There is an extra charge for all X-Venture activities.

 Extras: An 18-hole miniature golf course called Putt Around the Park, extra charge, that features miniature versions of amusement park attractions, including a roller-coaster hole.

 Season: April through October.

 Operating hours: Opens daily at 10:00 or 11:00 A.M. Closing times vary.

Admission policy: Pay-one-price, under $31; includes Pioneer Village, waterpark, and "dry" rides. Parking charge. Park discount coupons are easily found at sponsoring retail stores.

 Top rides: The Rocket, 200-foot-tall free fall; a 153-foot-tall gondola Ferris wheel; Rattlesnake Rapids, river rapids; Dracula's Castle, a dark-ride; Samurai, a twisting vertical thriller; Cliffhanger, a 360-degree flipping ride; Flying Carpet, a 360-degree swinging platform; Tidal Wave, a pendulum pirate ship; a train ride around the lagoon and through a small zoo.

 Roller coasters: Spider & The Fly, spinning coaster (S); Wild Mouse, family (S); Fire Dragon, 2-loop (S); Roller Coaster (W); Jet Star II, family (S); Puff, kiddie (S).

 Plan to stay: 8 hours.

 Best way to avoid crowds: Sunday and Monday are the slowest days of the week. Saturday is the busiest.

 Directions: Located off I–15, 17 miles north of Salt Lake City and 17 miles south of Ogden. Take the Lagoon Drive exit.

Raging Waters

1200 West 1700 South
Salt Lake City, UT (801) 972–3300
www.ragingwatersutah.com

Not quite as big (or salty) as the Great Salt Lake, but here's a crystal-clear alternative for getting wet in this famous city. With more than 22 water activities and a lot of fresh, cool water, this is a top-notch place for that hot summer afternoon.

The H2O Roller Coaster, a slide that resembles the action of a real roller coaster, is popular, as are the Acapulco Cliff Dive and Waimea body slides. There's plenty of water going over the Shotgun Falls slides, the lazy river is a fun journey, and there's always a lot of action in the wave pool. An adult hot tub is quite popular.

Two children's play areas, Dinosaur Beach and the WaterWorks, are filled with interactive and whimsical activities for the kids.

Open daily, Memorial Day weekend through Labor Day, 10:30 A.M. to 7:30 P.M. Free unlimited soft drinks throughout the day. Admission, under $18.

Utah Fun Dome
4998 South 360 West
Murray, UT (801) 265-FUNN
www.fundome.com

This is thrill convergence at its finest. Traditional rides are mixed with extreme rides, indoor attractions are mixed with outdoor thrills, and kiddie rides are mixed with heavy-duty teen and adult rides. The only thing missing here is waterpark rides.

It's a park with an attitude and is surely what the large family fun centers of the future will end up modeling themselves after. Three large glass towers mark the entrance to the 250,000-square-foot fun center. Inside there are 13 rides, including a family roller coaster, a Himalaya, a Tornado, a Sizzler, a motion-based ride simulator, a double-deck carousel, bumper cars, and a go-kart slick track.

Also indoors are a 3-D theater, a huge laser tag arena, a 30-lane bowling center, miniature golf, and a large arcade with redemption center. Outside there are 5 extreme ride attractions including a bungee jump and a reverse bungee. There's another miniature golf course outside.

Open daily year-round, but not all activities are open everyday. Call first to make sure what you want to do is in operation. There is free admission, with everything priced separately, or there are numerous money-saving combination packages available. Located 20 minutes south of downtown Salt Lake City.

 Roller coaster: Dragon Coaster, family (S).

VERMONT

Santa's Land

Route 5
Putney, VT
(802) 387–5550/(800) SANTA99
www.santasland.com

Kids and kids-at-heart will enjoy this Christmas-themed park nestled in the foothills of the Green Mountains. Tucked in among the quaint Alpine buildings is a family-friendly lineup of varied activities.

The park's main attraction is the train ride that puffs its way through Santa's tunnel. There are also a carousel, an iceberg-shaped giant slide, a petting zoo, a playground, and an animatronic show. The little ones won't want to miss a chance to meet Santa, Mrs. Claus, and the workshop elves in the rear of the park. Their house is open for all visitors, so the kids can make sure they get Santa's ear before Christmas.

The Igloo Pancake House is a great place to enjoy breakfast any time of day. It has pancakes, waffles, and delicious fresh maple syrup. Be sure to stop by the Candy Shop and pick up some fudge. The park has several shops with great gifts, so you can do your Christmas shopping early as the kids play.

Open from May through Christmas Eve; closed Thanksgiving day. Pay-one-price, under $15.

VIRGINIA

Busch Gardens, The Old Country

Route 60
Williamsburg, VA (757) 253–3350
www.4adventure.com

The folks at Busch Entertainment have done a masterful job of mixing authentic-looking sixteenth-century architecture

"Ireland," Busch Gardens, Williamsburg, Virginia
Photo by Tim O'Brien

with some of America's most breathtaking and high-tech thrill rides to create one of the most interesting and successful theme parks in the country.

TiM'S TRiViA

Known for its beauty, Busch Gardens Williamsburg was designed to complement the natural terrain of the magnificent countryside in which it is located. However naturally beautiful the area is, a bevy of Busch gardeners must help out a bit. The park's landscape features more than 150,000 annuals, 80,000 tulips, 6,000 mums, and 700 container gardens, not to mention thousands of trees and shrubs.

Each of the six Old World European hamlets looks as if it has been there for centuries. Ireland was added in 2001 and was the first new "land" created here since 1980. The Celtic area features the music, dance, architecture, shopping, and, of course, the free spirit of the Irish people. Grogan's Pub is the neighborhood bar where a pint of your favorite beer is always available. The Irish dance show in the Abbey Stone Theater is the best show in the park.

Extras: *R.L. Stine's Haunted Lighthouse,* a 4-D attraction, is a real hoot! It stars Christopher Lloyd and "Weird" Al Yankovic. A special "Shopper's Pass" is available if you want to enter the park only to shop in the stores.

THE AMUSEMENT PARK GUIDE

 Season: April through October.

 Operating hours: Opens at 10:00 A.M. daily, closing times vary from 6:00 to 11:00 P.M., depending on season.

 Admission policy: Pay-one-price, under $43. A 3-day ticket is good for unlimited use of Busch Gardens and its sister park, Water Country USA, under $67. Parking charge.

 Top rides: Escape from Pompeii, a themed, indoor-outdoor shoot-the-chute; The Land of the Dragons, an interactive children's play area with several kiddie rides and play elements; 3 different steam locomotives; Roman Rapids, a raging-rapids ride; a scenic boat cruise down the Rhine River; a 1919 Allan Herschell carousel.

 Roller coasters: Alpengeist, inverted (S); Apollo's Chariot, twister (S); Big Bad Wolf, suspended (S); Loch Ness Monster, 2-loop (S); Wilde Maus (S).

 Plan to stay: 10 hours.

 Best way to avoid crowds: Come in spring or fall, when crowds are fewer. During the season, midweek is best.

 Directions: Take I–64 east to exit 243A, which will lead you directly to the park.

Motor World—Your Place to Race

700 South Birdneck Road
Virginia Beach, VA (757) 422–6419
www.vbmotorworld.com

A complete makeover took place for this park in 2002, including a new name (it was formerly known as Virginia Beach Motor World). The new owners want to create a go-kart heaven, so they've removed 4 old tracks and most of the park's thrill rides and replaced them with 5 new go-kart tracks.

The park still has 3 kiddie rides, a Himalaya, bumper boats, 2 miniature golf courses, and an arcade. But the new emphasis is on go-karts, and the place now has more than 250 of them, with 14 different body styles! The 8 tracks include 2 kiddie tracks, 2 two-seater tracks, sprint cars, stock cars, and European bullet cars. The Road Racer Track features an extra-long ½-mile track with up to 40 cars racing at once. The new kiddie track allows young drivers as small as 36 inches tall to try their hand behind the wheel.

Now open year-round, weather permitting, the park operates from 10:00 A.M. to midnight during the summer season. There's no parking or admission charge, and ride tickets are sold individually for $1.00 or in discounted ticket books, with attractions requiring from 2 to 6 tickets.

TiM'S TRiViA

The world's first air-powered roller coaster opened at Paramount's Kings Dominion in Doswell, Virginia, for the 2001 season. The Hypersonic XLC accelerates riders from 0 to 80 mph in 1.8 seconds.

Paramount's Kings Dominion WaterWorks

Route 30
Doswell, VA (804) 876–5000
www.kingsdominion.com

The new millennium has certainly brought about a lot of new attractions here! In 2000 the park opened Pipeline Peak, a 4-slide waterpark attraction that lets guests drop down a 77-foot tower, and in 2001 it rolled out the world's first compressed air–launched coaster, the Hypersonic XLC, which blasts guests at 80 mph up a 165-foot tower. In 2002 it debuted the park's twelfth coaster, Ricochet, a "wild mouse" family coaster, and Meteor Attack, a motion simulator. In 2003, the park is set to introduce the Drop Zone Stunt Tower, a 305-foot tower drop ride, and the whimsical family ride SpongeBob SquarePants.

THE AMUSEMENT PARK GUIDE

For those looking for a tamer thrill, the park offers 39 non-coaster rides, including 20 that the young ones can ride.

The kids will love KidZville. It's a neat little family town where the entire family can ride and have fun together. It's also where the Hanna-Barbera characters, including Scooby Doo, Boo Boo, Huckleberry Hound, and George Jetson, hang out. Over in Nickelodeon Central, you'll find all the Nickelodeon stars, from Blue to the Rugrats.

WaterWorks is a 19-acre waterpark with a variety of water activities, including a huge wave pool, a 4-story water fun house, speed slides, tube slides, and a lazy river. Lil' Barefoot Beach and the Surf City Splash House feature an interactive playground for the entire family.

 Extras: The 6,500-seat Showplace Amphitheatre offers top-name entertainers on a regular basis throughout the season. There's a charge for these concerts in addition to park admission. The most wooden roller coasters and the most high-speed launch coasters of any park in North America can be found here.

 Season: End of March through mid-October.

 Operating hours: 10:30 A.M. to 8:00 or 10:00 P.M.

 Admission policy: Pay-one-price, under $42. Parking charge.

 Top rides: Drop Zone, free fall; SpongeBob SquarePants, 3-D simulator; Meteor Attack, motion simulator; White Water Canyon, a raging-rapids ride; Shenandoah, a log flume; Berserker, a 360-degree rotating pirate ship; Diamond Falls, shoot-the-chute; a 1917 Philadelphia Toboggan Company carousel.

 Roller coasters: Hypersonic XLC, air-launch (S); Volcano, the Blast Coaster, LIM inverted (S); Ricochet, wild mouse (S); Rebel Yell, twin racing (W); Scooby Doo Ghoster Coaster, junior (W); The Grizzly (W); Shockwave, stand-up (S); Anaconda, looping (S); Hurler (W); Flight of Fear, indoor (S); Avalanche Bobsled (S); Taxi Jam, junior (S).

 Plan to stay: 10 hours.

Best way to avoid crowds: Tuesday is the least busy day. Get there early and head to the major rides first.

 Directions: Located 20 miles north of Richmond. Take exit 98 (Doswell) off I–95; the park is right there.

Water Country USA

Route 199 & I–64
Williamsburg, VA
(757) 253–3350/(800) 343–SWIM
www.watercountryusa.com

Remember the Beach Boys, Jan & Dean, the Safaris? The 1950s and '60s surf-scene theming here may have you longing for those days all over again, that is, of course, if you were around back then! Everything from the music to the food is based on that era, and you can immerse yourself in them amidst a wonderful Virginia forest. And you know it's going to be done right because this park is owned by Busch Entertainment!

As the mid-Atlantic's largest themed waterpark, the facility features 35 water attractions and activities, including more than a dozen slides. The newest, a be-boppin' bobsled adventure known as Meltdown, provides up to four riders at a time a fast adventure down a twisting water chute. And be sure to ride Aquazoid, a special effects raft ride where four-person tubes zoom down dark tunnels and through water curtains while laser lights and sound effects add to the wild atmosphere. Rounding out the slide selection are Jet Scream, where quadruple flumes speed riders down 415 feet at 25 mph; Nitro Racer, a six-person racing slide; and Big Daddy Falls, a river-rafting adventure that zips riders through 670 feet of twists and turns.

Cow-A-Bunga and H_2O UFO are two large, interactive play areas for kids, featuring water slides, heated pools, waterfalls, gushing geysers, and water cannons, all fantastically themed.

The park is adjacent to Busch Gardens. Open May through early September at 10:00 A.M., closing times vary. A 1-day admission to the waterpark is under $30, and a 3-day combination pass with Busch Gardens sells for under $67.

THE AMUSEMENT PARK GUIDE

WASHINGTON

Enchanted Village
Wild Waves

36201 Enchanted Parkway South
Federal Way, WA (253) 661-8000
www.sixflags.com

Since becoming a Six Flags property in 2000, the park has received a dozen new rides and attractions and plenty of new amenities. As the Northwest's largest amusement facility and still growing, this waterpark/ride park offers up a diverse lineup of rides, slides, and coasters. TimberHawk, the park's first wooden coaster, was to be added in 2003.

Enchanted Village, built on the side of a hill overlooking the waterpark, is the amusement park, featuring 30 wooded acres of rides. Among the rides is Lumberjack Falls, a 50-foot-tall shoot-the-chute that opened late in 2002. Also on the ride list are the Timber Axe, a 360-degree high-velocity ride; Hang Glider, a circular swing where riders lay flat horizontal with the ground; Ring-of-Fire; Red Baron planes; and a Pirate Ship.

The nostalgic centerpiece of the rides is the 1906 Parker carousel. Known for their sweet-faced expressions, the 36

Enchanted Village Wild Waves, Federal Way, Washington
Photo by Tim O'Brien

jumping horses are lined up in 3 rows. The ride has been in this park since 1980.

Wild Waves is the largest waterpark in the state, with 9 water slides, a wave pool, a raging-river ride, and Hook's Lagoon, a play area full of ropes, slides, water cannons, and interactive water elements, including a dump bucket that promises to get everyone in the area cooled off.

 Roller coasters: TimberHawk (W); Klondike Gold Rusher, wild mouse (S); Wild Thing, looping corkscrew (S); Kiddie Coaster, kiddie (S).

Both parks open daily from late May through Labor Day at 11:00 A.M. In addition, the amusement park is open on weekends from mid-April through May and in September and October. Closing times vary with season. Pay-one-price for both parks, under $31.

Fun Forest

Seattle Center
370 Thomas Street
Seattle, WA (206) 728–1585
www.funforest.com

You know you're in Seattle when there's a Starbucks coffee shop in your favorite amusement park. Located under the famous Space Needle icon, this free-admission park was the fun zone for the 1962 World's Fair and is a part of the 20-acre Seattle Center, which also houses, among much more, the new Experience Music Project interactive music museum, the Seattle Children's Theater, the Children's Museum, and some great outdoor sculpture.

The park has 20 rides, 10 of which are for the kiddies. The wheel is in the shadow of the much taller Space Needle, and the fantastic purple reflective exterior of the Experience Music Project is the backdrop to the Wild River flume. There are midway games, fast-food outlets in an indoor food court, and the year-round pavilion houses a video arcade, a miniature golf course, a roller-coaster simulator, kiddie rides, bumper cars, and several food outlets.

 Extras: The Seattle Center is chock full of fun venues, fountains, gardens, theaters, and public performance venues. The monorail runs from the

Ferris Wheel and Space Needle, Fun Forest, Seattle, Washington   Photo by Tim O'Brien

Center to Westlake Mall in the downtown area of the city, just a few blocks from the active wharf activities.

 Special events: Bite of Seattle, a food fair, mid-July; Bumbershoot, a music festival with lots of arts and crafts, Labor Day weekend.

 Season: March through October.

Operating hours: Opens daily during summer at noon; closes at various times. Entertainment pavilion containing bumper cars, miniature golf, laser tag, games, and a MaxFlight rollercoaster simulator opens daily at 11:00 A.M. year-round.

Admission policy: Free gate, with rides and attractions on a pay-as-you-play basis. Pay-one-price available during the week only, under $21. Parking charge.

Top rides: Gondola Ferris wheel; Jet Spin; Wild River, a log flume; Orbitor; Inverter; Galleon, a swinging pirate ship; bumper cars; a carousel.

 Roller coaster: Windstorm, family (S); Roller Coaster, kiddie (S).

 Plan to stay: 4 hours.

 Best way to avoid crowds: The park gets very crowded during festivals and special events but is less busy during the early part of the week and during fall.

 Directions: Take exit 167 (Mercer Street) west off I–5, and continue for 1 mile. The park is located adjacent to the highly visible Space Needle.

Riverfront Park

507 North Howard Street
Spokane, WA (509) 625–6600
www.spokaneriverfrontpark.com

A beautiful 1909 Looff carousel has been operating here and entertaining the locals since 1975. It has 54 hand-carved jumping horses and 2 menagerie animals. The ring machine operates and riders can grab for the brass ring each time they ride; if you're really lucky you'll catch it on a day the 1907 Ruth & Sohn band organ is cranked up. Both the ride and the organ were completely restored in 1990.

Located downtown along the Spokane River, this 100-acre park was the site of the 1974 World's Fair. Beautifully land-scaped, the park now has an IMAX theater, miniature golf, and several amusement rides in addition to the carousel. Among the rides are a Spider, Sizzler, Crazy Cars, a Dragon family coaster, an SR-2 ride simulator, and a Ferris wheel.

 Roller coaster: Dragon, family (S).

Unfortunately, due to bridge construction over the river, the park's gondola ride over the spectacular Spokane Falls had to be closed down. It will reopen when the bridge is completed, sometime in late 2004 or early 2005.

THE AMUSEMENT PARK GUIDE

Admission to the grounds is free, and all attractions are on a pay-as-you-go basis. A pay-one-price ticket is available, which includes all attractions, including the IMAX theater and golf, under $16. Most attractions are open from March 1 through mid-October; however, the IMAX and carousel operate year-round. For specific times, call first.

WEST VIRGINIA

Camden Park

Route 60 West
Huntington, WV (304) 429–4321
www.camdenpark.com

Here's a perfect example of the many hometown parks that at one time dotted the country's landscape. Camden Park has been around since 1903 and has the classic midway with games, food, and a canopy of trees.

There are 23 attractions, including 8 for children. The park's classic Big Dipper roller coaster opened in 1958 and its original N.A.D. coaster trains are some of the most beautiful in the country. The Haunted House is a gravity-powered darkride featuring effects from the Pretzel Company and Bill Tracey. The park's Whip is another classic ride that should not be missed. With other unique attractions, such as 2000-year-old Indian burial ground, this 26-acre park packs a lot within its fences.

 Season: May through September.

 Operating hours: Weekdays, 11:00 A.M. to 10:00 P.M.; weekends, 11:00 A.M. to 10:00 P.M. Closed Mondays.

 Admission policy: Pay-one-price, under $15. Special rate on Fridays, after 6:00 P.M., for $6.

 Top rides: Kite Flyer; Bumper cars; Kiddie Whip; Hand Karts; carousel; West Virginia Logging Company, a log flume.

Roller coasters: Big Dipper (W); Lil' Dipper, junior (W); Thunderbolt Express, shuttle loop (S).

 Plan to stay: 6 hours.

 Best way to avoid crowds: Come on Tuesdays.

 Directions: Take exit 6 off I–64, go 300 yards, and turn left onto Highway 60 West. Go 3 miles to the park.

WISCONSIN

Bay Beach Amusement Park
1313 Bay Beach Road
Green Bay, WI (920) 391–3671

Unless there's an amusement park out there that gives away free rides, there aren't any less expensive than Bay Beach. Tickets here cost 20 cents each, with each ride taking 1 or 2 tickets.

That means you can take a ride on the Tilt-A-Whirl, Ferris wheel, Yo-Yo, Scat, bumper cars, giant slide, Scrambler, and 9 other rides for 40 cents or less. They don't come any cheaper than that! There's also a train that takes you on a journey around the park and along Green Bay. Parking is free, admission is free, and you get a great free view of the lake.

In addition to rides, this city-owned park offers a wading pool, softball diamonds, volleyball courts, and a wildlife sanctuary with a nature center, hiking trails, and educational programs. Didn't bring any athletic equipment? Ask the staff members and they'll lend you whatever you need.

The wildlife sanctuary is open year-round, but the rides only operate from May through September, from 10:00 A.M. daily. They close at either 6:00 or 9:00 P.M.

Take exit 187, Webster Avenue, off I–43 and head north for 1 block to Irwin Avenue. The park is on your right, next to Kastle Kart go-kart track and miniature golf.

Big Chief Kart & Coaster World

Highway 12
Wisconsin Dells, WI (608) 254-2490
www.bigchiefcarts.com

By far, this is one of the most aggressive and diverse fun centers ever created! With 17 themed go-kart tracks, 3 wooden roller coasters, batting cages, kiddie rides, and bumper boats, this place stands out from the rest here in the Dells, which is quite hard to do in this summer resort area.

 Roller coasters: Cyclops (W); Pegasus, junior (W); Zeus (W); Little Titans, family (S).

The Trojan Horse go-kart track is the coolest around! The all-wooden track, which reaches a 6-story elevation, goes through the belly of the giant all-wood horse, then down under the parking lot through a 500-foot tunnel. The Poseidon go-kart track takes you under water.

Kiddie Wonderland features 7 rides that parents can enjoy with the smaller members of the family. Among the rides is a steel roller coaster, a kid-friendly tower drop, Red Baron airplanes, and a Rio Grande train.

Admission is free and all rides are on a pay-as-you-go basis, with each ride taking one token. Pay-one-price available, under $33. Open May through October. Hours and days of operation vary, depending on season and weather.

Circle M Corral Family Fun Park

10295 Highway 70 West
Minocqua, WI (715) 356-4441
www.circlemcorral.com

Horses, boats, karts, and trains all serve as modes of fun at this family-owned and -operated Western-themed family fun center.

Attractions include a train ride through the scenic pines, go-karts, junior go-karts, bumper boats, junior bumper boats, miniature golf, a kiddie splash area, a water slide, batting cages, pony rides, and trail rides.

You can buy individual rides, different blocks of rides, or a ride on everything, including a trail ride, for $35. Open Memorial Day weekend through September. Hours vary; call first.

Extreme World

100 Wisconsin Dells Parkway
Wisconsin Dells, WI
(608) 254–4111/ (608) 254–7565
www.extremeworld.com

Great name for a park that offers only extreme thrills! Here, in one park, you'll find some of the best extreme experiences in the Midwest. In addition to bungee jumping, an ejection seat, a 100-foot-tall Skycoaster, go-karts, wall climbing, and alligator feeding (they had to have something for the little guys in the family), there is one tall, awesome ride called Terminal Velocity. You take an elevator to the top and are dumped off the platform, unattached, for a free fall into a soft net. It's a total free fall! It's quite an experience.

The park is open daily at 10:00 A.M., May through September, with closing times ranging from 5:00 P.M. to 1:00 A.M. Free admission, with all activities on a pay-as-you-go basis. Free Parking.

Little A-Merrick-A

Highway 19
Marshall, WI (608) 655–3181
www.littleamerricka.com

Named for its owner and founder, Lee Merrick, this fun park was built in 1991 to house and show off Merrick's collection of ⅛-scale trains, one of the largest such collections in the world.

It has grown into a full-scale amusement park, featuring 21 rides, including a monorail. The train ride is a 2½-mile journey around the park and through the countryside.

There are also a go-kart track, a railroad-themed miniature golf course, and the Haunted Shack attraction. The train collection consists of 5 steam engines, 4 diesel locomotives, and 25 cars.

 Roller coasters: Mad Mouse, family (S); Swiss Toboggan, family (S); Little Dipper, kiddie (S).

Open daily Memorial Day through Labor Day, noon to 6:00 P.M. Admission is free, with the option to buy individual ride tickets, or the all-day pay-one-price unlimited pass for approximately $13, which does not include go-karts or miniature golf. In October, ride the Pumpkin Train out to the patch to pick out a pumpkin. From Thanksgiving, ride the Christmas Tree Train out to the woods to get your tree. Call for times and prices.

Noah's Ark

1410 Wisconsin Dells Parkway/ Highway 12
Wisconsin Dells, WI
(608) 254–6351
www.noahsarkwaterpark.com

By the numbers, here's what's inside the park that bills itself as "America's Largest Waterpark." You'll find 2 wave pools, 2 endless rivers, 36 slides, 4 kiddie water play areas, a Go-Gator kiddie coaster, kiddie bumper boats, miniature golf, 12 restaurants, 5 shops, and 1 candy store that makes fresh fudge and caramel apples daily!

For 2003, a cool non-water-based ride was added: Noah's Incredible Adventure. Walk in, take an imaginary elevator ride, and then climb aboard a German-made mystery swing.

The twin sidewinder-style slides, known here as Sting Ray, are as much fun to watch as ride. What really sets this waterpark apart from the rest, however, is Flash Flood, a shoot-the-chute ride that's usually found only in the country's largest amusement parks.

Open daily, Memorial Day through Labor Day weekend, 9:00 A.M. to 8:00 P.M. A pay-one-price admission, good for all rides, slides, and activities, is available, under $37.

Riverview Park & Waterworld

Highway 12
Wisconsin Dells, WI (608) 254–2608
www.riverviewpark.com

It takes a lot for a major attraction to stand out from the rest in a resort area such as the Wisconsin Dells. There are hundreds of fun things to do and attractions to visit. But if there is such a thing as a one-stop thrill shop, something to amuse everyone in the family, this is it.

The park has 13 mechanical rides, 20-plus water activities, and nearly a dozen go-kart opportunities, or U-Drive 'Ems, as they call them here, all on 35 acres. Among the rides are bumper cars, a Tilt-A-Whirl, a Scrambler, a Ferris wheel, and a Himalaya.

 Roller coaster: The Galaxi, family (S).

Grand Prix racing, junior go-karts, and mini-Indy racing are all available, as are speed slides, tube slides, interactive play areas, a wave pool, and the Hurricane Water Coaster in Waterworld. If you get worn out running from one thing to another, stop by the Hydro-Spa and put some warm jet-streams on your muscles!

Open daily at 10:00 A.M., Memorial Day through Labor Day. Closing times vary. Waterworld closes earlier than does the amusement park. Free admission, with attractions on a pay-as-you-go basis. An unlimited "Ride, Slide & Drive" pass is available, under $19, and a waterpark-only pass is on sale, under $13. A money saving nighttime pass is also available, under $10.

Located near the boat docks on Highway 12, just south of Highway 13. Take exit 87 (Highway 13) off I–90/94 to Highway 12, and turn south.

CANADA

Canada, like the United States, has a varied selection of amusement parks. Some are big corporate parks, others are smaller family operations, but each has its own personality and its own following.

Operation- and attractionwise, Canadian parks don't differ much from U.S. parks. The goal is the same: to create an environment in which kids of all ages can have fun.

Following is a sampling of Canadian parks, by province, that will give you a good idea of what the country has to offer.

Note: All prices are in Canadian dollars.

ALBERTA

Calaway Park

Trans-Canada Highway at Springbank Road
Calgary, AB (403) 240–3822
www.calawaypark.com

The magnificent Canadian Rockies serve as a backdrop to western Canada's largest outdoor family amusement park. Founded in 1982 just 6 miles west of Calgary, this 60-acre park features 27 rides, including 12 just for the little ones. The name of the park comes from the fact the park is "away" from Calgary, thus "Calaway."

You'll also find a very neat Western-theme miniature golf course right in the middle of the park. Next to the mini-golf is the classic Eli Ferris wheel, located on a platform out in the small lake. Other attractions of note are the Shoot-the-Chute flume ride, the Ocean Motion pirate ship, the Haunted Mansion walk-through haunted house, and the several play areas set aside for the little kids.

The park has a lot of water in it, and in one area, trout fishing is offered.

Roller coasters: Corkscrew, 2-loop (S); Superjet, family (S).

There's plenty of good food at various locations, and there are several live stage shows and street entertainment daily. Opens in late May and runs through October. In July and August, it operates daily from 10:00 A.M. to 8:00 P.M. Weekend spring and fall hours vary.

A pay-one-price admission includes all rides and shows, under $23. A special family-of-four ticket is available for $60.

Galaxyland Amusement Park

8770 170th Street
Indoors at West Edmonton Mall
Edmonton, AB (780) 444–5300
www.galaxyland.com

Galaxyland is the "real" amusement park inside North America's largest indoor shopping mall, but the entire mall, with all of its entertainment and eating offerings, is virtually one big, wonderful, fun, and amusing complex.

 TiM'S TRiViA

You certainly won't go hungry while visiting Galaxyland Amusement Park or the World Water Park inside the West Edmonton Mall. There are more than 110 eating establishments inside the mall. Also, there's no need to go home if you get tired. Fantasyland Hotel is a 355-room establishment inside the mall. It features 118 themed suites where you can sleep in an igloo, in the back of a pick-up truck, in Polynesia, or in Africa.

The 9-acre Galaxyland has 22 rides and several attractions, including the Haunted House and the Galaxy Kid's Playpark soft-play area. Among the rides is The Mindbender, a 14-story-tall, triple-looping roller coaster. Other rides of note are the Space Shot free-fall tower and the perilous Pendulum Swinging Ship.

Nearby in the mall are other attractions, such as World Water Park; Professor Wem's Adventure Golf Course; Deep Sea Adventure, featuring 4 sea-worthy submarines; Ice

Palace, a regulation-size ice-skating rink; Dolphin Lagoon, a dolphin show; and Blue Thunder Bungee.

 Roller coasters: Mindbender, 3-loop (S); Auto Sled, family (S); Dragon Wagon, family (S).

Admission to the park is free, with rides on a pay-as-you-go basis, or a pay-one-price ticket is available, under $31. An all-day family pass for four is available for $70. The hours are basically the same as those in the mall. Free parking.

Heritage Park

1900 Heritage Drive SW
Calgary, AB (403) 268–8500
www.heritagepark.ca

The past unfolds here at Canada's largest historical village. The 66-acre park features more than 150 exhibits, including homes and buildings representing western Canada prior to 1914.

In keeping with the nostalgia theme here, the park has an area it calls the Antique Midway, which features several classic amusement rides, including a Ferris wheel, a Whip, a Caterpillar, a swing ride, and a circa 1904 Herschell/ Spillman carousel. The 3-row portable carousel has 36 jumpers and 4 chariots and has been here since 1969. In addition, there is a steam train ride that circles the park and a stern-wheeler boat ride that plies the waters of the reservoir. The kids will love the cute little Baby Eli Ferris wheel.

Open daily mid-May through early September, 9:00 A.M. to 5:00 P.M., and on weekends in spring and fall. Pay-one-price admission, which covers everything, is under $22.

World Water Park

8770 170th Street
Indoors at West Edmonton Mall
Edmonton, AB (780) 444–5300
www.westedmontonmall.com/entertainment/
waterpark.shtml

There's a 5-acre tropical water wonderland inside the world's largest entertainment and shopping mall. You've got to see it to believe it! The waterpark has more than 20 water activities, including speed slides, tube slides, and a great family interactive play area known as Little Caribbean. The Blue Thunder Bungee Jump is here as well. The Tropical Typhoon is a new bowl-style body slide that is quite a thriller.

The park is huge and it looks even bigger under glass. Spread out over an area equivalent to five professional football fields, the park offers a large wave pool, a lazy river, and hot tubs. For sun worshipers, the large glass dome over the wave pool allows sunbathing along the beach, without the outdoor heat, bugs, or humidity. Snowing outside, who cares?

Park opening ranges from 10:00 A.M. to noon, and closing is from 6:00 to 9:00 P.M., depending on the day of the week. Admission is under $32 for unlimited use. Come in during the last 3 hours of operation and get a nice discount, under $20.

All Fun Recreation Park

2207 Millstream Road (Off Highway 1)
Victoria, BC (250) 474–3184
www.allfun.bc.ca

The name pretty well sums it up. There's plenty of action and lots of family fun here, including 16 water slides, an 80-person hot tub, miniature golf, batting cages, 2 go-kart tracks, beach volleyball, a driving range, and Western Speedway, an oval stockcar racing track. Vancouver Island's largest swap meet is held here every Sunday morning, March through October.

The waterpark, with slides for all members of the family, is open mid-June through August, from 11:00 A.M. to 7:00 P.M. Admission to the slides is with either a full-day pass or an afternoon pass, good from 3:00 P.M. to closing time. An "observers" pass is also good for the hot tub and beach volleyball courts. The rest of the facility is open April through September.

Burnaby Village Museum

6501 Deer Lake Avenue
Burnaby, BC (604) 293-6501
www.city.burnaby.bc.ca

This living history museum features life as it was in the area in 1925, complete with costumed guides, replica architecture, and authentic events. However, the real star here is the circa 1912 C. W. Parker carousel. It's Number 119 out of the Parker camp and is a 3-row, portable unit with 36 jumpers, 4 standers, and 1 wheelchair-accessible chariot. Music is provided by a circa 1925 Wurlitzer band organ. It was restored and moved here in 1993 after spending 32 years at the nearby Playland Park. Open May through September, and again in December for the holidays. Located 20 minutes from downtown Vancouver.

Dusty's DinoTown

53480 Bridal Falls Road
Rosedale, BC (604) 794-7410

You'll think you've walked back 2,000 years when you enter the front gates of this wonderful little children's park, just east of Vancouver.

The 11-acre park specializes in "people-powered" rides, including paddleboats, pedal cars, and hand-powered bumper cars. Other features include a children's playground, complete with treehouse; a dinosaur park, where little ones can climb on big statues; miniature golf; a "liquid playground"; and a cartoon train ride around the prehistoric city.

A live music and dance show, featuring Dusty Bones and the Bones Family, takes place several times each day. And when they aren't performing, the characters roam the park.

There are several walk-up food stands, and management encourages families to bring their own lunches and make a day of it. The park has a number of nice picnic areas where barbecue grills are permitted.

Open from Mother's Day through September, 10:00 A.M. to 5:00 or 7:00 P.M. Admission is pay-one-price, under $15, and parking is free.

Playland Family Fun Park

East Hastings Street
In Exhibition Park
Vancouver, BC (604) 255–5161
www.pne.bc.ca/playland

There are plenty of family thrills waiting for you just 6 miles from downtown Vancouver. Here's where you'll find the largest collection of amusement rides in British Columbia. The 30 rides, including 11 for the kids, become the cornerstone of Canada's largest fair, the Pacific National Exhibition, in late August each year.

The rest of the year, the park is open with great thrills for the entire family. Among its top rides are the Drop Zone Skycoaster; the Hellevator free fall; and the Revelation, where you sit on one end of a 160-foot-long arm, someone sits at the other end, and you start spinning like a high-speed propeller!

In addition to those thrillers, there is a good selection of standard park attractions, including the Wild Wasserbahn log flume, a Ferris wheel, and a well-supervised kiddieland with more than a dozen attractions. There's miniature golf, batting cages, and a climbing wall.

 Roller coasters: Wild Mouse, family (S); Roller Coaster (W); Corkscrew (S).

The park is open from Easter Sunday through first week of October. Pay-one-price available, $21, but does not include Drop Zone Skycoaster or the Revelation. Hours vary; call first.

Splashdown Park

4799 Nulelum Way
Tsawwassen, BC (604) 943–2251
www.splashdownpark.ca

A 10,000-gallon, 100-degree hot tub awaits you if the weather seems too chilly to partake of all the other activities here at greater Vancouver's largest outdoor water facility. The centerpiece of the 7-acre park is a tall mountain from which 6 body slides, ranging from tame to wild, and a 320-foot-long tube slide descend. Off in the corner of the park are 2 enclosed tube slides for those 48 inches and taller, and adjacent to that is a kids' splash area with various pee-wee activities, including 5 slides.

The park opens the last weekend of May and runs through August daily, with weekend operation in September. Ticket prices are based on all-day usage or twilight usage, which goes into effect 4 hours before closing time, which varies between 4:00 and 7:00 P.M. Park opens daily at 10:00 A.M.

Stanley Park

Downtown Vancouver (604) 257–8400
www.seestanleypark.com

This city-owned public park near downtown is a haven for fun-seeking families. The 1,000-acre facility houses, among other attractions, the Vancouver Aquarium, several beaches, a waterpark, an adventure playground for the kids, a totem pole park, a petting zoo, and a mile-long scenic train ride through the forest. The railroad has 2 C. P. Huntington locomotives and a locally built replica of the first locomotive to enter Vancouver. The use of the 3 locomotives is rotated during the summer months, and all 3 are used during the popular Ghost Train at Halloween event and the Christmas Train during the Christmas holidays.

Park entrance is free, with each of the attractions charging nominal fees. Park is open year-round with attractions open on a seasonal basis.

NEW BRUNSWICK

Crystal Palace

499 Paul Street
Dieppe, NB (506) 859–4386
www.crystalpalace.ca

Tucked in among an 8-screen cinema, McGinnis Landing restaurant, a 120-room Ramada Inn, and a Starbucks, this indoor/outdoor park offers 6 indoor mechanical rides and an outdoor area with go-karts and several additional rides.

The 1.3-acre indoor area lies under a high glass dome and includes a Wave Swinger, Krazy Cars, a Red Baron, a carousel, a Rio Grande train, and the Bullet family coaster. Also indoors is a 1,500-square-foot Lazer Runner Battle Arena, a large video-game and games-of-skill arcade, and a miniature golf course.

Outdoors, the ride lineup changes a bit each year, but you'll usually find a Ferris wheel, a swinging ship, bumper boats, and go-karts in operation.

 Roller coaster: Bullet, family (S).

Open daily, year-round. Admission is free, with rides on a pay-as-you-go basis, a pay-one-price bracelet, or a 4-month season pass. Free parking in mall lot; a shuttle bus operates between Crystal Palace and the main entrance of the mall.

NOVA SCOTIA

Atlantic Playland

Lucasville Road
Halifax, NS (902) 865–1025
www.playland.ns.ca

There's a plate full of activities here, from miniature golf to water slides to a ride on a Ferris wheel. The waterpark slides are the tallest around; the arcade, with a large redemption center, has more things to play and do than anywhere else in Nova Scotia; and the wax museum offers a great view of the Last Supper.

The 8 rides include a Ferris wheel, a Tilt-A-Whirl, bumper cars, and a small kiddie roller coaster. There are batting cages, bumper boats, go-karts, miniature golf, and a funky gravity house attraction.

 Roller coaster: Rockin' Roller Coaster, kiddie (S).

Open daily, 10:00 A.M. to 8:00 or 10:00 P.M., from Victoria Day weekend to Labor Day, and weekends in the fall. Everything

THE AMUSEMENT PARK GUIDE

is priced separately, but an all-day pass, under $20, is inclusive of most attractions for at least one ride or activity. Located on Lucasville Road, between Hammonds Plains Road and Highway 101.

Upper Clements Amusement Park

Old #1 Highway
Upper Clements, NS (902) 532–7557
www.upperclementspark.com

Huge trees, beautiful grounds, and rustic buildings serve as a backdrop to an amazingly unique entertainment complex way up here in a wooded, rural area of the province.

Although the park first opened in 1989, its rustic beauty and maturity make it appear that it has been here for years. There are rides, daily shows, weekly themed festivals with live music, indoor and outdoor miniature golf courses, a great artisans' village featuring local arts and crafts, and some fabulous eating at the full-service restaurants that serve up full menus, from salmon to steak.

There are 11 rides, including the Sissiboo Sizzler, a flume ride; antique cars; carousel; Fundy Splash Water Slide; The Tree Topper, a wooden roller coaster; and a train excursion. There are several kiddie rides as well. The outdoor miniature golf course is on a Nova Scotia–shaped island in the park's lake, giving you a chance to putt around the province!

In addition to the rides and other activities, the park is considered the largest live-entertainment venue in summertime Nova Scotia. Approximately 150 acts appear each season, most performing traditional Nova Scotian music. In addition, there are magicians, storytellers, and a few Canadian pop artists.

 Roller coaster: The Tree Topper (W).

General admission is $6 and permits a guest to listen to the shows and enjoy the park. If you want to ride, a $12 pay-one-price ride pass is available. The park closes at dusk every night during its peak summer period.

ONTARIO

Centreville

Centre Island
Toronto, ONT (416) 625–2351
www.centreisland.ca

The first ride you'll need to take when you visit this unique family facility is a ferry ride out to Centre Island. Hop on, and before you know it you'll be stepping onto a 640-acre island, which has been turned into a beautiful, lush city park.

Near the ferry dock is the 14-acre amusement park, which was designed to resemble a turn-of-the-twentieth-century Ontario village. There are 21 family rides, including antique cars, a log flume, a Scrambler, bumper cars, and a train ride around the park. A circa 1900 Dentzel carousel is in operation, featuring 16 jumpers, 10 standers, a wonderful menagerie of 21 animals, and 2 chariots. The ride began its life at Bushkill Park, Easton, Pennsylvania, and was brought here in 1965.

 Roller coaster: Toronto Island Monster, family (S).

The 7 food stands in the park serve a variety of foods, from steaks to fried chicken to hot dogs. Make sure, too, to stop by the fabulous O. Bumble ice-cream parlor for a wonderful ice-cream treat. Island Paradise and the Carousel Cafe are two full-service family restaurants.

There are many other activities on the island that you may wish to partake of while visiting. Among them are a swimming pool, bike trails, boating, and fishing.

The entire complex here is low-key and offers a good way to spend a quiet, relaxing afternoon with your family.

Open May through September, 10:30 A.M. to dusk. Rides are pay-as-you-play; a pay-one-price is available, under $23. An all-day, unlimited-use pass for a family of four, under $75.

Chippewa Park

Highway 61B
Thunder Bay, ONT (807) 625-2351

Overlooking Lake Superior, this 260-acre municipal park has all the fun stuff any municipal park is supposed to have, with a zoo, playing fields, a sand beach, and picnic areas, plus a tidy little amusement area.

A family roller coaster, bumper cars, and 4 kiddie rides are among the 8 rides featured here. In addition, a circa 1915 C. W. Parker carousel is in operation. The 2-row carousel, with 28 jumpers and 2 chariots, has been in the park since 1934, when it was purchased from a traveling carnival that was going out of business.

The park is open year-round, while the amusement area is open daily from late May through Labor Day. Rides are on a pay-as-you-go basis; each costs between $1.50 and $2.00.

 Roller coaster: Roller Coaster, family (S).

Marineland of Canada

7657 Portage Road
Niagara Falls, ONT (905) 356-9565
www.marinelandcanada.com

Killer whales, dolphin and sea-lion shows, and high-tech amusement rides co-exist here to create a fun-filled entertainment package for the entire family. Originally a marine park, it now has 14 rides, including two just for the little ones.

In 2003, a triple-tower 300-foot-tall free fall was built on a man-made mountain that is 150 feet high. That makes the ride 450 feet above the park. What a view!

A castle-like structure in the middle of the 300-acre grounds houses a deer-petting park, and a huge, man-made mountain in the back of the amusement park contains the Dragon Mountain, a roller coaster that has one of the most interesting ride entrances in North America, complete with cave.

 Roller coasters: Dragon Mountain, looping (S); Tivoli Coaster, junior (S).

The park is currently involved in a $160 million expansion program, most of which is dedicated to new and improved animal habitats. Arctic Cove, which opened in 2003, is a 2.5-million-gallon home for beluga whales, and a 20-acre aquarium complex, which officials say will be the world's largest, will have one large dome in the middle, surrounded by three other domes. There will be interactive exhibits and educational programs, and the domes' 6 million gallons of water will house dolphins, sharks, and numerous other aquatic creatures.

Pay-one-price admission, under $32, and parking is free. *Note:* The rides and attractions are spread out, with a great deal of space in between, so you should plan to do a lot of walking.

Ontario Place

955 Lakeshore Boulevard West
Toronto, ONT (416) 314-9811
www.ontarioplace.com

Don't let the tranquil city park atmosphere fool you. This place is much more than an impressive 96-acre greenway on the shores of Lake Ontario in downtown Toronto. On second glance, you'll find this is one of the most rocking places in the city. There are street performers all over the place, colorful flags, and numerous places to eat, rest, and watch other people.

By day, it's a family oasis, with a waterpark, a children's area, a ride area, miniature golf, and a great family arcade with challenging video and virtual-reality games. At night, the complex comes alive as one of the hottest adult night spots around, with live music, dance clubs, and great restaurants. Most venues offer a magnificent nighttime view of the Toronto skyline.

Soak City Waterpark features a children's water play area and a bowl ride where you body-slide off a tower down a water trough and then spin around in a funnel-like bowl until you slow down enough to plop through the hole in the middle into a pool below. The waterpark also offers Rush River family raft ride and Pink Twister & Purple Pipeline, a pair of tube slides.

Children's Village is an entire "village" of activities and play areas for kids 12 and under. In another area of the park, you'll find a challenging MegaMaze, with optical illusions, and laser and sound effects. There's an IMAX theater, a Mars Simulator Ride, and the Wilderness Adventure Ride, a fully animated water flume trip through the scenic forests and canyons of northern Ontario.

The various areas all have their own admission prices. Many are on a pay-as-you-go basis, and there are several combination passes you can buy. Most of the restaurants and entertainment venues stay open year-round, with seasonal activities running during the summer only.

Paramount Canada's Wonderland
Splash Works

9580 Jane Street
Maple, ONT (905) 832–8131
www.canadaswonderland.com

You'll be doing plenty of walking in Canada's largest park, that's for sure. There are more than 300 acres and more than 60 rides in eight themed areas. The 20-acre Splash Works waterpark, which is included with admission to the theme park, has the country's largest outdoor wave pool; a quarter-mile lazy river; an interactive "sprayground" for the kids; a bowl slide where the rider goes round and round as if in a funnel, until dropping out the hole at the bottom; and 16 different slides.

In addition to the 11 roller coasters, there are some great thrill rides here, including the new and humongous Sledge Hammer thriller, which takes you up and over and back down again, kind of like you're sitting on the end of an umbrella being opened and closed. Other flat and high rides include Drop Zone, a 230-foot-tall free fall; the Psyclone, a tall pendulum thriller; and Shockwave, a ride that will twist you in directions you didn't think you could go!

One of the first things you'll see as you enter is the spectacular International Fountain, especially dazzling after dark, when the computerized light show begins. Just beyond the fountain is the 150-foot-high Wonder Mountain, a man-made mountain that contains the Thunder Run coaster.

Roller coasters: The Fly, wild mouse (S); Dragon Fire, corkscrew loop (S); Mighty Canadian Minebuster (W); Wild Beast (W); Ghoster Coaster, junior (W); SkyRider, stand-up (S); Thunder Run Mine Train (S); The Bat, looping (S); Silver Streak, junior inverted (S); Vortex, suspended (S); Top Gun, inverted (S); Taxi Jam, junior (S).

Scooby Doo's Haunted Mansion, a 7,000-square-foot interactive darkride, is fun for the entire family as is the new ride simulator, SpongeBob SquarePants.

For the kids, there's Hanna-Barbera Land. This is where you'll find the antique car ride, the carousel, and your favorite Hanna-Barbera characters, including Scooby-Doo.

The ZoomZone is an all-new family area featuring 3 rides the family can ride together. The Silver Streak is the world's first suspended kids' coaster, the Jumpin' Jet is a fun Crazy Bus–style ride, and the Blast Off is a kid-size free-fall ride. KidZville is another kids' area with a lot of fun things to do.

Plan to spend the entire day if you want to see and do everything. Admission is pay-one-price, under $50. The major season runs from early May through mid-October.

Santa's Village

Santa's Village Road
Bracebridge, ONT (705) 645–2512
www.santasvillage.on.ca

If you're in search of Santa and heading to the North Pole, you're on your way there when you stop by this neat little village founded in 1955. Located on the 45th parallel, it's exactly halfway between the equator and the North Pole!

There are 7 family rides, including a reindeer roller coaster, airplanes, a train ride around the park, a carousel, and a Ferris wheel with gondolas in the shape of Christmas ornaments. Santa's here every day, and there's a great interactive sing-along on Santa's Stage. On Elves Island, you'll find a Lego play center, a ball bounce, and a net crawl as well as other fun activities. Mature trees and landscaping abound and Bavarian and Alpine architecture is dominant.

At the adjacent Sportsland, you'll find go-karts; Babe Rudolph's Batting Cages; Mister Rudolph's Birdies and Bogies miniature golf course; a Lazer Runner arena and Rudy's Rollers, an in-line skate trail.

Admission to Sportsland is free, with attractions on a pay-as-you-play basis. Admission to Santa's Village is pay-one-price, under $20. Both parks are open daily from mid-June to the first week in September, and weekends through the end of September.

 Roller coaster: Roller Coaster, family (S).

SportsWorld

100 SportsWorld Drive
Kitchener, ONT
(519) 653–4442/(800) 393–9163
www.sportsworld.on.ca

Weather won't stop you from having fun around here! This is one huge entertainment center that truly has something for everyone, and a good part of it is indoors.

Inside you'll find the region's largest indoor golf driving range, batting cages, a rock-climbing wall, a video games arcade, and go-karts. If you're hungry, the whimsical Moose Winooski's is a fun place to eat for the entire family. The owners say the eatery offers a "Northern adventure in dining."

In the great outdoors, you'll find the 4.5-acre Hawaii H_2O Waterpark complete with a wave pool, slides, and interactive play areas. Additional rock-climbing walls, miniature golf, a ¾-mile go-kart track, and an amusement rides area are also located outside. Among the 11 rides are a 70-foot-tall Ferris wheel, bumper cars, a Tilt-A-Whirl, a carousel, swings, and 6 rides for the smaller kids.

The indoor activities are open year-round; most of the outdoor activities are in action from spring through fall only. There is no admission fee to the complex and most attractions are on a pay-as-you-play basis. A pay-one-price ticket is available for the waterpark, under $18, and for the amusement rides, under $15. Located adjacent to Highway 401, at the Highway 8 exit.

PRINCE EDWARD iSLAND

Rainbow Valley

Route 6
Cavendish, PEI (902) 963-2221
www.rainbowvalley.pe.ca

Throughout the summer, the park, one of eastern Canada's premier amusement parks, is alive with music, magic, and plenty of activities for the entire family. Founded in 1967, the park has a fun combination of traditional rides and water activities.

Among its 12 rides are a Tilt-A-Whirl, a Paratrooper, a Red Baron airplane ride, and a motion-based darkride that tells the story of the early rum-runners. A monorail takes you around the lakes, and the family roller coaster is a guest favorite year in and year out. There are several different boats, including rowboats, paddleboats, and swan boats, available for having fun on the 3 lakes. There's a petting barn, a shooting gallery, animal shows, and a cool flying saucer-shaped gift shop.

In addition, there are 6 different water slides and a water flume raft ride.

 Roller coaster: Bushwacker, family (S).

Sandspit Cavendish Beach

Route 6
Cavendish, PEI (902) 963-2626
www.sandspit.com

At first glance, the treeless park looks quite barren, but the green grass, other landscape elements, and ride placement make this park a fun, easy facility to get around in. Who needs shade this far north anyway?

There are 16 rides and attractions, including a 60-foot-tall Ferris wheel, a Scrambler, a Tilt-A-Whirl, bumper cars, a carousel, and several kiddie rides. In addition, there is a miniature golf course and go-karts.

 Roller coaster: Wildcat, family (S).

Open June through the first weekend in September, 10:00 A.M. to 11:00 P.M. Free admission, with rides on a pay-as-you-go basis. Pay-one-price available, under $20.

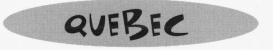

QUEBEC

La Ronde
Île Sainte-Hélène
Montreal, QC (514) 397–2000
www.sixflags.com

This is one of the coolest locations for a theme park in the world. Located on St. Helen's Island in the middle of the St. Lawrence River, the park was originally created for the 1967 World's Fair. Through the years it grew in popularity, and in late 2000 it was purchased by Six Flags, which immediately announced a multi-year, $90 million expansion.

The Vampire, an inverted, 5-inversion coaster, was the first major ride Six Flags built at the park during its first full year of ownership in 2002. A great deal of money is being spent yearly on renovating the infrastructure, restrooms, and restaurants and sprucing up all the buildings, as well as adding new rides and attractions. A new front gate area opened in 2002. In 2003, five new rides were added including new Tea Cups and a flying Carousel.

Meanwhile, a few of the oldies in the park are as popular as ever. Le Monstre, the tallest dual-track wooden coaster in the world, is still a favorite, as is the 150-foot-tall Ferris wheel that provides a magnificent view of the island and downtown Montreal. There is a total of 41 rides.

The park is host to the Montreal International Fireworks

Competition each summer, the largest multi-day pyro-musical competition in the world. It's a great show and a perfect time to visit the park. The Halloween Fright Fest is held weekends in October.

 Roller coasters: The Vampire, inverted (S); Le Monstre, racing (W); Zig Zag, family (S); La Boomerang (S); Le Dragon, enclosed (S); Le Super Manège, corkscrew (S); Le Petites Montagnes Russes, junior (S); Cobra, stand-up (S).

Make sure you bring a sweater or jacket, since the island gets quite chilly after dark, even in midsummer.

Rides and attractions don't open until 10:30 A.M., but they do stay open until 11:00 P.M. during peak season. The major season runs from late May through October. Admission is pay-one-price, under $30.

Mega-Parc
Galeries de la Capitale Mall
5401 Boulevard de Galeries
Quebec City, QC (418) 627–5800
www.mega-parc.com

As winter approaches, the folks around here are happy that Galeries de la Capitale exists, not just because of the indoor shopping, but also because of the extensive indoor theme park.

With 14 attractions, including 10 rides, the park is located on 3 floors overlooking an ice-skating rink. In addition to the carousel, Ferris wheel, bumper cars, family coaster, balloon race, and 5 kids' rides, there are a miniature golf course, Bowlingo bowling, a soft-play area with slides for the kids, as well as the Baby Jungle, a play area for the toddlers.

 Roller coaster: Capitale Express, family (S).

The family coaster is located on the third floor and runs around the entire top floor. Open year-round, during the same hours as the mall. The park's rides are priced by points. Each point costs 40 cents, with rides ranging from 2 to 4 points.

AMUSEMENT PARK INDEX

Note: Places in italics are located in Canada.

309

THE AMUSEMENT PARK GUIDE

AMUSEMENT PARK iNDEX

THE AMUSEMENT PARK GUIDE

AMUSEMENT PARK INDEX

THE AMUSEMENT PARK GUIDE

AMUSEMENT PARK INDEX

AMUSEMENT PARKS BY STATE AND PROVINCE

UNITED STATES

Alabama

Southern Adventures, Huntsville, 2

VisionLand Theme Park Bessemer, 3

Waterville USA, Gulf Shores, 4

Alaska

H2Oasis, Anchorage, 4

Pioneer Park, Fairbanks, 5

Arizona

Castles & Coasters, Phoenix, 5

Enchanted Island, Phoenix, 6

Old Tucson Studios, Tucson, 6

Arkansas

Burns Park Funland, North Little Rock, 7

Magic Springs and Crystal Falls, Hot Springs, 8

California

Adventure City, Stanton, 9

Anaheim Boomers, Anaheim, 10

Balboa Fun Zone, Newport Beach, 10

Belmont Park, San Diego, 10

Bonfante Gardens Theme Park, Gilroy, 11

Castle Amusement Park, Riverside, 12

The Disneyland Resort, Anaheim, 14

Escondido Boomers, Escondido, 19

Fountain Valley Boomers, Fountain Valley, 19

Funderland, Sacramento, 20

Funderwoods, Lodi, 20

Knott's Berry Farm, Buena Park, 21

Knott's Soak City U.S.A.:
Buena Park, 23
Chula Vista, 23
Palm Springs, 23

Legoland California, Carlsbad, 24

Pacific Park, Santa Monica, 26

Paramount's Great America, Santa Clara, 27

Pharaoh's Lost Kingdom, Redlands, 28

Pixieland Park, Concord, 29

Raging Waters:
San Jose, 30
San Dimas, 30

Rotary Storyland & Playland, Fresno, 31

Santa Cruz Beach Boardwalk, Santa Cruz, 31

Scandia Fun Center, Ontario, 33

SeaWorld Adventure Park, San Diego, 34

Six Flags Hurricane Harbor, Valencia, 35

Six Flags Magic Mountain, Valencia, 36

THE AMUSEMENT PARK GUIDE

PARKS BY STATE AND PROVINCE

THE AMUSEMENT PARK GUIDE

PARKS BY STATE AND PROVINCE

THE AMUSEMENT PARK GUIDE

PARKS BY STATE AND PROVINCE

THE AMUSEMENT PARK GUIDE

PARKS BY STATE AND PROVINCE

WITHDRAWN

ABOUT THE AUTHOR

AS SENIOR EDITOR of *Amusement Business*, the world's number one business trade magazine for the amusement park industry, veteran news reporter Tim O'Brien literally travels the world's highways for a living. His specialty area of reportage is amusement parks, theme parks, and tourist attractions.

His interest in parks began early in his life as he was growing up across from Buckeye Lake Amusement Park, just east of Columbus, Ohio, and the love affair continues to this day.

Since joining *Amusement Business* in 1985, Tim has visited more than 500 amusement parks and has ridden more than 400 roller coasters in 17 different countries. He is quoted widely in the national press and is a sought-after guest for TV documentaries and news programs because of his vast knowledge of the business side of amusement parks and roller coasters.

A graduate of Ohio State University with a master's degree in journalism/film production, Tim is an accomplished photographer and public speaker. In 2001 he won the coveted Lifetime Service Award from the International Association of Amusement Parks & Attractions for his devotion and his "long-term achievements in the amusement industry." He was the first journalist to win this accolade in the association's 75-year history.

When he's not traveling, he's at home base in Nashville, Tennessee, where he lives with his wife Kathleen, and his two daughters, Carrie and Molly. His backyard koi pond and gardens continue to win kudos.

WITHDRAWN